FROM *Curiosity* TO DEEP LEARNING

Personal Digital Inquiry in Grades K–5

**JULIE COIRO,
ELIZABETH DOBLER,
and KAREN PELEKIS**

FOREWORD BY
STEPHANIE HARVEY

Stenhouse Publishers
Portsmouth, New Hampshire

Stenhouse Publishers
www.stenhouse.com

Table 3.2/Appendix E is adapted from the Cultures of Thinking Self-Assessment Tool from *Creating Cultures of Thinking: The 8 Forces We Must Master to Truly Transform Our Schools* by Ron Ritchhart © 2015. Reprinted by permission of Wiley Publishing.

Figure 5.3 ReadWriteThink Alphabet Organizer © 2013. Reprinted by permission of ReadWriteThink and The National Council of Teachers of English.

Bulleted list on page 175 in Chapter 8 is excerpted from The WWWDOT "Approach to Improving Students' Critical Evaluation of Websites" by Shenglan Zhang, Nell K. Duke, Laura M. Jiménez © 2011. Reprinted by permission of Wiley Publishing.

Every effort has been made to contact copyright holders and students for permission to reproduce borrowed material. We regret any oversights that may have occurred and will be pleased to rectify them in subsequent reprints of the work.

Library of Congress Cataloging-in-Publication Data

Names: Coiro, Julie, author. | Dobler, Elizabeth, 1963- author. | Pelekis, Karen, author.
Title: From curiosity to deep learning : from curiosity to deep learning : personal digital inquiry in grades K–5 / Julie Coiro, Elizabeth Dobler, and Karen Pelekis.
Description: Portsmouth, New Hampshire : Stenhouse Publishers, [2019] | Includes bibliographical references.
Identifiers: LCCN 2019006612 | ISBN 9781625311566 (pbk. : alk. paper) | ISBN 9781625311573 (eISBN)
Subjects: LCSH: Inquiry-based learning. | Digital media—Study and teaching (Elementary) | Curiosity in children.
Classification: LCC LB1027.23 .C645 2019 | DDC 371.3—dc23
LC record available at https://lccn.loc.gov/2019006612

Cover design, interior design, and typesetting by Gina Poirier, Gina Poirier Design

Manufactured in the United States of America

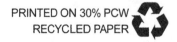

PRINTED ON 30% PCW
RECYCLED PAPER

25 24 23 22 21 20 19   9 8 7 6 5 4 3 2 1

For Charlie, Meghan, Sarah, and my parents, Fran and Charlene
— whose love and support encourage me every day.
—J.C.

For the Ross Elementary fourth-grade reading group.
Thank you for teaching me at least one new thing every day for 180 days.
—B.D.

For my parents, siblings, Nicholas, Stephanie, Jim, and my students,
thank you for all of your help along the way.
—K.P.

CONTENTS

Foreword

You'd be amazed at the number of classrooms I've visited where kids are scattered around the room *alone,* devices in hand, earbuds wired for sound, eyes laser-focused on bright screens, thumbs filling in bubbles and blanks at warp speed. There is a rising backlash against the situation that is reflected in headlines across the nation, *Silicon Valley Parents are Raising their Kids Tech Free. . . .Parents in Overland Park Kansas Fed Up. . . .Get Kids off Screens. . . .Cupertino, CA Parents Petition Schools to Limit iPad Use. . . .The Kids Look Like Zombies. . . .*And several of these concerns come from the very places that conceived and developed digital devices! It's no wonder many parents, teachers and kids have thrown their hands up in frustration with these worksheets on the screen and this notion of personalized learning. If you are looking for a guide to that kind of personalized learning, you may as well close this book.

However, if you want an in-depth exploration of what real and genuine personal learning is all about, you've come to the right place. Julie, Elizabeth, and Karen understand what the three words in the title, *personal, digital* and *inquiry,* represent. *Personal* is the belief that powerful learning springs from close personal relationships and experiences with human beings not merely with devices. *Digital* is the idea that the thoughtful use of digital texts and tools can take learners on journeys that print alone could not accomplish. And *inquiry* is the understanding that true education involves wondering about the world and believing that kids' questions are absolutely vital. As the authors state, "All that is needed to implement personal inquiry is space and time for learners to actively reflect, collaborate, and engage with personally meaningful ideas."

Personal Digital Inquiry (PDI) emphasizes personal relationships and collaboration, not solitude. In an era where personalized learning is often associated with isolated one-to-one device technology, we thirst for this personal, constructivist, and collaborative approach to digital inquiry. Technology guru, Alan November, reminds us that the term *one-to-one* is a misnomer. He notes that when every child has a device, "It is not one-to-one. But rather one-to-world." The role of technology is to connect people, not to isolate them.

Our authors suggest four practices for building a culture of inquiry within PDI. These include wondering and discovering, collaborating and discussing, creating and taking action, and analyzing and reflecting. As kids ask questions, they are given time to address them and discover answers. As they work collaboratively, discussions naturally emerge. As they create new ideas and share them, they want to act. Ultimately, they analyze their findings and reflect on them. The collaborative and organic PDI process stands in stark contrast to the solitary personalized learning movement. The PDI process is not rigid and linear, but rather dynamic, recursive, and even messy.

Messy yes, but not chaotic. This type of inquiry does not happen through osmosis. Too often when teachers jump head first into the inquiry process, chaos ensues. Our authors understand this and have found that careful planning will keep chaos from running rough shod over the most creative ideas. For example, Chapter 6 includes an accessible planning guide to PDI. This guide includes ideas for teachers to set expectations for teaching and learning, plan authentic opportunities for PDI, and make purposeful choices about digital texts and tools. Using this guide helps to move us ahead with inquiry and to resist the urge to contain the chaos and revert to traditional (and boring) state or animal reports.

When digging into classroom teaching, I need to know "how to do it." One of my favorite aspects of this book is that each chapter begins with a chapter overview and a bulleted list of the chapter's strategies, practices, techniques, and tips. Chapter 4, "The Nuts and Bolts of Creating a Culture of Inquiry" is a great example of this. In this chapter, the authors share ways they make time for inquiry, organize space, foster collaboration, teach foundational routines, and use text, tools and technologies to facilitate inquiry. They share inclusive language and model explicit phrases for working together. As a reader, you will find new ways to encourage kids to adopt and adapt our teaching language as their learning language. How exciting it is when we hear kids using the language with each other that we have modeled and shared!

From Curiosity to Deep Learning: Personal Digital Inquiry in Grades K-5 is all about the importance of student voice and choice, the significance of personal relationships, the power of collaboration, and the role of technology to enhance learning and the need for continuous analysis and reflection. As this book shows, if curiosity is at the core of our curriculum, inquiry-based teaching and learning can and will flourish. As Sir Ken Robinson says, "Curiosity is the engine that drives creativity." This book is a prime example of that. I wish you the best as you read and wonder about the pages within.

Yours in curiosity,
Stephanie Harvey

Acknowledgments

Welcome readers! Thank you for joining us on our journey to dig deeper into personal digital inquiry. This book stems from our wondering: How can we bring our own understandings and rich experiences together into a format that will inspire and deepen the understanding of interested educators? Just like the saying, "Everyone learns from everyone," making the story of personal digital inquiry come alive in a book became an opportunity for us to learn from each other as authors. Equally important are the many lessons we learned from the generous teachers and children who agreed to share their thoughts and work with us. With heartfelt thanks, we would like to recognize these teachers and library media specialists, and beg forgiveness from the ones we inadvertently left out. Thank you to Jeremy Guski, Deb Krisanda, Tracy Noble, Gracy Baker, Tracy Austin, Tyler Gill, Christina Brunfield, Allison Preston, Ann Au, Liz Martinez, David White, Elizabeth Gonzalez, Elena Valencia, and all of the many children that provided wonderful opportunities for us all to continue learning.

We are also thankful to Renee Hobbs, Kara Clayton, Amanda Murphy, and the many other educators and faculty members at the University of Rhode Island's annual Summer Institute in Digital Literacy who were willing to try out our ideas and share their creative interpretations of personal digital inquiry across so many different contexts. In addition, thank you to Barbara Miller, Sue Luft, Barbara Johnson, Ari Orefice, and Ila Berry—we are inspired by their energy and passion for teaching and learning and we appreciate their insightful feedback and suggestions to guide us toward the final versions of the book. And to Stephanie Harvey, a huge thank you for writing the foreword to our book—your work with comprehension and inquiry has greatly inspired our own thinking and your support means the world to us!

Finally, we are grateful to Stenhouse, and in particular to our editor, Bill Varner, for his guidance on this writing journey to our production editor, Amanda Bondi, for her amazingly responsive feedback; and to other members of the Stenhouse production team, especially Stephanie Levy, Jay Kilburn, Shannon St. Peter, Gina Poirier, and Cindy Black for making our ideas become a reality.

Introduction

Welcome to *From Curiosity to Deep Learning: Personal Digital Inquiry in Grades K–5*. We (Julie, Beth, and Karen) invite you to join us on a journey that seeks to envision ways of designing personal digital inquiry experiences for young learners. We wrote this book to share an emerging vision of how to cultivate personal digital inquiry (PDI) in ways that foster rich learning, active participation, and creative expression with digital texts and tools.

Our aim is to provide a resource, supported by research and filled with real examples, that serves as a practical guide for others to understand and flexibly use PDI in a variety of educational settings. Here, we begin by discussing the research showing the importance of inquiry and briefly peeking inside Karen's classroom to illustrate how PDI can transform teaching and learning in powerful ways. Then we explore our reasons for writing this book, describe how the book is organized, and discuss the major questions that guided our thinking along the way.

Why Inquiry?

Inquiry is the essence of what many describe as twenty-first-century teaching and learning. Inquiry-based experiences prepare learners for a fast-changing world in which they will need to deal with problems that we cannot yet even define. Offering learners in classrooms and libraries space to generate their own wonderings about such problems helps them connect their own interests to real-life issues in ways that can lead to real change (Alberta Learning 2004). In turn, opportunities for purposeful, self-directed inquiry become personally fulfilling learning experiences (Pink 2009).

Researchers are finding that elementary school students engaged in technology-embedded inquiry practices have begun to demonstrate many of the twenty-first-century skills called for by international thought leaders, business leaders, and educational researchers alike. In addition, studies have documented dramatic increases in elementary student performance in literacy and numeracy as well as in high school graduation rates (Clarke et al. 2014). Teachers in these inquiry-based settings also began to appreciate the different ways that learners gain knowledge and skills in a digital world.

There are also calls for increased opportunities for students to practice these global survival skills in ways more closely connected to their own lives. Policy makers recommend inquiry-based teaching practices that make learning relevant, encourage metacognitive reflection and teamwork, and use technology to support learning while fostering creativity and collaboration (Saavedra and Opfer 2012).

These recommended learner needs and associated teaching practices are closely aligned to the four core sets of practices embedded into our PDI framework, ensuring all students have more opportunities to wonder and discover, collaborate and discuss, create and take action, and analyze and reflect. Throughout this book, you'll learn much more about these ideas.

Why Personal Digital Inquiry?

A Teacher's Reflection

I (Karen) have always wanted my students to become the strongest learners and citizens they can be. This means that they are curious about the world, ask insightful questions, collaborate meaningfully with others, find answers, express themselves effectively, and thoughtfully reflect on their studies to better develop essential academic and social-emotional skills. This prepares them to more confidently and successfully pursue their interests, navigate changes throughout their lives, and thrive in and out of school.

From my first day of teaching, it was important that I build a trusting relationship with my class. We strive to foster a caring community where we listen to each other, feel comfortable taking risks, and work productively together. I need to know my students individually to help each one grow, and this means tailoring instruction at times to include student interests. Since cultivating classroom relationships is central to my teaching, the personal component of digital inquiry is essential.

Over the years, I have explored different ways to teach my students. As digital tools became available, I wanted to see how I could incorporate them. Having few computer skills, I was fortunate to be able to collaborate with creative, supportive colleagues. We started by enriching a unit on the continents by having students work with partners to study videos. My first graders felt like they were traveling around the world. They were also able to learn more, because the videos provided information they could understand but was too hard for them to read independently in books. As a result, they were inspired to draw, write, and read more about geography. Meaningful uses of technology changed how I taught and how my students learned.

It took more time to realize that incorporating technology was only part of the reason why my students were more engaged and learning better; the bigger impact came because they were doing inquiry work. Although digital tools opened up opportunities for inquiry, my class was primarily benefiting from the intricate combination of enriching experiences, including asking thoughtful questions, having informed discussions, taking action to find answers, and reflecting on new discoveries. The inquiry work was making the difference, and it was strengthened by my choices of digital and nondigital tools, as well as tailoring learning to meet the personal needs of my students.

Meanwhile, while my colleagues and I were busy developing curriculum for students, we recognized that our professional collaboration was also a powerful inquiry experience for us as educators. We saw how our combined strengths made it possible to achieve something we could not have done individually. These positive experiences made me want to continue the challenge of integrating inquiry and digital literacy into my teaching. As a result, personal digital inquiry has transformed my instruction, how the students learn, and our process for designing curriculum.

Why Write a Book About Planning for Inquiry?

From our own experiences and our work with other educators and researchers, we have come to realize that building opportunities for PDI into the culture of elementary school classrooms can be challenging. Encouraging children to ask questions is one thing; finding ways to plan thoughtful lessons, support diverse learners, and make intentional choices about technology use aligned to those questions is something quite different.

Implementing PDI experiences means carefully building a culture of inquiry in your classroom community and intentionally aligning your teaching with meaningful goals for learning and participation while guiding students to pursue their own inquiries. PDI requires knowledge about sound teaching techniques and a lot of reflection and risk-taking to venture into the unknown.

Our conversations with teachers have taught us that using PDI is more effective and manageable with careful planning. Years of experience and workshops with educators led Julie to develop a comprehensive planning guide that makes it easier to pull all of these pieces together to create cohesive inquiry practices. We hope that this book can serve as a guide to help educators better understand the elements of PDI and use it to establish inquiry teaching in their learning environments, individually or with others.

How Is This Book Organized?

In this book, we seek to document our learning around PDI practices and reflect on the challenges encountered along the way. Some stories come from our own classrooms, and others come from teachers with whom we have worked.

The book is organized in two parts. Part I is structured to help you build an understanding of PDI practices one layer at a time. By design, Chapters 1–6 are relatively short chapters, allowing you to process each layer before building on it in the next chapter. In Chapters 1 and 2, we examine what's at the core of PDI and why each of four sets of practices is important to pursue. In Chapter 3, we model ways of cultivating personal inquiry through a process of analysis and self-reflection, and in Chapter 4, we offer strategies to inform your planning, implementation, and renewed practice of inquiry-based opportunities. Chapter 5 weaves relevant practices together into the PDI triangle, a framework that integrates intentional inquiry-based teaching decisions geared toward student ownership and learning with intent. Finally, in Chapter 6, we guide you through the details of planning authentic opportunities for PDI while mapping your plans along a continuum of thinking processes most likely to foster students' deep understanding and active engagement.

We also provide several visual tools and frameworks in Part I to guide and support your planning and implementation of PDI; these include the PDI framework, PDI self-reflection tool, PDI questioning tool, PDI triangle, PDI planning guide, and the PDI knowledge continuum. We introduce these planning supports, one at a time, in the context of several inquiry experiences, and we provide examples and think-alouds that demonstrate how teachers have used them as part of their planning.

The second part of the book is designed to provide clear and detailed examples of how teachers and librarians in grades K–5 have creatively orchestrated PDI practices in their school contexts. Chapter 7 includes two complete examples of the PDI planning process as part of two different units of study. In Chapter 8, we zoom in on the four core sets of PDI elements to more deeply examine related intentional teaching practices. Then, in Chapter 9, we offer three more examples of what PDI looks like in different elementary school contexts. We close by offering ideas for how to continue your own journey and inspire others in transforming teaching and learning at your school.

To provide you with additional opportunities to ask questions, explore new ideas, and deepen your knowledge of PDI practices, we have also created a companion website that you can access at bit.ly/PDInquiry. At the website, you will find digital versions of student artifacts, other PDI resources, and a study guide for each chapter. Whether you are reading this book with a book study group or on your own, the book discussion guide includes prompts for taking our ideas and making them your own. The beginning of each chapter includes an icon reminding readers of the discussion guide questions and prompts available on the companion website. We hope you find these useful.

From Curiosity
to Deep Learning:
Personal Digital Inquiry
in Grades K–5
Companion Website

What Questions Guide Our Thinking?

Our goal for this book is *not* to describe one best way to cultivate PDI in your classroom. Instead, we strive to share an emerging vision of what might be, informed by a set of questions, important educational theories, anecdotal stories, and, when available, evidence-based research. Some of the major questions guiding our thinking include:

1. What do we mean by PDI, and what makes it worth embracing in classroom settings?
2. What role do teachers play in the inquiry process, and what responsibilities do students have as learning becomes more self-directed?
3. What informs the selection and use of digital texts and tools as part of PDI?
4. How can teachers flexibly plan developmentally appropriate learning opportunities that connect and engage learners with real-world experiences?
5. How do PDI practices impact learners over time?

If you are grappling with some of these same questions, whether you are a first-year educator, a veteran teacher, or an administrator seeking to transform teaching and learning in your school, this book is designed to guide your thinking as you move forward. If you are in a place where some of these questions might be too overwhelming, this book is also for you—to encourage you to safely peek into other classrooms and get a sense of what might be possible. Either way, we welcome you to join us on a journey to uncover and describe productive ways of connecting with and engaging young learners.

PHOTO: VICTORIA PRESSER, SCARSDALE PUBLIC SCHOOLS

PART I

Building an Understanding of
Personal Digital Inquiry
Practices, One Layer at a Time

T he frameworks, visual tools, think-alouds, and reflections featured in Part I are designed to support your planning and implementation of PDI practices one layer at a time. We hope these ideas help to build an understanding of why and how flexible inquiry-based practices in your own learning environments can move students ever closer to becoming curious, creative, and self-directed learners.

1

Understanding Personal Digital Inquiry

In this chapter, you will learn about

* the natural process of inquiry as part of learning

* how personal digital inquiry (PDI) is defined

* four core sets of PDI practices and related questions to guide your planning of PDI

Find additional ways to engage with these ideas in the online study guide for Chapter 1.

bit.ly/PDIstudyguide

Inquiry Is a Natural Part of Learning

As we begin to explore PDI, it is helpful to think about how we use the inquiry process all the time as educators, as well as in our everyday lives. As the following three examples from each of the authors show, inquiry can be part of schooling, from graduate students to our youngest learners, and can extend to all environments, including libraries and classrooms. Let's look together at these examples to see how inquiry is part of learning.

Julie teaches reading and digital literacy courses at the University of Rhode Island. Recently, she wondered how to actively engage her undergraduate preservice teachers with generating ideas about effective instructional strategies for addressing sociocultural and linguistic differences among students in their future classrooms. First, they were asked to view and take notes from a set of three teaching videos for homework. Next, they held a question-and-answer session with an international graduate student who had been in the United States for one year as a non-native English speaker. Then, during class, groups of three students were assigned to learn more about one of eight different questions they generated. Each group was given fifteen minutes to collaboratively integrate the most important points into a single slide on a class slideshow. Finally, the group members shared their new understandings with the class. Together everyone generated a set of evidence-based practices from their readings and discussions to share with other preservice teachers in their program.

Beth, in her work as an elementary school media specialist, wondered how she could encourage students to check out and read more nonfiction books. Information and ideas were gathered from other librarians through participating in two online discussion groups, by reading a professional book, and from asking students directly. She then created nonfiction book displays, gave nonfiction book talks, and hosted an after-school Books and Cookies activity for teachers, featuring the new nonfiction books in the library.

And, finally, Karen, a first-grade teacher from Scarsdale, New York, regularly explores different ways of keeping her first graders engaged with important curriculum goals while pursuing topics related to their interests. Twenty years of wondering about how to foster young children's deep understanding of phenomena in science, math, and social studies while encouraging reflection, creative expression, and collaboration has led her on a teaching journey with many stories to share and learn from.

A picture tells a thousand words, and the photo in Figure 1.1 of Karen's students engaged in their plant inquiry beautifully depicts our vision of PDI in action: learners actively engaged in flexible opportunities to wonder and discover about topics related to the life cycle of plants in a garden, collaborate with others as they discuss personally relevant

FIGURE 1.1 Students engaged in plant inquiry

connections, closely analyze and regularly reflect on their discoveries, and cre-atively express their new knowledge in ways that lead to action in their school community (see Figure 1.1).

As you can see, working through the inquiry process is already an integral part of our lives. If you pause to think about things that you are genuinely inter-ested in (as educators or in your personal lives), efforts to explore those ideas, talk with others, share solutions, and reflect on what you learned often happen quite naturally. This is what we mean by PDI. For all three of us, and most likely for you, when fueled by personal curiosities and needs, we connect with people and ideas as we discover new ways of thinking about living, teaching, and learning in today's interconnected world.

What Is Personal Digital Inquiry?

So, what exactly do we mean by "personal digital inquiry," or what we'll often refer to in this book as PDI? Briefly, our vision of PDI is one that engages teachers and students in collaborative discussion, analysis, and reflection that leads to knowledge building, knowledge expression, and personal action. Based on these ideas, a PDI project includes regular opportunities for every learner to wonder and discover, collaborate and discuss, create and take action, and analyze and reflect. Learners may move through these opportunities in varied sequences with varied levels of support and varied amounts of technology use, but we have found that successful inquiry-based experiences make room for all four core sets of practices. Throughout this book, you'll learn much more about each of these practices and how they work together for children of various ages.

We intentionally placed the term *personal* at the forefront of our vision of PDI for two reasons. First, and foremost, our emphasis as educators is on building personal relationships. The affective quality of teacher-student relationships is a central and critical motivator of student engagement and performance. Educational theory and years of research suggest that positive interpersonal relationships with students are the building blocks of productive interactions within a classroom and the larger learning community (Wubbels, den Brok, van Tartwick, and Levy 2012). For example, in her rigorous study across 581 classrooms, Kristy Cooper (2013) found that a personal and emotional connection to the teacher, to content, and to instruction increased student engagement more than *seven* times as strongly as academic rigor or lively teaching. That is, teachers who convey care, provide affirmation, demonstrate understanding, use humor, promote the relevance of students' learning experiences, and enable self-expression help to create personal meaning for academic work. Teachers working toward PDI honor their students by listening to them, learning about their interests and personalities, and valuing their contributions in their classroom community. By focusing on building relationships, everyone has a sense of belonging and caring for each other to meet everyone's fullest potential.

The second reason for placing personal at the forefront of our vision of PDI is to emphasize the importance of engaging children as partners in learning. Children bring important and creative ideas from their experiences outside of school and are very willing to share with others when given a space to shine during the school day. Children also bring personal preferences and questions that drive their own curiosities about the topics we are expected to teach. When describing PDI, we do not suggest teachers fully relinquish their role in directing learning pathways to blindly follow their students' personal wonderings. Rather, we seek to consciously consider ways to vary support for children while planning instruction aimed to foster active participation and student agency around ideas that matter in the real world.

Importantly, our use of the term *personal* in our vision of student-guided inquiry is not to be confused with the movement to personalize learning that has gained popularity in some schools. From our perspective, most proponents of personalized learning approaches advocate top-down models of learning through technology via digital playlists, for example, that are designed to serve up learning based on a formula of what teachers (or a computer algorithm) thinks a particular learner needs most. Students may have some control over the sequence and pace they move through customized playlists, but they typically work independently with few opportunities to jointly construct ideas and collaborate with others. Finally, personalized learning approaches usually require that the learner interacts with a computer.

Personal learning experiences, however, "involve something *human* whereby the learner initiates and controls at least a part of the learning process" (Coiro 2016). Often, this type of learning emerges from actively engaging and talking with others about one's personal wonderings. Typically, these wonderings are sparked by a topic or problem encountered in school, at home, or in the community. These personal learning experiences offer students opportunities to generate questions and create products that connect their own interests to real-life concerns in personally fulfilling ways, and learners are not constrained by what teachers make available to them on the computer. All that is needed to implement personal inquiry is space and time for learners to actively reflect, collaborate, and engage with personally meaningful ideas.

The *digital* component of our vision reflects the important role that digital texts and tools have come to play in both learning and teaching through an inquiry process. You will notice that we are careful to not suggest that all inquiry must involve technology. Rather, we recognize the range of ways that technology can expand how children access, build, and express new ideas about topics fueled by personally relevant wonderings and teacher-guided supports. Woven into this book are examples of how and why teachers select specific texts and tools from which children can build their understanding of key concepts. In addition, you'll be introduced to a range of digital resources that elementary-aged children can use to share their ideas and have access to a wider range of authentic audiences. Weaving digital media into inquiry-based learning experiences helps develop children's capacity to access, analyze, create, and engage in critical thinking. Through this deep thinking, children can work toward becoming responsible citizens in both real-world and digital contexts.

Finally, although the term *inquiry* comes third in our label, inquiry lies at the core of our PDI framework. Like John Dewey ([1938] 1997), we wholeheartedly believe that learners grow and change with opportunities to identify problems in their community, generate personal wonderings, and engage in collaborative dialogue around these problems. When learners apply their new knowledge by reflecting on and acting out solutions in ways that transform thinking, learning becomes relevant and lasting. Children learn to revisit and reconsider their thinking as they encounter new perspectives and different ways of doing things, with

In their paper, *A Rich Seam: How New Pedagogies Find Deep Learning,* Michael Fullan and Maria Langworthy (2014) invite readers to think much more about how purposeful technology use and learning partnerships between students and teachers can activate "the deep learning goals of creating and using new knowledge in the real world" (3). These ideas align quite a bit with our PDI framework.

Michael Fullan and Maria Langworthy's paper A Rich Seam: How New Pedagogies Find Deep Learning *bit.ly/fullanrichseam*

and without technology. Encouraging children to reflect, question, analyze, and hypothesize develops higher-level thinking and problem-solving skills.

Through modeling and the careful selection of instructional supports, students learn about the inquiry process and their own preferences and abilities. Gradually, teachers incorporate more flexibility into their planning as students are motivated by projects about their personal interests. Central to this process is the relationship that teachers have with their students and the climate teachers create in their classroom so that students feel comfortable taking risks and exploring their interests. Effective teachers strive for a balance of child-guided and adult-guided interactions in large-group, small-group, and choice time activities.

In this book, we spotlight educators who work to plan and cultivate opportunities for PDI as a regular part of their elementary classroom practices. These teachers and media specialists are beginning to transform teaching and learning in ways that promote deeper understanding and increased engagement.

Curiosity Is the Foundation of Personal Digital Inquiry

Curiosity involves a natural inclination to think about and question the world around us; it often leads to discovering answers to our questions and seeking out additional information. When curiosity is welcomed and nurtured in the classroom, a sense of wonder blossoms among both students and teachers. In education, teachers can encourage and extend curiosity in many ways:

- introducing new ideas
- showing a known concept in an original way

With John Dewey's work as a starting point, our inquiry process led us to the National Research Council's 2000 report entitled *How People Learn: Brain, Mind, School Experience* (Committee on Developments in the Science of Learning 2000). This document provides a rich description of effective teaching practices for promoting inquiry-based education.

NRC 2000 report How People Learn: Brain, Mind, Experience, and School
bit.ly/naphowpeoplelearn

- setting up activities that foster investigation
- asking guiding questions
- promoting student questions

An ability to ask questions, in particular, is essential to learning, reasoning, and understanding. As Dewey ([1938] 1997) proposed almost a century ago, when curriculum is built around learner instincts to talk, investigate, construct meaning, and express new discoveries with others, meaningful and transformative learning happens quite naturally.

Teachers can foster curiosity by sharing books, videos, and other resources that prompt questions. Students then learn how to find answers to their questions through research. Experiences that involve students observing artifacts or engaging in hands-on activities can help students better understand abstract concepts and remember what they have learned (see Figure 1.2). "Intentional opportunities to capitalize on the natural sense of curiosity that lies within each of our students is the essence of what drives learning forward. . . . Helping students learn to satisfy their own curiosities gradually empowers them to tackle the complex problems they will face in our rapidly changing digital world" (Coiro 2015, 192).

Curiosity and questioning play a crucial role in promoting the PDI process. For some children, rich questions that elicit deep thinking come naturally. For

FIGURE 1.2 Kindergartners actively satisfying their curiosity by dissecting owl pellets as part of their inquiry about animals and their habitats

others, instruction and modeling, along with engaging experiences, are needed to develop an ability to generate thought-provoking questions that go beyond the literal. To encourage curiosity and deep thinking that connect to other core PDI practices, consider the following questions about your teaching:

- How might the activities you design prompt more or richer questions while offering flexibility in how learning evolves in response to these new wonderings?

- How and when might you intentionally build in time for children to revisit and fully develop new ideas informed by their questions?

- What hands-on activities can provide authentic reasons for children to notice, discuss, collaborate, and share their thinking about these experiences with others?

- How might you weave in time for observing and journaling to practice analysis and reflection while giving enough time for children to explore the topic sequentially in an unrushed manner?

- How might you sequence activities and instruction to help children actively deepen their understanding by connecting to and building on what they learned previously?

Building a Culture of Inquiry

Underlying these questions is our firm belief that implementing PDI experiences requires purposefully building a culture of inquiry in your learning community. Our PDI framework is designed to help visualize and plan for regular opportunities for four core sets of practices as part of PDI before you implement these experiences with children. Here, we very briefly introduce each core set of PDI practices (see Figure 1.3). Then, in the chapters to come, we explore these opportunities more fully with stories from various settings in grades K–5.

- **Wonder & Discover:** All learners have opportunities to engage with content and experiences that prompt their own questions about a topic and time to explore resources and discover new ideas about the world around them.

- **Collaborate & Discuss:** All learners have opportunities to engage in joint conversations around shared interests, discuss interpretations, make connections, and negotiate differences in their thinking.

FIGURE 1.3 Personal digital inquiry framework

- **Create & Take Action:** All learners have opportunities to express their interests and new understandings through creative work designed to start conversations, raise awareness, take action, or change minds in their learning community or beyond.

- **Analyze & Reflect:** All learners have opportunities to analyze content to build their understanding of challenging information and reflect on their choices and what they've learned at multiple points (e.g., before, during, and after) of their inquiry process.

We chose to divide these core PDI practices into what appears to be four separate sets of elements to make it easier to focus on each one in its own right. We also chose to label each PDI element as a pair of reciprocal processes that reflect authentic inquiry in action. For example, authentic opportunities to *wonder* are naturally paired with time to actually *discover* answers to these wonderings. Working *collaboratively* with others typically leads to thoughtful *discussions* about what has been discovered along the way. *Creating* and sharing new ideas provides tangible ways for learners to turn their knowledge into *action*. And, finally, public and private *reflection* are deeply entwined with opportunities to *analyze* and think critically about new ideas.

Importantly, there is no specific hierarchy or order to how the four core sets of elements work together in our PDI framework. Learners may move back and forth through these experiences in varied sequences with varied levels of support and varied amounts of technology. At times, in a group setting, all of the practices may even interact simultaneously. We'll share lots more about planning for these elements as we move through the chapters of this book.

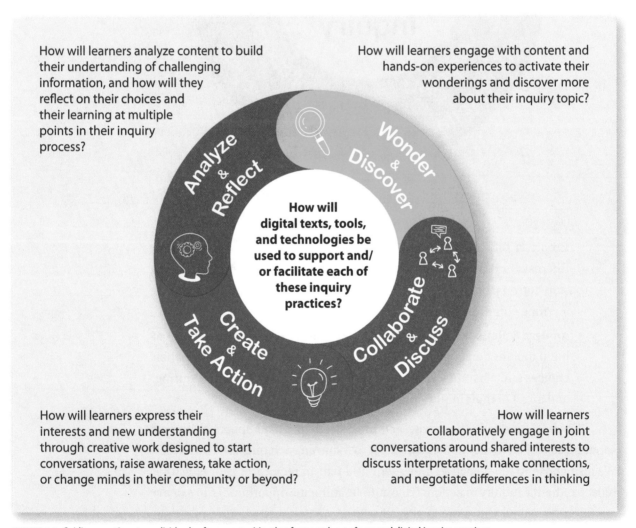

How will learners analyze content to build their undertanding of challenging information, and how will they reflect on their choices and their learning at multiple points in their inquiry process?

How will learners engage with content and hands-on experiences to activate their wonderings and discover more about their inquiry topic?

How will digital texts, tools, and technologies be used to support and/or facilitate each of these inquiry practices?

Analyze & Reflect

Wonder & Discover

Create & Take Action

Collaborate & Discuss

How will learners express their interests and new understanding through creative work designed to start conversations, raise awareness, take action, or change minds in their community or beyond?

How will learners collaboratively engage in joint conversations around shared interests to discuss interpretations, make connections, and negotiate differences in thinking

FIGURE 1.4 Guiding questions to explicitly plan for opportunities that foster each set of personal digital inquiry practices

We also want to stress that the messiness of inquiry-based learning rarely happens in four isolated steps or phases. In reality, these four sets of key PDI practices overlap and weave in and out of varied inquiry experiences. Discussing new ideas collaboratively, for example, gives rise to new questions and ways of exploring that overlap with dimensions of wondering and discovery. Likewise, as children turn their knowledge into action and share their digital creations with a real audience, their new insights are likely to promote lively discussions or future collaborations among others with similar interests.

The reciprocal and overlapping nature of the PDI elements is especially true for analysis and reflection. In fact, it's hard to imagine a classroom of children collaboratively discussing and generating new questions without first examining, or analyzing, something that prompts talking and thinking. Kindergartners may analyze a pumpkin, including the shell, seeds, and fibrous strings, before a shared writing experience. Fifth graders may analyze a narrative and informational text about bullying before creating an antibullying infomercial. Similarly, as children make plans to design their creations and then present their work to others, it's natural to think about, or reflect on, the quality of their work and how it was received by the audience. From our perspective, analysis and reflection represent the deep-level thinking and metacognition that is ultimately embedded into *all* of the other elements of PDI.

Guiding questions aligned to each of these interconnected PDI practices (see Figure 1.4) can serve to support your initial planning of one or more of these sets of practices without being constrained by the use of technology. The question in the center encourages you to then consider the role that technology may, or may not, play in the teaching and/or learning connected to these experiences. As you generate ideas, keep in mind the most powerful learning opportunities have personal relevance and purpose; this means letting students be successful from the beginning but also striving to enrich their knowledge and understanding in new ways. In Chapter 2, we'll introduce a number of ideas for how you might differentiate the levels of support and enrichment you provide to meet the unique needs of learners in your classroom.

Varying Levels of Supported Inquiry

In any new learning situation, skilled teachers make intentional decisions about how much support to offer, when to offer it, and to whom it should be offered. Planning for teaching that supports learning within an inquiry-based model is no different. At first we give lots of support through modeling, thinking aloud, and working together. When students are able, they begin to move through the inquiry process with less guidance and more independence. As we will explore, this gradual release of responsibility may occur within a single lesson or unit or over an extended time.

As the teacher varies the intensity of support, learners transition through the levels of modeled inquiry, structured inquiry, guided inquiry, and open inquiry (see Table 2.1). These levels provide initial, flexible guidelines for how you might tailor your inquiry and digital experiences depending on the amount of openness and the cognitive demands required. Over time, and with assistance, learners of any age become more creative, more positive, and more independent in how they conduct their inquiries in ways that prepare them for problem solving in the real world.

Find additional ways to engage with these ideas in the online study guide for Chapter 2.

bit.ly/PDIstudyguide

TABLE 2.1

LEVELS OF INQUIRY THAT GRADUALLY RELEASE RESPONSIBILITIES TO THE LEARNER	
Modeled Inquiry	Learners observe models of how the leader (a teacher or another student) makes decisions. This might be the sole purpose of an inquiry experience or the leader might model specific practices while explaining to learners what is expected of them in less supported phases of inquiry.
Structured Inquiry	Learners make choices that depend on guidelines and structure given by the leader. Structure often varies according to learner age, abilities, and interests.
Guided Inquiry	Learners make choices in the inquiry that lead to deeper understanding guided by some parameters given by the leader.
Open Inquiry	Learners make all of the decisions, and the focus is based primarily on their interests, wonderings, and goals. There is little to no guidance from the leader.

In many ways, this gradual release of responsibility mirrors phases of comprehensive literacy instruction that are used to guide learners through modeled, shared, guided, and independent reading experiences matched to their individual needs (see Pearson et al. 2007). This continuum also parallels supports for young children through stages of modeled, interactive, guided, and independent writing processes. As you choose to incorporate digital texts and tools into these reading and writing practices, additional considerations emerge. Together, these four levels of inquiry can provide tangible approaches for how to structure and facilitate classroom-based digital inquiry experiences for a variety of learners.

Understanding the Levels of Inquiry in Practice

Let's look at each of these levels of inquiry in practice to see how different levels serve different purposes in the learning process. First, notice how within a single unit of study, these levels can be interwoven to meet student needs. Ari Orefice, a kindergarten teacher, integrated a series of smaller inquiries into a four-week unit in November and December focused on animals and habitats. She designed many opportunities for children to collaboratively read, explore, and discuss books about fish and tadpoles, owls, and wolves. Two questions that guided their inquiries were (1) How do animals form communities, work together, and use and adapt to their environments? and (2) What are some differences between fiction and nonfiction texts?

Across their inquiry experiences, Ari intentionally varied the levels of support she provided to accomplish different purposes. For example, she used *modeled* inquiry practices to explicitly demonstrate how to get different kinds of information from informational and narrative texts to answer their questions. Other days, Ari used *structured* inquiry practices, such as when she encouraged children to read whichever books they wanted, but then offered them a graphic organizer on chart paper to help structure their class discussion and sharing of findings into four categories (food, characteristics, habitat, and other). She also attached student work to the bottom of the class chart (see Figure 2.1), to remind her students that they are partners in learning and encourage them to extend the class outline by incorporating their own emerging ideas.

In other parts of the same unit, Ari structured her imagination station center activities (see Figure 2.2) to include index cards labeled with specific vocabulary students were learning about. However, children were free to bring in other materials and creatively express their emerging understanding of animal habitats in much more open-ended ways. Her kindergartners brainstormed suggestions about what furniture and props to keep in the area, what to remove, and what would be needed to transform the center from a house/school area into a woodland.

FIGURE 2.1 Graphic organizer for structured inquiry

Over several days, a pond was added as a place for acting out the life cycle of the frog, and children made additional props for the woodland area. Then, after reading about the life cycle of salmon, a river was added, to extend their learning even further through active play and conversation. Eventually, children created trees in the area as well. Quite naturally, they asked for more index cards to label the additional items they added to their woodland habitat.

These teaching decisions and learning experiences aligned more with *guided* inquiry practices, in which the teacher guides the learning with some parameters, and then invites children to make personal choices as they interact with materials in ways that lead to deeper understanding of important content. Importantly, not at all inquiry practices need to involve technology to give children agency in their learning.

FIGURE 2.2 Imagination station center with children's construction of a woodland habitat

Now in her third year of integrating inquiry-based practices into her classroom, Ari is exploring ways of moving toward *open* inquiry for those kindergartners who are ready for that degree of independence. She encourages students to use informational books and classroom activities as a springboard to research, draw, and write about topics and questions they are interested in. Sometimes students work individually and other times in small groups. As projects and products emerge, Ari thinks of ways to link and display these together under a common theme on their class website or hallway bulletin board. Talking about these connections helps her kindergartners bridge their understanding from personally generated ideas to larger concepts in their world. Chapter 9 offers a closer look at Ari's classroom inquiry into animals and their habitats.

Scaffolding Levels of Inquiry Experiences over Time

Discovering the most effective ways to prepare students for more independence means considering the range of inquiry experiences students will have over time. Contemplating the optimal levels of support and learning is beneficial for individual lessons and longer units, as well as across the year. Teachers acknowledge what is developmentally appropriate, they consider how best to progress with teaching important skills, and they strive for ways to gradually release responsibility to students. Ari's weaving of leveled inquiry practice into a single unit, as described previously, represents one way that PDI plays out in elementary school classrooms.

In this next example, Jeremy Gusky, a fifth-grade teacher, took a more holistic approach for planning toward inquiry by systematically decreasing levels of support across the school year. Like many schools, Jeremy's district requires that all fifth graders create a capstone project at the end of the year; this is where each student researches a self-selected topic, creates a project, and then presents it to a large audience. Starting with the end in mind, Jeremy's planning involved (1) identifying the learning needs of his students, (2) creating a yearlong progression of skill-building units of study, and (3) designing a process that would result in students gradually solidifying their research abilities and the sustained focus needed to complete the capstone and turn their knowledge into action. As you read, notice how Jeremy progressively released responsibility to his students over the course of the year, as PDI practices flowed from modeled and structured inquiry practices toward guided and open inquiry.

Jeremy began the school year in September with a *modeled inquiry* experience designed to introduce, talk through, and reinforce research skills as his students worked to answer the question, How are people shaped by the world around them at various stages in their lives? Using a specific, detailed example (the life of Jackie Robinson), Jeremy followed the biography outline, including the place of birth, childhood, middle years (including school experiences), and adulthood/new family, and influences throughout this person's life. Jeremy's explicit modeling helped students learn about the inquiry process and important online reading skills: using keywords to search, understanding the layout of different websites, using a website's internal search features, and realizing the differences between search engines and the search features of a specific website. These demonstrated practices then served to lay the foundation for future research.

Jeremy intentionally narrowed the scope of this inquiry project so students could focus primarily on structured outlining and research skills. Students needed to follow his biography model, but they were able to select the person they wanted to study. Jeremy purposely did not ask students to create a formal presentation in this phase, and he chose not to formally grade students on this assignment. Instead, he offered constructive feedback in a conference setting, and students worked in small groups to review, compare, and reflect on a few other students' projects. Then, his fifth graders informally shared their work with parents, as well as with their first-grade buddy class.

By November, most of Jeremy's students were ready to choose which type of outline they would use to organize their information. He introduced an inquiry study focused on the question, How have inventors turned their ideas into realities? This unit fluctuated between *modeled and structured levels of inquiry*, depending on individual student needs. Jeremy began by modeling the creation of a schematic web and then discussing alternative ways that students might outline their project depending on their topic. This gave students the opportunity to take on a bit more ownership by deciding which note-taking structure best aligned with their topical study.

As part of this two-month inquiry, Jeremy also sought to strengthen students' research skills by focusing on specific strategies, such as cross-referencing, creating a proper works cited page, and recognizing the differences between .com and .org websites. He suggested ways to find the most useful resources, reviewed how to paraphrase informational texts, and taught about suspicious elements to watch for on fake websites—effectively blending instruction in print and digital literacy practices.

Students were asked to use note cards to visually organize what they learned on trifold boards, as shown in Figure 2.3. As they worked, Jeremy shared tips on the thoughtful placement of images and how to neatly use colored borders for visual appeal. As they prepared for their oral presentation, students were taught oral presentation skills, such as keeping their eyes on the speaker, watching their speaking pace, and crafting a compelling ending. Students received a grade only on their trifold board. Jeremy wanted students to grow and practice their oral presentation skills at this point in the year, so he gave students suggestions rather than a grade for that portion of the project.

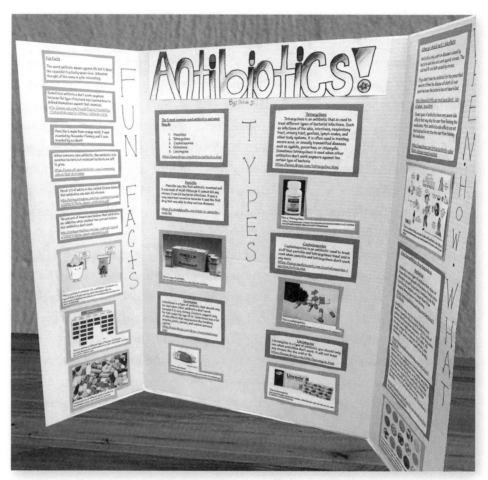

FIGURE 2.3 One fifth grader's incredible invention project

In February, Jeremy began a *guided inquiry* study during which students investigate how an animal's physical characteristics allow it to survive in the environment. Armed with a number of practiced skills, his students were now responsible for selecting an animal of interest, generating open-ended research questions, designing their own outlines, independently conducting research, and sharing what they learned in a well-designed slideshow and oral presentation. Building on previously taught skills, Jeremy urged his students to paraphrase rather than copy sources, giving a brief reminder lesson on this topic. To guide students toward success, he asked them to create a shared digital document for each section, with the URL from each source copied and pasted into the document. As Jeremy monitored project progress, he checked whether students were using their own language, and then had students delete these links in their final version.

At this point in the year, Jeremy also taught students how to embed video clips and create slides with fewer words from their note cards. They were reminded to stay focused on their essential question and to judiciously use special effects to enhance the quality of the slideshow, rather than cause distractions. They enjoyed learning how to effectively use the laser pointer and the forward button and how to show items in diagrams. Students collaboratively analyzed and reflected on practice performances, as they watched and gave feedback to each other. Students then received a grade on both their visual slideshows and their oral presentations.

In May and June, students engaged in the culminating capstone *open inquiry* experience. By then, they were able to put into action the thinking, research, creation, and presentation skills built from the previous inquiry projects. To begin, each student completed an interest inventory to identify a personal interest or curiosity to explore. As students analyzed their inventory, they discussed ideas with Jeremy and their classmates to derive their essential question.

Students were expected to produce a structured project timeline, which included completing the interest inventory, creating a curriculum wheel organizer, finalizing the selection of an essential question, conducting research from a range of sources, synthesizing work, reflecting on the inquiry process, making a project proposal, developing the slideshow, and presenting it to an audience. Although students worked on their own topic, they also connected with their peers to share websites and other resources as part of their personal inquiries. Each student proudly presented a ten-minute multimedia slideshow to a large group of parents, followed by a celebration where the audience had an opportunity to look at student materials.

Looking across these sequenced inquiry experiences, Jeremy intentionally planned ways to scaffold, support, and empower students to have more agency in their learning. Through opportunities to wonder, collaborate, reflect, and share their work, he facilitated their large-group, small-group, and eventual personal inquiries in ways that gradually decreased the amount of modeled structures and explicit supports. In doing so, his students were able to handle the demands of research, enjoyed creating multimedia projects that expressed their thinking, and were excited about presenting to a larger audience.

Designing Opportunities for Agency

As you seek to understand the teacher's role in supporting levels of inquiry, it's also critical to clarify what role students will play in their learning. In her article, "Seven Rules of Engagement: What's Most Important to Know About Motivation to Read," Linda Gambrell (2011) summarizes research that suggests giving children opportunities to choose what they read and how to engage with these materials allows them to take ownership of their learning and leads to increases in competence, understanding, intrinsic motivation, and academic performance. In addition, teaching children how to find and choose real-world learning materials connected to their own interests fosters feelings of autonomy and personal responsibility.

At each level of inquiry, we can improve learning and foster personal engagement by giving young children some degree of choice and responsibility for some aspects of their own learning. During modeled inquiry, for example, elementary-aged children can help generate an initial set of wonderings about the topic in question; in turn, these wonderings can serve as the focus of a minilesson where a teacher *models* a certain part of the inquiry process (e.g., how to use a search engine to find a video about those wonderings; how to use a digital comic book tool to illustrate what you've learned about those wonderings; how to fine-tune your questions as you reflect on initial discoveries). In this way, even modeled inquiry can offer opportunities for children to take part in the questioning process. Similarly, as part of a *structured inquiry* experience, children may be required to read the same texts and discuss the same ideas or they may choose from one of several different thinking prompts you crafted and select any three of the five texts you curated to scaffold their discussion around the inquiry topic.

In *guided* and *open* inquiry, children may have opportunities to choose which of three digital tools might work best, for example, or to decide, with a partner, whether to express ideas through writing a poem or creating video. Over time, and with support, children learn how and why to select texts and tools to meet their interests and needs. Bound choice opportunities can slowly be unbound and opened up to encourage more choice and responsibility, which in turn engages children as active partners in learning.

Although the four levels of inquiry are useful by themselves, most inquiry experiences don't really fit cleanly within a single category—especially when our aim is to gradually release more responsibility to learners when they are ready.

Plans for a project might initially be framed as one level of inquiry, but as work begins, it becomes apparent that some students may need (or want) a different amount (intensity) of support. Teaching for authentic inquiry often demands moving flexibly across the levels of support depending on the situation and the purpose (Friesen and Scott 2013).

So, the challenge then becomes determining where in the inquiry process we can gradually begin to let go, while still offering support when needed. Is there only one "right way" to release responsibility? How do differences across classrooms, students, and inquiry projects influence where in our plans we provide more (or less) structure?

Although the answer is complicated, there are at least four questions to consider as you look for opportunities for students to have more agency—opportunities to be actively engaged, make choices, share their preferences, and ultimately take ownership of their learning as part of the PDI process. These questions include:

1. Who *generates* the question or problem that guides the inquiry experience?

2. Who *selects* or *designs* the resources and tools used at different phases of the inquiry?

3. Who *selects* or *designs* the procedures taken and the products created as part of the inquiry?

4. Is the answer to the inquiry question known in advance?

Answers to the first three questions draw your attention to ways of progressing along a continuum from teacher-guided to learner-guided practices. We've depicted these ideas on our diagram for weaving student agency into inquiry (see Figure 2.4). A response to the fourth question is influenced by the idea that often inquiry units in elementary school address curriculum-informed questions to which teachers will likely know the answers. Such questions are completely appropriate, at times. However, ultimately, exploring problems where no one, even the teacher, quite knows all of the answers more closely resembles authentic open inquiry.

The dotted lines on each continuum in our diagram represent a progression that is more fluid, and less rigid, because there are many factors involved in differentiating supports for all students. The top row of the figure and gradual shading of colors across each row from darker (more support) to lighter (less support) is a reminder that often, teacher-guided practices occur as part of modeled or structured levels of inquiry, and more learner-guided practices reflect movement toward guided and open inquiry. Overall, the diagram is designed to encourage purposeful but flexible decision making about when and how we empower learners as part of PDI.

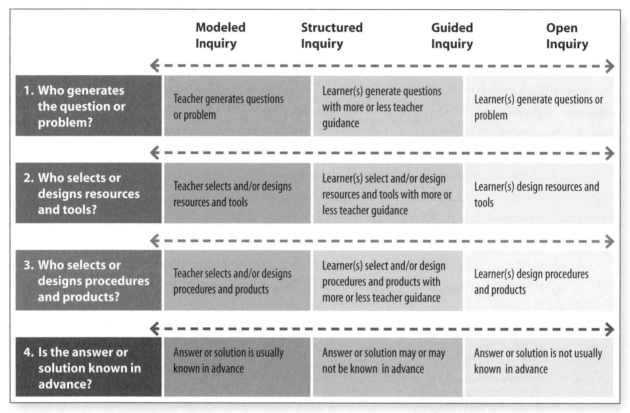

	Modeled Inquiry	Structured Inquiry	Guided Inquiry	Open Inquiry
1. Who generates the question or problem?	Teacher generates questions or problem	Learner(s) generate questions with more or less teacher guidance		Learner(s) generate questions or problem
2. Who selects or designs resources and tools?	Teacher selects and/or designs resources and tools	Learner(s) select and/or design resources and tools with more or less teacher guidance		Learner(s) design resources and tools
3. Who selects or designs procedures and products?	Teacher selects and/or designs procedures and products	Learner(s) select and/or design procedures and products with more or less teacher guidance		Learner(s) design procedures and products
4. Is the answer or solution known in advance?	Answer or solution is usually known in advance	Answer or solution may or may not be known in advance		Answer or solution is not usually known in advance

FIGURE 2.4 Four locations for gradually weaving learner agency into levels of inquiry

Adapted from Marie Kellow's (2006) interpretation of Marshall Herron's (1971) work

Our thinking about student agency in relation to inquiry levels as represented in Figure 2.4 is greatly informed by Jan-Marie Kellow, an educator from New Zealand who is passionate about digital inquiry and the way digital technologies and inquiry-based learning can make a difference for students. In her report *Inquiry Learning in an ICT-Rich Environment*, Jan-Marie sums up her research on how information and communication technologies were used to implement inquiry-based learning with primary school students. You can find her report online at bit.ly/kellowinquirylearning. Jan-Marie's ideas about varied levels of support build on original work by Marshall Herron, who developed the Herron Scale to evaluate the amount of inquiry in science lessons in relation to four levels of inquiry. You can read more in Herron's (1971) article, "The Nature of Scientific Enquiry," published in *School Review*.

Jan Marie Kellow's Inquiry Learning in an ICT-Rich Environment bit.ly/kellowinquirylearning

Tailoring Digital Inquiry Practices to Match Your Students' Needs

Throughout this book, you will see how different teachers and students at different grade levels engage in PDI practices using varied levels of support. At times, efforts to assist children with digital inquiry projects may logically cluster around one level of inquiry for most learners. In our previous examples from Jeremy, we saw that he focused on modeled inquiry during the first two months of school. At other times, children's own interests and experiences with digital inquiry projects may demand varied levels of support for different learners working within the same classroom. When Jeremy's students tried out a new technology tool to convey their learning, some students needed extra support, even though all were working in an open inquiry time. In these ways, Jeremy varied his level of support depending on the students' learning needs.

Your own comfort level and experience teaching at each level of inquiry and your expectations about what learners can do at each level also influence your decisions about the level of inquiry. Other influences include school district views, parents' attitudes, and beliefs held by the students in your classroom. But it's hard to argue against the deep and lasting learning that occurs when students are engaged and constructing knowledge.

To learn more about personal agency, Barbara Bray and Kathleen McClaskey (2016) have written a useful guide titled *How to Personalize Learning: A Practical Guide for Getting Started and Going Deeper.* In their book, they help clarify the multiple dimensions of agency, including voice, choice, engagement, motivation, ownership, purpose, and self-efficacy and how teachers can gradually move from teacher-centered to learner-driven experiences to foster agency. Kathleen McClaskey's website also has an extensive set of resources around learner agency, including visual continuums of each element of learner agency (see www.kathleenmcclaskey.com/continuums/) and a companion crosswalk of learning through agency across the stages of personalized learning environments (see www.kathleenmcclaskey.com/crosswalk-of-learner-agency-across-the-stages/).

Kathleen McClaskey's website Make Learning Personal www.kathleenmcclaskey.com

Laying the Foundation for Personal Digital Inquiry

In this chapter, you will

* learn about the cultural forces that can work together to transform the culture of your classroom

* use a self-reflection tool to intentionally guide your purposeful planning of PDI practices

* consider ways of cultivating inquiry to meet the unique needs of your students with tips for managing the learning environment, developing skills and routines, and working with texts, tools, and technologies

Find additional ways to engage with these ideas in the online study guide for Chapter 3.

bit.ly/PDIstudyguide

In Chapter 1, we introduced the four core sets of elements that we believe are critical in successfully promoting PDI practices: wonder & discover, collaborate & discuss, create & take action, and analyze & reflect. In Chapter 2, we discussed the four flexible levels of inquiry designed to gradually release responsibility to students to foster agency. In this chapter, we focus on the what, why, and how of creating classroom culture for students to experience these opportunities.

In his book *Creating Cultures of Thinking*, Ron Ritchhart (2015) argues that learning how to be curious, collaborative, and reflective happens through immersion in a culture that values and reinforces these traits. Ron explains how schools, and teachers, "send important messages about what learning is, how it happens, and what kinds of learning is of value" (20). Ron's work helps us understand how these messages are reflected in what he calls "a story of learning." That is, the beliefs, expectations, values, and routines that we promote as part of learning are important indicators of our classroom culture. If we seek to transform our classrooms into spaces that build upon and benefit from a culture of inquiry, it is important to clarify how to create and sustain such a culture with young learners.

With that in mind, we use an adapted version of Ron's framework of the cultural forces for transforming schools to help us articulate how these forces underlie our vision of PDI. From our perspective, some forces work together to provide the foundation for building a culture of inquiry in your classroom: high *expectations*, precise *language*, a preliminary *timeline*, and *modeled* ways of thinking and acting as part of inquiry.

Once this foundation has been established, it's time to consider how to orchestrate the remaining four cultural forces likely to help transform teaching and learning. This involves flexibly designing regular *opportunities* for PDI practices as part of learning and thoughtfully shaping features of the *environment*, classroom *routines*, and *interactions* to further cultivate a spirit of PDI.

In his book, Ritchhart defines opportunities as "a set of conditions or circumstances that make it possible to do something" (2015, 141). He explains that great teachers create opportunities to think deeply, to engage with others, and to create meaning—"in short, opportunities to learn." Importantly, these opportunities focus on the process as well as the products of learning. Next, we provide concrete definitions for each of these cultural forces (as pictured in Figure 3.1) to help better

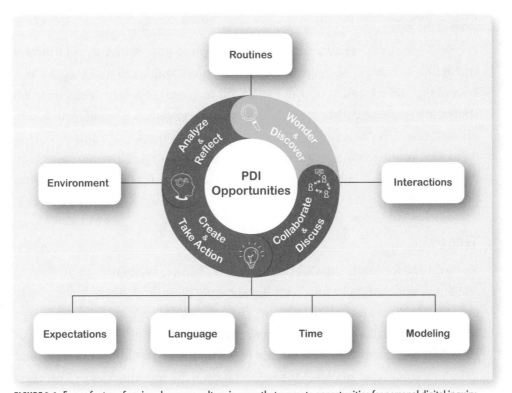

FIGURE 3.1 Forces for transforming classroom culture in ways that promote opportunities for personal digital inquiry

understand each on its own before we turn our attention to how they can work together to enrich the PDI experiences in your learning environment.

Cultural Forces for Grounding Personal Digital Inquiry

Expectations

Teachers and students who value PDI practices expect that school will be about learning and understanding rather than just going through the motions of accumulating skills and completing assignments. Teachers expect students to focus on deep learning and creative application; these teachers embrace challenge and mistakes as critical parts of learning. They also strive to act in ways that empower rather than control students to move them toward independence. Learning from mistakes and accumulating successes fosters an appreciation of what students have individually and collectively accomplished as part of their inquiry.

Language

Words shape our experiences and draw attention to important ways of thinking and acting. Teachers use language to notice, name, and highlight PDI practices. Describing and modeling how to use digital texts and tools are likely to enrich students' discovery, collaboration, creation, and reflection. Through words and actions, teachers communicate respect for and interest in students and what they bring to the learning community. Comments from teachers and peers can move learners toward productive identities as readers, writers, collaborators, and problem solvers.

Time

Finding time for inquiry is always a challenge. The key is not to *wait* for time to open up in your busy schedule. Teachers who truly value the power of inquiry *make* time for children to talk about, critique, and reflect on ideas across the school day. Building in choice, as a center option or short blocks of time at the beginning or end of a week, can also provide natural opportunities for children to wonder and talk about things that matter to them. Over time, with opportunities and practice, an inquiry mind-set builds among all in the classroom.

Modeling

Teachers who value inquiry regularly model their love of learning and openly share their wonderings and passion for certain topics. Rather than worrying about not knowing the answers to everything, teachers demonstrate PDI practices by sharing their own questions and inviting students to be co-learners as they seek out new knowledge. This helps students understand that everyone is a learner as they ask questions and practice their research skills together. Over time, the children develop a mindset that values inquiry and curiosity as integral for learning.

Cultural Forces for Growing Personal Digital Inquiry

Once a set of high expectations, precise language, a preliminary timeline, and an understanding of modeling is established as a foundation, putting the next set of cultural forces into action can more intentionally help transform teaching and learning. This process involves designing regular opportunities for the PDI core elements—wonder & discover, collaborate & discuss, create & take action, analyze & reflect—while thoughtfully shaping features of the environment, classroom routines, and interactions to further cultivate a spirit of PDI.

Opportunities

Guided by our PDI framework, teachers intentionally design learning opportunities to promote the PDI core elements to foster more student-directed inquiry. These opportunities focus on the process as well as the products of learning. Importantly, there is no specific hierarchy or order to the four core elements in our PDI framework. Learners may move back and forth through these opportunities in varied sequences with varied levels of support and varied amounts of technology use. At times, in a group setting, all of the practices may even interact simultaneously.

Environment

The physical environment conveys key values and messages for promoting the four core elements of PDI. The ways teachers arrange the furniture and what is on the wall and on the shelves can help construct spaces that support PDI.

Tables or small groups of desks enable students to easily talk and share their work with others. Brainstorming tools such as sticky notes, markers, photo collections, and wonder boards remind children their questions are important and worth saving. Anchor charts help children make connections across key ideas and prompt discussion and reflection over time.

Routines

Explicit ways of letting students know expected routines for learning and thinking as part of inquiry can support children in the early stages of PDI. Later, these same routines can be used as tools for children to take control of and use themselves while wondering, collaborating, creating, and reflecting. Time set aside to regularly reflect on these routines clearly communicates to children how and why they do things in their classroom.

Interactions

The positive ways that students interact with teachers and with each other lay the foundation for building a culture where learning is valued. Children can begin to feel empowered and confident in their growing ability to control their own learning decisions with support from their peers. In addition, time spent developing personal connections with individual students supports growth in their identity as a valued member in their classroom learning community. Positive interactions between teachers and students include focused listening and thoughtful questions. Taught through modeling and practice, these expected behaviors support collaboration and form the building blocks of a classroom culture of thinking.

On any given day, these eight forces may be alive and well in your classroom. You likely model during lessons, make strategic decisions about room arrangement, and value positive interactions. Now let's consider these forces as a unified foundation for creating a learning space that promotes the construction of knowledge. Guided by these ideas, it's time to dig in and think about how to get started with your inquiry plans.

Beginning with Self-Reflection to Guide Your Personal Digital Inquiry Practices

Although often considered the final element in an inquiry experience, reflection can also be viewed as the beginning, and most critical part of inquiry. Ideally, inquiry should lead to a learner's next burning question (Thomas and Brown 2011). So, it makes sense to start planning your journey toward PDI with close analysis and reflection about your own values and practices. In this context, analysis and reflection involve a thoughtful process of examining your practices while comparing, critiquing, evaluating, interpreting, and perhaps reenvisioning what learning and teaching look like in your classroom, and possibly in your school.

We encourage you to talk and exchange ideas with other educators who are integrating inquiry-based approaches into their classrooms or library settings. These might be colleagues at your school or they may be educators you have met online—both can serve as useful sounding boards to inspire new ideas. As part of your reflection, two important questions can help guide your work with PDI: (1) What is driving you toward PDI? and (2) Where should you focus your energy first?

What Is Driving You Toward Personal Digital Inquiry?

The first phase of your reflection involves assessing your purpose. Here, it is important to recognize that there are many different purposes and starting places from which to begin your journey. In his book *Drive*, Daniel Pink (2009) reminds us how our personal motivations drive what we do, giving us a sense of purpose and relevance to our work. The personal motivations that drove you to pick up this book and keep reading are likely to be unique to your previous experiences, your questions and interests, your current educational setting, and the changing needs of the learners with whom you work. Of course, there is no single blueprint and no two people will have exactly the same contexts and motivations. Beth and Karen elaborate on what made them want to pursue PDI in their own work contexts.

Beth's Reflection

I (Beth) see my role as a media specialist as one who supports readers as they search for answers to their personal questions. These answers may appear in a picture book or a novel that speaks to a reader's own experiences and emotional needs or a nonfiction book or a website with just the right information needed for a class project. I often share my motto with students: I am here to help you find the information and books that are important to you! At first, the students did not quite know what to make of my media center motto. It took time for us to build trust and for them to know that I meant what I said—I am here to support the learning that is important to them.

When I started the year, I knew my heart was in the right place, but I also knew my experience with teaching students to be skilled at PDI was limited. I had lots of ideas, but little firsthand knowledge of whether these ideas would effectively support students. In addition, the students had limited experiences with PDI. Our school's basal reading program had an inquiry component, and the teachers who had been around a little longer knew of the time in the past when the school district expected the program to be followed with fidelity. But this was not the case now, because the district is transitioning into a new basal reading program with no specific inquiry component.

Although this situation may at first seem bleak, I found that it actually made for the perfect storm—a teacher-librarian, students, and classroom teachers all at a similar starting point (see Figure 3.2). I started the school year embarking

FIGURE 3.2 Personal digital inquiry led to new learning for both students and new practices for the media specialist.

on my own PDI, which centered around answering the question: What are the skills and strategies students need to be able to ask questions, search for and locate information to answer their questions, understand the information, and share their new knowledge with others?

Karen's Reflection

Why PDI? I am motivated by the inquiry work, the creative possibilities of digital and nondigital tools, and being able to tailor my instruction to best meet the needs of my class. At first, I tried PDI because I wanted to improve my teaching. After seeing how PDI positively impacted student learning, I have continued to find ways to integrate it in my classroom.

Inquiry work helps my students become stronger learners because they are better able to create and articulate their own understandings. For this kind of teaching, I need to thoughtfully incorporate rich tasks or problem solving into my lessons. The goal is for my first graders to have to think more deeply and to have the agency to figure out answers themselves. To that end, my role is to provide them with the necessary background knowledge and time to discuss, wonder, analyze, and share and, then, to help facilitate the learning that unfolds.

For example, when we hatched chicks in previous years, I would introduce the incubator to the whole class, describing all of its features and explaining how it met the needs of the growing embryos, because it was designed to take the place of the hen. This year, instead, I turned the lesson into an inquiry investigation. First, I discussed with the whole class what jobs the hen had to do to take care of her eggs, and that this machine was created to do those jobs. I had two machines operating in the room, as well as the boxes they came in. Students were asked to work in pairs to observe an incubator, draw a picture of it, and figure out how it operated to replace the hen. By shifting the focus, the class truly studied how an incubator works. As a result, my students were more engaged than in previous years, and they had better questions, observations, illustrations, and discussions.

Another important reason I use PDI is because it opens up innovative possibilities by incorporating digital and nondigital tools, which makes teaching more interesting for my students and for me. Some options I like to use are creativity software, mixed-media resources, video conferencing, digital posters, and screencasting. For example, to add some much-needed energy to our chicken life cycle unit, I decided to create a ChickyWiki, which is an organized, digital resource for students I created in Google Docs that contains videos and information about chickens and related topics. This resource complements our books and hands-on activities and offers experiences beyond the classroom, such as seeing other animals hatch from eggs and observing the behavior of hens and roosters.

The third reason I use PDI is that it respects the art of teaching. Students, circumstances, and curriculum change from day to day and year to year. Since numerous interruptions and difficulties are built into working with a class of children, a teacher needs to optimize the opportunities for learning and capitalize on the teachable moments that happen each day. PDI makes it possible to flexibly find ways to teach my students and make the best choices for them, in ways that cannot be achieved with scripted, step-by-step programs. It gives me more freedom to tailor learning to meet the needs of my class and gives students opportunities to pursue passions and experiment with ideas.

For example, when studying about the chicks, I have my students research an area of interest and create a poster. One group of students wanted to learn more about combs and wattles, and they worked hard to research the topic, choose which facts to include, determine how they would take turns making the poster, create illustrations, and combine the drawings with digital text and graphics in Pixie (see Figure 3.3). The experts proudly shared their work with their parents and buddy classes.

Teaching is a challenging, complex, and meaningful vocation. When it works, it means enjoying that hum in the room of productively engaged students who are learning at a deeper level than I would have thought possible, and that's why I use PDI.

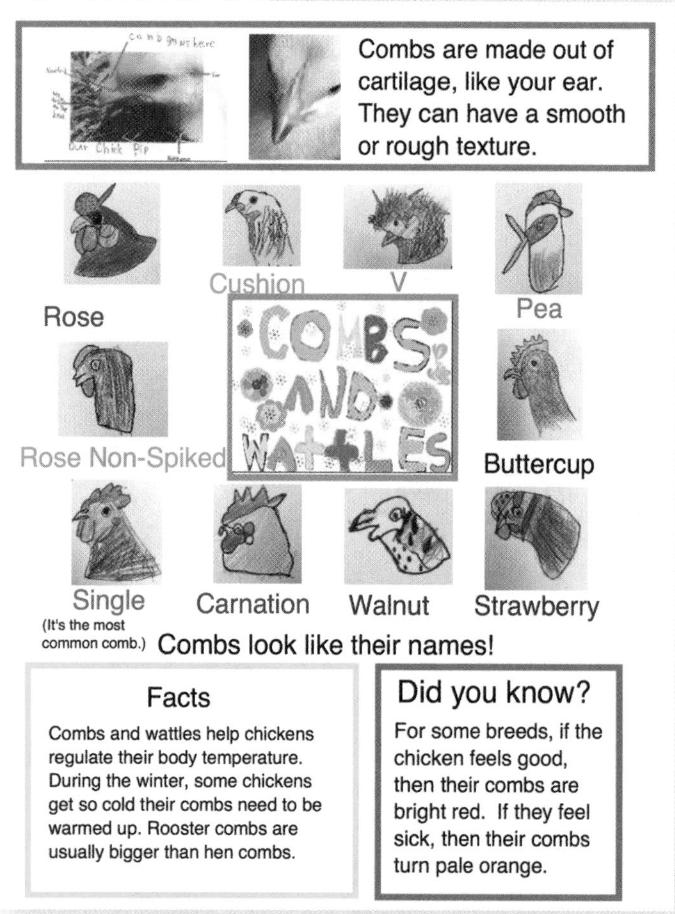

FIGURE 3.3 Poster of combs and wattles created by students studying the chicken life cycle

Why do you integrate inquiry into your instruction? Table 3.1 briefly identifies the motivations of three elementary school teachers. These teachers were asked to consider what first intrigued them about cultivating inquiry-based practices

TABLE 3.1

MOTIVATIONS FOR GETTING STARTED WITH PERSONAL DIGITAL INQUIRY	
What motivated you to consider an inquiry-based approach to instruction and what guided your exploration of personal digital inquiry?	**What seemed like a realistic starting place to explore personal digital inquiry?**
Ari (kindergarten teacher) **Motivation:** My students were frustrated and/or bored with content, and I was given the opportunity to explore how a new inquiry-based curriculum might help. **Guiding Question:** How can I re-envision my curriculum to promote children's creativity and their ability to collaborate and think critically?	I worked closely with the other kindergarten teacher at my school. Over the summer, we looked at big picture ideas, and then we planned for our first unit. We explored as we went, one week at a time, adjusting our timing and the activities we planned in response to what intrigued our students most. Then, we reflected and planned the next unit, and we just kept on learning along with our kindergartners.
Amanda (third-grade teacher) **Motivation:** My district had mandated efforts to integrate student-directed, personalized approaches to learning with technology into our teaching. **Guiding Question:** Why and how should my teaching change to incorporate strategies for personalizing learning?	I started by reading more about what student-directed learning looks like in elementary school and trying to understand how to intentionally adjust my teaching while considering students' own interests. I also started talking with other teachers to think about how to use technology so that students took on more responsibility for their own learning.
Jeremy (fifth-grade teacher) **Motivation:** My students were expected to complete a large, open-ended inquiry project at the end of the year, and I wanted to set them up for success. **Guiding Question:** How can I organize inquiry projects throughout the year to best prepare my students for an open inquiry capstone project at the end of it?	I developed a set of sequential steps with spiraling units that built up over the year into a culminating project. Each of these units focused on particular inquiry skills I wanted students to develop, so they would gradually be prepared to handle the work necessary for their final, and future, projects more independently and with greater confidence.

in their classroom and what they envisioned as a realistic starting place toward PDI. These examples, from teachers across grade levels who have grappled with many of the same issues you may be facing, remind us that many paths can lead up the same hill. Embarking on a journey to learn about PDI will likely be fraught with twists and turns, but know that you are not alone in striving to make learning meaningful, engaging, and relevant for your students.

Where Should You Focus Your Energy First?

A second phase of analysis and reflection involved in planning for PDI connects to Steven Covey's (1989) guiding principle of beginning with the end in mind. For educators, this means we begin planning by considering what we want students to know and be able to do by the end of the activity, project, or unit. The ultimate goal of PDI is to build a strong culture that values inquiry. Nested within this culture is a teacher's intentional work toward cultivating PDI practices designed to develop children's knowledge and facilitate self-directed and purposeful learning.

Yet, we all know that building and refining the culture of learning in your classroom is a huge task, and certainly not one that happens overnight! We have found that much like tackling anything big, it's helpful to break things into smaller tangible chunks that are easier to digest to help determine where to start first. This is where analysis and reflection can again play a role in the PDI planning process.

To begin, imagine that you've stepped into a learning environment that values PDI—this might be a classroom, a media center, or a space for small-group support. As you mentally look around this learning space, consider the following questions:

- What exactly would the learning space look like or sound like, and how would the space make people feel, as teachers and learners?

- What is valued in this learning space, and how do you know?

- What are the children doing, and how do they interact with classmates, peers, teacher(s), and other adults?

- What do the children and visitors remember most when they step out of this space and into the school or the community?

All of the things you imagined—the way the learning space looks and sounds, how the children and adults feel and interact—are outward signs of the culture of the learning space. This culture comes about through careful decisions made by the teacher, based on a collection of values about teaching and learning.

Using the PDI Self-Reflection Tool

One way you might explore the culture of inquiry in your own learning space is through self-reflection. The PDI self-reflection tool (see Table 3.2 and Appendix E) is designed to help guide your thinking about these ideas. To create this tool, we adapted details from Ron Ritchhart's (2015) guide for assessing teacher actions in a culture of thinking to identify the eight forces that can lead to more closely aligned actions that reflect the spirit of PDI. These eight forces work together to characterize a culture of any learning environment and, in particular, a culture designed to foster curious, thoughtful, and self-directed learners.

An important phase of your planning for PDI entails zooming in to closely analyze details of these eight cultural forces and then zooming out to appreciate how they all work together to shape and define learning in your classroom. This process helps clarify and deepen your understanding of the overlapping nuances of PDI. You can begin to acknowledge your accomplishments in each area, identify points of challenge, and decide where to focus your energy next. As teachers, we tend to be hard on ourselves, so talking with others can shed new light on your efforts from another perspective.

TABLE 3.2

PERSONAL DIGITAL INQUIRY SELF-REFLECTION TOOL

Imagine if someone stepped into your classroom on any random day and stayed for at least an hour. How likely would this visitor notice each of the following actions described here? For each statement, assign a rating between 5 and 1 using the following scale.

5 = Hard to miss it
4 = Highly likely to notice
3 = Hit or miss depending on the circumstances
2 = Not very likely to notice
1 = I doubt anyone would notice

EXPECTATIONS	Rating
1. I stress to students that solving problems and developing understanding, not only acquiring knowledge, are the goals of classroom activity and lessons.	
2. I make a conscious effort to communicate to students that using or acting on what they learn in creative ways is valued.	
3. I actively establish a set of expectations for student independence so my students are not dependent on me to answer all questions and direct all activity.	

LANGUAGE	Rating
1. I try to notice and name the thinking and learning occurring in my classroom, saying things like, "Alex is generating specific questions to guide his inquiry" or "Letitia is reflecting on whether or not that document sharing tool was useful."	
2. I give specific, targeted action-oriented feedback (oral or written) that guides students toward taking initiative in future efforts and actions, rather than generic praise comments ("good job," "great, brilliant," "well done").	
3. I use inclusive, community-building language, talking about what "we" are learning and "our" inquiry, while listening and clarifying ideas generated by the group.	

Adapted from the Cultures of Thinking Self-Assessment Tool from *Creating Cultures of Thinking: The 8 Forces We Must Master to Truly Transform Our Schools* by Ron Ritchhart ©2015. Reprinted by permission of Wiley Publishing.

TABLE 3.2 *(continued)*

TIME	Rating
1. I make a conscious effort to weave time for building relationships into everyday routines and project schedules.	
2. I provide the time and space for students to listen, reflect on their own ideas, extend the ideas of others, and share their contributions.	
3. I try to sequence activities in ways that allow students to make connections and build on what they learned previously to anticipate what they might learn in the future.	

MODELING	Rating
1. I display open-mindedness, taking risks, reflecting on my learning, and a willingness to consider alternative perspectives.	
2. I demonstrate my own curiosity, passion, and interest to students.	
3. My students and I regularly ask questions and explain our thinking as we discover new things and solve problems together.	

OPPORTUNITIES	Rating
1. I focus students' attention on discovering, discussing, analyzing, and reflecting on meaningful connections between their work and important ideas in their worlds outside of school.	
2. I provide students with opportunities to direct their own learning and become independent learners.	
3. I encourage students to use or act on their creative learning products to start conversations, raise awareness, take action, or change minds in their classroom, learning community, or beyond.	

TABLE 3.2 *(continued)*

ROUTINES	Rating
1. I use explicit routines and flexible structures to organize age-appropriate lessons that ensure we can all use technology to help us learn (e.g., use digital devices, find digital resources, work in shared documents, publish work).	
2. I set up ways to regularly document, share, and celebrate our important work with peers, with families, with the local community, and, when appropriate, with relevant audiences in the real world.	
3. I regularly share with students the purpose(s) for learning with or without technology and explain how the skill sets we are using can help to inspire curiosity, answer questions, and think deeply about our world.	

INTERACTIONS	Rating
1. I ensure that all students show a genuine interest in and respect for each other's thinking. Students are pushed to elaborate on their thinking beyond a simple answer or statement. Ideas may be critiqued or challenged, but people are not.	
2. I view students as partners in learning and encourage them to share what they know or have learned with multiple audiences whenever possible.	
3. I listen in on groups and allow them to make mistakes and collaboratively grapple with ideas, rather than always inserting myself into the process.	

ENVIRONMENT	Rating
1. I arrange the physical and digital learning spaces of my classroom to facilitate thoughtful interactions, collaborations, and discussions that vary flexibly to accommodate learner needs.	
2. My wall displays and planned activities are ongoing and flexible to invite sustained inquiry and connections across lessons and topics throughout the year.	
3. A visitor can easily recognize what I care about and value with respect to learning.	

REFLECTIONS

Which PDI practices am I especially proud of at this point in the year and why?

Which PDI practices are not as likely to be noticed at this point and why?

Which PDI practice(s) would I most like to focus on next and why?

What are my next steps to get started?

Listen in as Beth and Karen assess their own values, beliefs, and actions relative to details in the PDI self-reflection tool and then reflect on next steps toward building a stronger PDI culture in their classrooms. We all continue to be learners, and there are ways we can help ourselves improve.

Beth's Personal Digital Inquiry Self-Reflection

The beauty of being a teacher-librarian is that I get to teach the same lesson four or five times in a week, and in a way, the students are teaching me by the ways they respond to a lesson. Through reflection and tweaks, I can inch closer to making the lesson a success. With so many opportunities for do-overs, being reflective in my teaching is imperative, or I am doomed to repeat, in Groundhog Day fashion, a less effective lesson several times.

After using the PDI self-reflection tool to think back on my teaching, one area I feel good about is my creation of a learning space that encouraged thoughtful interactions, collaborations, and discussions. I think of this learning space as my classroom, the media center, and the online learning spaces I created for students. While I was responsible for teaching a myriad of standards and skills (i.e., library and technology, English language arts), I also taught social skills. Turn taking, appropriate voice level, and a posture for listening were all a part of the media center lessons. Students knew our learning space was to be a positive, safe, inviting space, where classmates could share their ideas and ask questions. Every day I reminded students of what it would take for us to learn together. I also applied these same concepts to the digital learning spaces that I created within Google Classroom, Google Drive, and Seesaw. We developed routines for appropriate ways to give classmates feedback and how to add information to a Google Doc, without changing or deleting what others have added (we learned from our mistakes!). I also came to realize that what occurs in the digital learning space can carry over into the physical space, and vice versa, so both spaces must be cultivated with clear expectations to ensure success.

Karen's Personal Digital Inquiry Self-Reflection

One aspect I like about teaching is getting the chance to reflect on my experiences from the prior year, decide on important changes, and start again with a new class. The PDI self-assessment tool confirmed my ongoing efforts to support student relationships and interactions by having a caring, respectful classroom where students feel comfortable sharing and taking risks.

Within the PDI self-reflection tool, there are several references to reflecting and taking action. Reflecting is the most important area that I want to improve. I need to schedule more time for it and preserve that time, as well as include it during activities, rather than saving it for the end. Reflecting can be hard for first graders, but it is essential work. Building in reflection pages in their journals, making a point to have students express their reflections in small groups as they work, and using screencasting as another opportunity for this learning will help ensure that these skills are practiced.

As for taking action, I grapple with this concept as it pertains to my young students. How much of taking action is really authentic or necessary with first graders? What is appropriate for them to be exposed to outside of the classroom, and what boundaries do I set regarding their privacy in a digital world? In the past, our taking action has consisted of sharing our learning with buddy classes and parents, as well as showing our projects in the hallway bulletin board and school library. In addition, the students have interviewed experts in our community. But I wonder what ways I could have students safely take action outside of our school, because I value the foundational skills it teaches for civic responsibility.

Our PDI self-reflection tool is designed to encourage you to identify your strengths and areas for growth. Recognizing what you can improve sets you on the path of your own professional inquiry. Ground this search in your purpose for exploring PDI, and you have a plan for moving forward. Reflecting on your purpose and aligning this to the current culture in your classroom and the four sets of core practices can directly inform the steps you take to plan and implement inquiry-based experiences with your students. By relying on your reflections to guide your growth, you are able to tailor your goals to the areas of PDI that match your own learning needs, which is the personal element of PDI.

4

The Nuts and Bolts of Creating a Culture of Inquiry

In this chapter, you'll learn

* strategies to help prepare and manage your learning environment in ways that cultivate inquiry-based learning

* techniques for developing foundational skills and routines associated with personal digital inquiry

* tips for working with a wide range of texts, tools, and technologies to facilitate the inquiry process

Find additional ways to engage with these ideas in the online study guide for Chapter 4.

bit.ly/PDIstudyguide

Moving forward in your PDI practice has been compared to a journey, and we have reflected on our personal journeys in the previous chapter. Preparation is an important way to ensure a successful journey, and this chapter focuses on specific strategies to support embarking on the PDI journey with your students, in your learning space.

In this chapter, we describe ways to prepare and manage the learning environment by letting all who enter your learning space know what is valued: questioning, deep thinking, discussing, creating, sharing, and reflecting. To this, we add descriptions of foundational skills and routines that will put students into the mind-set and promote the actions of constructing knowledge. A third element in the mix entails the use of texts and tools, including digital resources, which facilitate those actions we value (see Table 4.1).

Creating a culture of inquiry begins with our modeling and expectations shared on the first day of school and nurtured every day thereafter. As you read through this chapter, watch for the ways we are implementing the eight forces into the process of creating a culture of inquiry (expectations, time, language, modeling, opportunities, routines, interactions, and environment).

TABLE 4.1

STRATEGIES TO SUPPORT YOUR PERSONAL DIGITAL INQUIRY JOURNEY	
Preparing and Managing Your Learning Environment	• Make time for inquiry. • Organize a learning space. • Develop an attitude that values learning. • Foster trust and risk-taking. • Use helpful words. • Make good choices about partners. • Encourage expertise. • Consider digital options.
Developing Foundational Skills and Routines	• Develop underlying skills. • Teach communication skills. • Scaffold while resolving disagreements. • Teach ways to organize and give credit for information. • Teach visual literacy skills. • Think deeply about new learning.
Working with Texts, Tools, and Technologies	• Explore and practice with texts and tools. • Work with tools to support collaboration. • Check students' digital skills before beginning a project.

PREPARING AND MANAGING THE LEARNING ENVIRONMENT

A teacher makes literally thousands of decisions in a day, about everything from what to teach, how long to teach, where to stand, what to say, who to look at, and what to read, just to name a few. Many of these decisions can have a positive effect on promoting the four core sets of PDI elements: wonder & discover, collaborate & discuss, create & take action, and analyze & reflect. Some of your inquiry-related decisions will focus on physical elements, such as the room arrangement or the display of texts. Other decisions will seek to support social/emotional skills, such as attitudes, values, and communication, which work together to help students interact effectively and see learning as valuable. All work together to create an environment where students, guests, and the teacher know inquiry is valued.

The PDI self-reflection tool can serve as a guide for what to focus on when it comes to creating an environment that supports inquiry. Read on as teachers, during their self-reflection, share a few of the ways they create a productive learning environment:

- *I stress to students that solving problems and developing understanding, not only acquiring knowledge, are the goals of classroom activity and lessons (expectations).*

- *I use inclusive, community-building language, talking about what we are learning and our inquiry, while listening and clarifying ideas generated by the group (language).*

- *I listen in on groups and allow them to make mistakes and collaboratively grapple with ideas, rather than always inserting myself into the process (interactions).*

- *I arrange the physical and digital learning spaces of my classroom to facilitate thoughtful interactions, collaborations, and discussions that vary flexibly to accommodate learner needs (environment).*

Consider these and other elements of the self-reflection tool much like a road map on your GPS, providing a suggested path for your journey. The following strategies can support forward movement along this path.

Make Time for Inquiry

Early on, it's helpful to develop a general idea of what you want your students to experience and how much time will be allotted to the overall unit or activity. Consider opportunities for students to engage in real-world experiences that inspire authentic questions, and then make time in your planning for students to generate these questions. If time is only available for a mini-inquiry project (one or two lessons rather than an entire unit), be sure to build in a shared experience, such as reading an informational picture book, viewing a video clip, or discussing real objects, all of which can activate students' curiosity. Then, as a class, brainstorm a list of questions for possible further study. As you become more familiar with embedding inquiry into your teaching, it becomes easier to incorporate it in a variety of subjects and studies. It is important to be flexible, because sometimes students will become very engaged in a study, bringing true opportunities to do deeper work.

Organize a Learning Space

Think strategically about how to arrange the different large-group, small-group, and individual spaces in your classroom in ways that allow for talking and sharing as well as for thinking and creating. Use grouping strategies that already work for you, like a workshop model, rotating groups, and differentiated assignments or supports. Strive to help students understand how to access, use, and store books, materials, and technologies they will need to be more independent in their learning. If possible, set up two computers next to each other so that one can be used for research and the other for responses; this naturally promotes collaboration and conversation. Stock writing and research centers with a range of print and digital tools to encourage choice and creativity. Organize student work in shared folders, grouped by areas of inquiry or exploration.

Develop an Attitude That Values Learning

What we say and what we do conveys to our students what is important. At times, specific lessons about trust and community building are appropriate, and at other times, teaching occurs through conversation, feedback, and modeling. Some phrases to encourage both students and teachers to collaborate and discuss could include:

- We all learn from each other.
- Let's do this together.
- Two heads are better than one.
- Would it be all right if I give you a suggestion?
- How can we figure this out?
- How about if you do this part, and I do that part?
- Let's talk through this problem together.

The process of creating a classroom culture requires explanation, modeling, a gradual release of responsibility, and opportunities for ongoing practice. Once the expected behaviors and attitudes become more natural, occasional refresher activities may be needed to remind students of behavior that is valued and expected for collaborating and discussing.

Foster Trust and Risk-Taking

Creating a project and sharing it with others involves students taking a risk. Do I have something of value to say? What if my project isn't very good? What will happen if I circulate my idea to others in my class or beyond? Will others laugh at my attempts? Do I have the skills needed to create my project, whether these are nondigital (i.e., drawing or handwriting skills) or digital (i.e., knowing how to use a certain digital tool). Actually, the whole process of creating is fraught with opportunities for others to criticize our work, which can be scary. However, a skilled teacher can mitigate some of these emotions by creating a classroom culture of acceptance. Explicitly tell students about the culture of acceptance you expect to see in the classroom, with attention to specific qualities of their work. Model phrases of acceptance, such as, "I like where you are headed with that drawing"; "Remember, it's okay if your project doesn't look exactly like you planned, as long as you have the key components"; "When you see a classmate's project, be sure to give a positive comment and a gentle suggestion." Then, expect students to use positive phrases when they interact with each other.

Use Helpful Words

Make the concepts and vocabulary of collaborate & discuss an integral part of your teaching. During explanations and modeling, use words such as *conversation, dialogue, turn taking, consensus, listening posture*. Continually explain behavior expectations through this language. As a class, develop a list of discussion reminders (Almasi 1995), which might include:

- Stay focused.
- Be serious.
- Give encouragement.
- Take turns.
- Help, if needed.
- Don't interrupt.

Explain and model each reminder. Display a list of these in the classroom, and return to the list before, during, and after collaboration time. Once the collaborative discussion ends, it's a good time to take a few minutes to debrief about the discussion process. Model for students how to self-assess their own participation or the success of their group in following the discussion reminders. Learners can create a self-assessment checklist using the discussion reminders and ask students to spend three minutes checking themselves, and then writing a personal goal for their role in the next discussion.

Make Good Choices About Partners

For full-scale inquiry projects, determine topics students gravitate toward, and then pair students up based on interest and learning styles. For mini-inquiry activities, have students work with whoever is close by, since this activity will likely last only a few minutes. Develop a sense of how long conversations can last before they stop being productive. A teacher can revive the group by providing scaffolding at the moment through a comment such as, "I see your group is getting a bit off track. Let's refocus our thinking about the desert so we can complete part two of the project. Each person share with me one fact you have discovered so far. Then I want you to continue working for the next five minutes, and I will come back to check on your progress." We have found when all group members are interested and engaged with the topic, work teams seem to function better.

Encourage Expertise

Prompt partners or groups to see themselves as becoming experts. Emphasize the academic vocabulary of the content area being studied, so students begin to understand and use the words of the discipline in their discussions (i.e., teach the term *pollination* during a science unit; explain how to describe an object or locate characteristics during an observation). Talk to the partners/groups about the importance of developing expertise they can share with others, while also supporting each other's learning.

An environment that promotes learning is as much about the words and actions of people as the books and computers available in the space. All elements must work together to create a learning space where learners feel they can ask questions, search for information, read and analyze, and share with others.

Consider Digital Options

Before integrating technology into your inquiry instruction, it's good to know your options. First, consider what you would like to accomplish. Firm up in your mind how you envision your students using the technology to support the inquiry process. Many of the activities we suggest in this book can be done with a variety of texts, tools, devices, and configurations, including teacher demonstration, small groups, pairs, or one-to-one devices. Explore what is available in your school and district by talking to the technology support staff. Find out what devices are available, when, and for how long. Peruse the apps and programs that the district or school makes available. Become familiar with the process for accessing apps or programs not presently available. Learn more about the district's network, whether Wi-Fi or hardwired. For those just starting out, all of this information can be a bit overwhelming, so start small if you need to. Talk with your colleagues and find one good app that facilitates your students' inquiry, and give it a go.

For those seeking more guidance, Appendix A outlines specific questions to consider with respect to the kinds of digital devices, digital applications, and tool features as you plan for digital tools to enhance your classroom inquiries. We encourage you to discuss these questions with others in your district as you consider what would be most useful in supporting your vision of PDI.

Most important, keep in mind that digital texts and tools are constantly changing and evolving; as familiar ones disappear, new (and often better) ones emerge. Remember to start small, choose wisely, stay focused on your teaching and learning through relevant inquiry experiences, and grow your collection of digital tools slowly.

DEVELOPING FOUNDATIONAL SKILLS AND ROUTINES

Our goal is to make inquiry a habit, so that wondering, collaborating, creating, and reflecting come as naturally to students as math facts and spelling words. Habits take time and practice to form. Skills provide a foundation for developing

inquiry into a regular part of teaching and learning. Examples of PDI self-reflection items that guide the development of foundational skills and routines include:

- *I regularly share with students the purpose(s) for learning with or without technology and explain how the skill sets we are using can help to inspire curiosity, answer questions, and think deeply about our world* (routines).

- *I display open-mindedness, taking risks, reflecting on my learning, and a willingness to consider alternative perspectives* (modeling).

- *I provide the time and space for students to listen, reflect on their own ideas, extend the ideas of others, and share their contributions* (time).

Reflecting on our teaching and making plans to implement additional strategies support teachers and students in the creation of a strong base for PDI.

Develop Underlying Skills

Give students practice with the underlying skills of

- improving their observations,
- describing their findings,
- asking questions to enrich understanding, and
- helping them know where to look for answers to their questions.

Students who are used to noticing details in books, adding description to their stories, clarifying their understanding with questions, and incorporating new words into their vocabulary will have more experience with these skills. Help students to understand that when they do ask questions, it is important to go to reliable resources to seek answers to conduct research.

Teach Communication Skills

Sometimes students must be specifically taught the skills they need to productively collaborate and discuss. These skills include listening effectively, taking turns, and speaking directly. Have students take turns in conversations for both listening and speaking. Begin by teaching this skill with partners, then expand to groups of three and four students. Some models of turn taking suggest the teacher set a timer for each speaker, thus ensuring that each person gets equal opportunity to share their ideas. Encourage students to notice their partners' interactions and to be sensitive to times when a person pauses to think, rather than jump in during a lull in the conversation. Teach students to be aware of their personal conversation style and that of their classmates. Also, teach students how to balance the group interactions by getting the quiet individual to speak up and the more dominant one to listen more. Encourage and practice the use of effective listening posture (i.e., sitting up, eyes tracking the speaker, head nodding). Model and encourage students to listen to each other's point of view as part of the process of coming to consensus.

Scaffold Through a Disagreement

Teach students how to resolve issues if group members cannot agree. This may entail providing scaffolding in the moment that guides students through a rough patch in the discussion. Model and have students repeat to their partner a statement such as, "I would like us to talk about another way to do this." It's also helpful to teach students strategies for resolving disagreements. The tried-and-true rock-paper-scissors is a problem-solving tool many children use and understand, and guiding children to this, or another routine, when an agreement cannot be reached can be a huge factor in a group's ability to move on and be productive.

Teach Ways to Organize and Give Credit for Information

Inquiry gives students opportunities to read, view, and analyze and then talk, write, and draw about their thinking—all activities that involve constructing new knowledge. Encourage the use of outlines, graphic organizers, and storyboards to help learners organize and share the information they collect. Teach students how to gather information through reading, listening, or viewing; how to analyze and sift out the important details; and how to use a paper-based or digital organizational tool to summarize and represent these details and their interpretation in their own words and creative format (see Table 4.2 for more ideas). In addition, it's helpful to teach students a system for organizing their work online using folders, tags, and a standard file-naming system. These organizational habits can be carried with them into their future digital work. Take time to model for students how to locate the name of a particular author or creator——and how to give them credit for their creative work.

TABLE 4.2

TOOLS FOR ORGANIZING INFORMATION	
Organizational Tool	**Format and Examples**
Mind Mapping and Note-Making Tools	Mind mapping, the process of making notes by using visuals, color, shapes, and lines to organize information, can be done on paper or with a graphic organizer tool, (i.e., Inspiration, Popplet, Mind Mash, and Timeline). Cornell Notes (Pauk and Owens 2010) and one-pagers (see McAndrews 2015) are specific ways to organize information. Effective note-making tools include the use of columns, numbers, bullets, headings, phrases, abbreviations, and sketches. A summary, written soon after making notes, will help to solidify an understanding of key ideas.
Annotating Tools	Making notes right on a text, or on a screenshot of a text, lets students leave tracks of how their thinking is being transformed by what they read. Sticky notes on paper work great for this process. Digital tools such as Seesaw, Explain Everything, ShowMe, and Easy Annotate let users highlight, draw, write, and make a voice recording about important information.
Storyboards	A storyboard provides a template for sequencing information or scenes in a story or organizing information and images to be presented in a slideshow or video or a dramatization. Storyboards can be drawn as a series of boxes on paper or created using digital storyboard apps such as Storyboarder and Directr.
Bulleted or Numbered List	Creating a list of the top ten, or so, facts facilitates the process of selecting the most important information and organizing into a succinct format. Lists can be created on paper, or digitally, using tools such as Padlet or Google Docs, where partners or a small group can collaboratively add their ideas to the shared list.
Images with Descriptive Text	Photos, sketches, and notes can serve as a useful collection of information, written in an interactive notebook, typed, or saved in a voice recording using apps such as Apple's Pages. Evernote lets users embed a voice memo within a document containing text and images and ThingLink makes it easy to digitally connect images, with text annotations, drawings, voice, video, or other forms of rich media.

Teach Visual Literacy Skills

Visual literacy is the process of interpreting meaning from a visual image or expressing an idea by creating a visual image. Diagrams, maps, charts, tables, timelines,
photos, and video give students the opportunity to think of ideas in a new way and
present information in a different format. Expressing ideas through visuals may
better match the learning needs of students who struggle with written or spoken
language. In their book *Discovering Digital Literacy: Teaching Digital Media and
Popular Culture in the Elementary School,* Renee Hobbs and D. Cooper Moore
(2013) focus on teaching children the skills for creating multimedia projects. In
addition to creating images, students can search for images online and repurpose
them to meet their needs. Your teaching can provide support as students:

- Use copyright-free websites, such as Creative Commons, to locate images
  for projects.

- Choose images in a thoughtful way, making sure that the image aligns
  with the inquiry focus and adds information to the project (see following
  example).

- Cite the creator/publisher of the image. Encourage students to look beyond
  resources such as Google Images or Pinterest, which serve as collection
  points, to locate the original source of an image so proper credit can be given.

An example from Beth's teaching:

During a fourth-grade library lesson, I taught students a process for close viewing
by analyzing images found online (see Figure 4.1). First, I modeled how to choose
an image of a yellow spotted lizard, an animal from the fiction book *Holes* that
the class was reading for a novel study. Using the Creative Commons website,
I searched for images labeled for noncommercial use with modification, and
selected an image with a variety of details in the background. While looking over
the image as a whole, I thought aloud, pointing out the details of the cactus, the
sandy ground, and the rocky hillside in the background. I described the way these
details helped me to understand more about a lizard's habitat. Next I closed my
eyes and described what I could see from the image in my mind's eye. Then I
took another look at the image, pointing out the path of my gaze, moving from
left to right and top to bottom. This time I pointed out a detail that I missed at
first glance—the lizard chose to sit in the sun, rather than in the nearby shade.

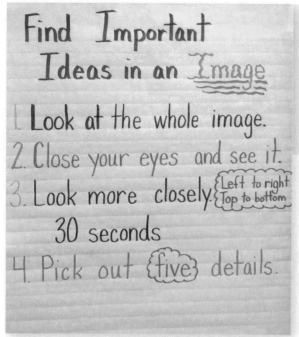

FIGURE 4.1 Finding important ideas in an image

Lastly, I made written notes about important details gleaned from the image. With this information, and the image itself, I was ready to create my slideshow. On each slide I included a URL, or web link, for the image, copying this in the lower right corner of the slide as a way to cite the source.

Think Deeply About New Learning

The skills for analyzing and reflecting must be taught directly, modeled in the context of real learning, and practiced often; the following strategies focus on ways for you and your students to reflect on learning, celebrate accomplishments, and plan for what comes next. "Deep learning happens when you examine your ideas from all sides and from other points of view" (Boss and Krauss 2007, 56).

Reflection can be woven into the school day. Thinking about how and what you learned begins with simple reflection activities and gradually moves to ones that demand more and deeper thinking.

- Your exit ticket to move from science to recess is to write down one new fact you learned today and whether you read it or viewed it.

- Draw a sketch of what you learned, label the parts, then explain your learning to your partner.

Focus on what students learned and how they learned it. Ask why and encourage students to elaborate. Give students opportunities to help create reflection questions. Make a space for students to think through problems they encountered while learning and how they tried to solve these.

To learn more about visual literacy, check out Steve Moline's book *I See What You Mean: Visual Literacy K–8* (2012), which provides lots of useful information and examples of visuals and graphic design elements, such as the effective use of layout, font, headings, and bullets to convey your message.

Our eventual goal is for students to analyze and reflect on their learning without our prompting, to internalize this reflection, and to use the ideas to learn more and in more effective ways. To do this, students must feel safe to admit when their work may not meet their own expectations. Honest reflection can occur in a classroom culture where students can take the risk of acknowledging their successes and failures.

Taking a candid look at your performance is not always easy, and at first, we find that young children often respond that their work is always good. Hopefully, in modeling your own reflections, you are taking that risk by being honest, rather than always positive, and emphasizing the process of learning, rather than only the final product. Below, we have provided a list of questions to prompt reflection.

Making inquiry a habit of thinking occurs more easily when inquiry is a routine part of the school day, whether through formal or informal opportunities to ask questions, searching for information, and sharing this with others. While we are on this journey of implementing PDI, consider the skills and routines much like a traveler considers a GPS and a cooler full of provisions—essential. Through instruction, modeling and practice, and a gradual release of responsibility, students can begin to see inquiry as a way of thinking and learning.

Sixteen Reflective Questions Every Learner Can Use

1. Define some of your most challenging moments. What made them so?

2. Define some of your most powerful learning moments. What made them so?

3. What would you say is the most important thing you learned personally? As a team?

4. When did you realize that you had come up with your final best solution?

5. How do you feel your solution relates to real-world situations and problems?

6. What do you feel most got in the way of your progress, if anything?

7. How well did you and your team communicate overall?

8. What were some things your teammates did that helped you to learn or overcome an obstacle?

9. How did you help others during this process?

10. Were your goals mostly met, and how much did you deviate from them if any?

11. What did you discover as being your greatest strengths? Your biggest weaknesses?

12. What would you do differently if you were to approach the same problem again?

13. What would you do differently, from a personal standpoint, the next time you work with the same group or a different one?

14. How can you better support and encourage your teammates on future projects?

15. How will you use what you've learned in the future?

16. How did you show the values of our classroom or school in your work as a team?

(adapted from Watanabe-Crockett 2017)

WORKING WITH TEXTS, TOOLS, AND TECHNOLOGIES

Inquiry is a process, but it relies on texts, tools, and technologies that facilitate this process. Texts may include a print book or magazine from the library, a digital book from the website Epic! (getepic.com), or an article from a kid-friendly website. Tools could be note cards, sticky notes, or a highlighter (pen or digital). Technologies would include websites and apps that support students' inquiry process, such as Google Docs (a document sharing site); a website for curating useful web links related to a topic (e.g., Diigo); or an app for recording a reflection (e.g., Flipgrid or Seesaw). The items from the PDI self-reflection tool remind us of elements we might expect to see in a classroom where PDI is a priority:

- *I actively establish a set of expectations for student independence so my students are not dependent on me to answer all questions and direct all activity* (expectations).

- *I focus students' attention on discovering, discussing, analyzing, and reflecting on meaningful connections between their work and important ideas in their worlds outside of school* (opportunities).

- *I regularly share with students the purpose(s) for learning with or without technology and explain how the skill sets we are using can help to inspire curiosity, answer questions, and think deeply about our world* (routines).

The tools, texts, and technologies form the backbone of inquiry work, but these are not an end to themselves. Reading an informational text is an important component of searching for information, and creating a digital slideshow lets us share ideas with others. But when reading is embedded within a process of inquiry, especially one based on students' own questions, the connections between what we do and why we do it become clear. The following strategies can support students' choice and voice as they seek information and share it with others.

Explore and Practice with Texts and Tools

In any part of the PDI process, provide opportunities for students to practice using both digital and nondigital tools as part of their inquiry such as those listed in Table 4.3 and Appendixes C and D.

TABLE 4.3

NONDIGITAL AND DIGITAL TOOLS	
Activities involving nondigital tools offer natural springboards for learning.	**Activities involving digital tools provide students with other creative ways to deepen knowledge, express ideas, take action, or reflect on their learning.**
• Exploration tools (using magnifying glasses or microscopes) • Measurement tools (measuring with rulers or protractors) • Digital procedures (logging into the computer, starting/stopping videos, taking/storing photos) • Information retrieval tools (reading a nonfiction book, searching for information with a child-appropriate search engine or a school library database) • Small, inexpensive materials can be studied for hands-on activities (like a seed or pollen)	• Creativity software (Pixie or Wixie) • Creative expression software (Stationery Studio, Glogster) • Graphic organizer (Padlet, Kidspiration) • Screencasting (Seesaw)

Practice with texts and tools (digital and otherwise) can lead to success with broader experiences. Some ways to devote time for tool exploration and practice as part of authentic inquiry may include the following:

- Create a discovery station in your classroom, where students can observe items at their own pace of interest over time.

- Use digital or print inquiry boards, notebooks, journals, or class books to record and honor questions; help students learn how to pursue answers, and to record and remember their previous work (including books, online resources, experts, interviews).

- Create a "What is it?" journal where students can deepen their knowledge about concepts in a fiction or nonfiction text.

- Set up manageable discovery experiences such as a mini science lab or a makerspace area with a reason for students to look for specific things or discover concepts on their own. Let students explore as a way to better understand concepts.

- Give students opportunities to zoom in (e.g., see what pollen looks like with magnifying glasses and flashlights).

- Collect information and ideas in a digital space (save and access files, create a shared document).

Work with Tools to Support Collaboration

A collaboration station could include clipboards, paper and pencils for note taking, sticky notes, scotch tape, staplers, glue sticks—supplies useful for jointly sharing and revising ideas. Knowing how to use digital tools could also be helpful. Students may be sitting in the same room, collaborating on a shared online document or interacting in a chat space or working from another site, such as the media center, special education classroom, or even away from school. Teach students proper screen etiquette (i.e., typing in all caps means a person is upset). Also teach how to create a shared document, using Google Docs or another shared space, and how to add information without deleting a teammate's work. At first, it's important to establish routines, such as the teacher creating the document and a designated space for each student to add his or her contribution. Show students how to look at the document history to see who has made changes. Talk about how it feels when someone changes your work and emphasize being respectful of each person's ideas, while also building on these ideas for a team project.

Demonstrate how to use an audio recording app, and encourage students to record a portion of their discussion, in case they need to be reminded later of the details. Model using a note-taking app (e.g., Apple Notes, Notability) or an app that lets students communicate, using video, audio, or chat. The use of online collaboration tools lets students participate in learning activities with community experts or with classmates who are away from school due to prolonged illness or travel. Designate a class or group expert who has additional knowledge about a particular tool and can support others. Select tools that aim toward higher-level thinking skills. Teach students the skills they will need to become more independent in their use of tools, especially digital ones. For example, model the sequence for logging onto a computer or tablet, starting/stopping videos, or taking photos with a tablet. Sharing useful tips for using digital tools sets students on a path towards being problem solvers for their own learning.

Check Students' Digital Skills Before Beginning a Project

Be careful about assuming that students know how to do more than they actually do when it comes to using digital tools. Research suggests that we overestimate the skills of younger and older students because they have grown up surrounded by digital texts and tools, when in reality, students are not always sure how to use them wisely in learning contexts (see Bennett, Maton, and Kervin 2008).

Additionally, students may overestimate their skills at using digital tools for learning, because they are excited to get started or want to seem proficient to the teacher or peers. When Beth started an activity for students to create a digital slideshow presentation, she asked students to raise their hands if they knew how to use Google Slides. Eighty percent of the students raised their hands. However, when she asked them to create a practice slide with a sentence and an image,

Digital Native Versus Digital Wisdom

Mark Prensky, the creator of the term *digital natives* (Prensky 2001), has recanted this line of thinking and replaced it with the need to more explicitly foster "digital wisdom" among both children and adults growing up in a digital world (Prensky 2011).

Prensky Digital Wisdom
bit.ly/PrenskyDigitalWisdom

the activity derailed when 90 percent of the students asked for help. You might consider trying one or all of these quick informal assessments to first determine students' skill level and then identify what you need to teach directly:

- Ask students to gauge their skill level by holding up one finger for *just learning*, two fingers for *knows a little but not a lot*, three fingers for *knows a lot,* and four fingers for *knows enough to teach others.*

- Ask students to demonstrate their proficiency by creating a quick practice sample using the digital tool. Provide the topic and the parameters, so students don't spend this time creating content. Observe the students while they are working and pause to question or listen to explanations as an extra check.

- Have students begin to create their project, and then pause and ask them to turn and talk, explaining to a peer what they did and how they did it. Listen in on these conversations and then debrief as a whole class. Remember, students can learn much from each other.

Karen shares an example of how she guides first graders towards using digital tools.

I find it helpful to have students practice with the tools they will be using before an inquiry study. If using creativity software, like Pixie or Wixie, give students opportunities to explore the various features and experiment with them, making it possible for them to later focus on their work for a project and better express their ideas. As students discover how to use different tools, they can teach each other how to use them. My students enjoyed trying out a feature where they could smudge their picture to blend the colors. This student later used this feature to enhance her picture of a flower (see Figure 4.2).

FIGURE 4.2 First grader's digital drawing of a flower using Wixie features

Selecting useful texts, tools, and technologies during inquiry hinges on recognizing a purpose for learning. Teachers can support the process of making the most efficient and effective choices to promote PDI. Your instruction, thinking aloud, and modeling are critical to the success of these practices. We will further explore the digital dimensions of PDI in Chapter 6.

5

Teaching with Intent to Promote Learning with Intent

In this chapter, you will learn

* three dimensions of teaching with intent, including engaging activities, thoughtful questioning, and meaningful feedback

* instructional practices that foster student ownership and learning with intent

* a framework that integrates intentional teaching practices and opportunities for deep and self-directed learning as part of PDI.

Find additional ways to engage with these ideas in the online study guide for Chapter 5.

bit.ly/PDIstudyguide

Teaching with Intent

As you begin to lay the foundation for inquiry in your classroom, your expectations, language, time, and modeling support learning opportunities that influence your classroom's environment, routines, and interactions. Teachers build on this base by planning and creating inquiry experiences with the goal of making it possible for students to carry out their own inquiries.

When teaching for inquiry, it's important to intentionally align your teaching with meaningful learning goals that seek to incorporate children's personal interests whenever possible. This involves multiple layers of intentional decisions and supports in a process that we call "teaching with intent." Generally, *teaching with intent* means intentionally designing flexible structures to create and manage learning experiences through engaging activities, thoughtful questioning, and meaningful feedback.

In the context of PDI, teaching with intent ideally means designing opportunities for children to build knowledge and transfer that knowledge into action through active participation and digital creation. Teachers plan for ways of working intentionally toward these goals. They adapt digital texts and resources to be developmentally appropriate, they scaffold transitions from large-group to small-group to partner and independent work, and they design tasks that foster collaboration, analysis, and reflection. They build in supported opportunities for children to explore, create, and remix print and digital media while encouraging them to assert their autonomy and ownership of new ideas.

During these intentionally planned inquiry experiences, children's increasing confidence and broadening knowledge base fuel their desire to share what they've learned with others. Creation and participation are essential for knowledge construction and identity development as inquiry shifts from learning about new things to realizing what fuels their passions. In turn, their inquiry becomes more personal and engaging and students begin *learning with intent*.

Listen in as Karen explains her teaching in a digital inquiry project about elephants to get a sense of what teaching with intent looks like in action. Then we'll step back and tease out some of the details, along with describing how the intentional teaching practices in this lesson could be adapted for other lessons and with students of varying age levels.

COLLECTIVE CLASS INQUIRY: WHAT MAKES ELEPHANTS SPECIAL?

To accomplish everything we need to do each year and to improve student understanding, I integrate subjects when I can. To meet science, social studies, writing, and reading goals, I planned a two-week informational reading comprehension and inquiry study for my students to learn about elephants. It was based on two books about elephants that I printed out and adapted from Raz-Kids (www.raz-kids.com), along with an accompanying reading journal that I created. The class also explored elephants online using an age-appropriate, multimedia resource that can read text aloud to them, called PebbleGo (www.PebbleGo.com).

The students heard elephants trumpeting, discovered new facts, and closely examined photos. They studied their Raz-Kids books, marked them up with sticky notes, and discussed their findings in small groups. They recorded their wonderings, compared information, designed maps, and completed diagrams in their elephant journals (see Figure 5.1). By the end of the second week, my first graders had finished the work I had assigned, yet they kept talking and asking more questions about elephants. The class had become fascinated with them and had to know more.

Typically, I have found that certain subjects will spark a collective interest, so that almost the whole class is excited about learning about it. One year it was understanding the life cycle of pumpkins; another year it was researching about bees. This year, it became increasingly apparent from their reactions and questions that it was elephants. When a collective class interest presents itself, I like to make it an opportunity to do additional inquiry work. At the beginning of school, I intentionally make my planning flexible so that we have the time (about three weeks) and ability to do one longer-than-expected follow-up inquiry study each year. So their avid curiosity this year led us to explore what became our guiding question: *What makes elephants special?*

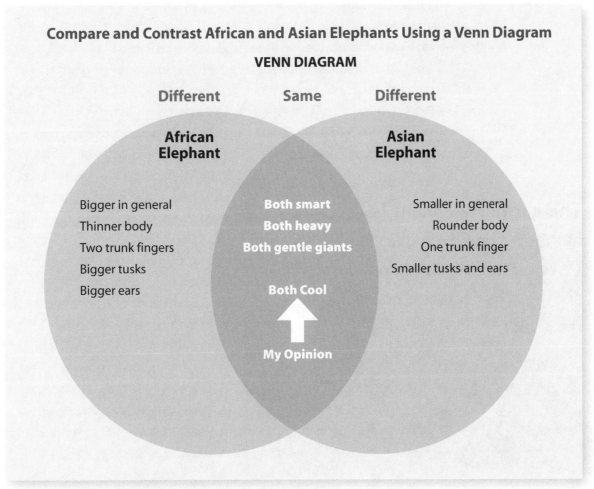

FIGURE 5.1 Venn diagram showing a first grader's opinion that elephants are cool

To build on the basic knowledge students had already acquired, I had my students take out lots of books on elephants from our school library to keep in our classroom. Since I knew that some books would be beyond their reading level, I made arrangements with our library media specialist or our fifth-grade buddy class to help them read these books.

Although it can take some time to search for appropriate and pertinent videos on YouTube, it is worth the effort. Based on the topics students thought were interesting, I found several videos that we studied to learn even more. We took a trip through the inside of an elephant's trunk, watched a mother elephant patiently help her baby with bent legs learn how to walk, and marveled at a mother elephant teaching her child how to move a rock. We stopped the videos and discussed, rewatched, and made new observations. Throughout, I encouraged my students to ask thoughtful questions, and they did. These videos served not only as resources but also as assessment tools. I was able to better gauge how much my students understood by seeing how they analyzed and synthesized important content.

The video resources answered some of their questions and also prompted them to raise new ones. I purposefully encouraged them to reflect on what they had learned and think about what else they wanted to know. With this foundation, my students were prepared for deeper learning. After modeling for the class how to select a topic of interest and conduct research on it, and reminding them of similar work they had done in the fall, I had each student work with a partner to learn about a particular area of interest. Some of the research they were able to do independently, and some required adult support.

Two students were intrigued with the fingers found at the tip of elephant trunks. One pair wanted to create a range map showing where elephants lived. Two others were interested in how elephant babies learn to use their trunks (see Figure 5.2). After conducting their research with a variety of resources and with assistance, students created digital pictures using

FIGURE 5.2 Digital drawing about baby elephants learning to use their trunks

Pixie creativity software (www.pixie.com) and designed short write-ups to show some of the things they had learned. I decided to differentiate support for this activity by evaluating the work students were doing, reflecting on what they were capable of achieving, scaffolding for groups that needed support, and encouraging those that I thought could do more by guiding their thinking through meaningful feedback.

Then, we needed to find a special way to combine this information to share with others. We decided to make a class ABC book, and we matched the alphabet to twenty-six topics, starting with the ones the students had previously researched. We created a few pages together as a class, and pairs of students worked creatively to complete the remaining letters of the alphabet. We chose to make the book as comprehensive as we could, by reviewing the variety of topics we had previously covered.

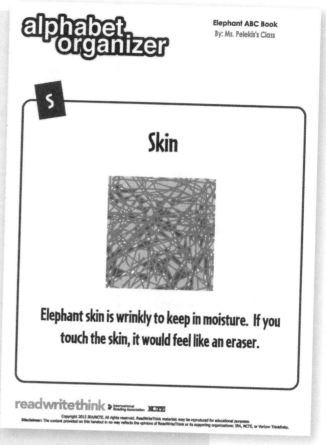

FIGURE 5.3 Student page from elephant ABC book

I debated about what format the ABC book should be. When using the online Alphabet Organizer (see Figure 5.3) from www.readwritethink.org, the students have to condense their research to a short statement to fit the text-length restrictions and the illustration space is small. The format is appealing, however, and the file-saving features are easy to use. If we created our own book, we would be able to make the size of the illustration larger and the text longer, but it would be a more difficult and time-consuming project. Given the amount of weeks this study had already taken, I chose to use the book from ReadWriteThink.

The students were proud and excited to share their considerable knowledge with their kindergarten buddy class, their fifth-grade buddy class, as well as their parents. After the presentation for parents, one father's reflection summed up our work: "My son is always talking about elephants at home. Who knew there was so much to learn about them?" Everyone got a copy of the ABC book in printed and digital form to keep and remember their experience.

As Karen discusses her teaching in this vignette, she offers a glimpse into the wide range of decisions and supports she had intentionally woven into her first graders' inquiries into the magical world of elephants. Throughout the unit, Karen teaches with intent; purposeful, thoughtful decisions are made about designing engaging activities, asking thoughtful questions, and giving meaningful feedback. Although Karen's unit is designed for first grade, many of the ways she teaches with intent could be used with older students, by making small adjustments. The process of intentional teaching entails purposefully making those decisions that guide students through the inquiry process, and this process actually varies little from one grade to the next. We believe intentional teaching, while at the heart of inquiry, should be the central focus of good teaching in general. We have found, though, in our own teaching that it takes constant vigilance to make your teaching intentional. It can be easy to fall back on old habits until new habits are firmly entrenched in our practices. To support this shift in thinking, we created Tables 5.1, 5.2, and 5.3 on pages 73–75, which identify specific ways to design engaging activities, ask thoughtful questions, and give meaningful feedback along with including suggestions for extending these ideas for intermediate-grade students.

For many, teaching with intent may not be a huge shift in current teaching practices. But when we get into the hustle and bustle of our daily teaching, it's good to remind ourselves of the impact seemingly small teaching decisions can have on the messages about learning we give to our students.

Learning with Intent

An intentional learner is someone who is motivated to learn, takes responsibility for learning, and actively engages in strategies that facilitate learning (Bereiter and Scardamalia 1989). Learning with intent encourages us to "consciously seek out new experiences; explore ways to apply new ideas; reflect on one's practice; share insights with others, be open to their perspectives, and together build on lessons learned" (Benest 2011, 18). Although intentional learners are self-directed, teachers play an important role in creating learning opportunities that encourage active participation, regular feedback, and metacognitive reflection. Our PDI framework integrates four core sets of PDI practices that are designed to foster students' intentional learning through intentional teaching. Over time, students internalize what is modeled and expected to begin learning with intent.

TABLE 5.1

DESIGNING ENGAGING ACTIVITIES

Build a foundation of understanding

- Explore books and digital/multimedia sources (video, audio, text, photos).
- Annotate print or digital texts with sticky notes and highlighters, and then discuss in small groups.
- Compare and contrast the information found in two texts.
- Design maps and create diagrams in journals.

Additional ideas for building foundational understanding for intermediate-grade students

- Compare and contrast information about the topic found in a text, a video, and a website.
- Define key content vocabulary and then encourage students to use these words in their writing and creating.
- Use annotations to summarize key ideas into one or two written paragraphs.

Deepen and extend understanding while creating opportunities for student-guided inquiry

- Analyze videos, sharing insights through whole-group and small-group discussion.
- Research follow-up topics of interest with a partner.
- Digitally record new learning (using creativity software, such as Pixie or Wixie, to illustrate discoveries).
- Write up new learning digitally with a partner to contribute to a class book.

Additional ideas for deepening understanding for intermediate-grade students

- Use a note-taking format to record information from a text, a video, or a website.
- Analyze two websites on the same topic. Discuss the website hosts' perspectives and ways this influences information that is present and missing.
- Create a digital or paper project to share new learning. Present the project to younger students or families and seek feedback.

TABLE 5.2

ASKING THOUGHTFUL QUESTIONS

Questioning prompts to structure students' inquiries

- Discuss book annotations.

  What did you discover on this page that made you put an exclamation mark sticky note on it? Why did it interest you so much?

- Compare information.

  How can you tell if this is an African or an Asian elephant?

- Analyze videos.

  How is the mother elephant teaching her baby to move that rock?

- Reflect on what students learned, what else they wanted to know, and how to find new information.

  The elephant life cycle does follow the same pattern as the plant life cycle. I like how you want to include how old the elephant is at each of the different stages on your diagram. Where can we find that information?

- Recall and connect inquiry processes to inform new research.

  Now that we know that an elephant's trunk has many muscles, what are some of the ways it can use its trunk?

- Discuss ways of sharing with others.

  We've learned so much about elephants. What are some ways we could put all our information together in one place to teach others?

- Model creation of class book page.

  What would be the best illustration to go along with the words you want to write? How can you label your drawings to extend the information you want others to learn?

Additional ideas for intermediate-grade students

- Encourage deeper digging, going beyond the basic facts.

  Tell me more than when Martin Luther King Jr. was born and died. Describe how he felt, the challenges he faced and who he loved.

- Create structured discussions for sharing information and asking questions with a shoulder partner.

  First, be a good listener. Second, let your partner know if a detail seems out of place or seems to be missing. Be a sounding board for your partner, helping him or her to recognize what work still needs to be done.

- Focus on comprehending the informational book, article, or website by using the structural guideposts (i.e., headings, captions, text features, key vocabulary).

  When you are reading the website, don't just click and scroll. Focus on the process of point, read, think, and then click.

TABLE 5.3

GIVING MEANINGFUL FEEDBACK

Prompts to encourage reflection about the process and product

- Reflect on previous learning.

  I see how your alphabet book page teaches the reader about your topic. Is there anything else you learned that might be helpful for you to include? This is your opportunity to teach someone else something new . . . Let's think of ways you could do that.

- Reflect on curiosities and feelings.

  Remember how excited you were when you learned about your topic? Let your reader discover that as well through your alphabet page.

- Offer encouragement to expand work.

  I like the way your alphabet book page starts to explain what you know. What other details could you include to give the reader an even better understanding of your topic? Those details could be in labels, pictures, or words.

- Help to clarify information and consider the audience.

  You already know a lot about your topic, and I see that in your work. Your reader probably doesn't know as much about it as you do. Are there any other descriptions you might include to make it easier for the reader to understand what you mean? Remember, we are going to share this with our kindergarten buddies, so we want them to be able to follow what you've done.

- Verify work is complete.

  You have a lot of good information here, but we have to make sure that everything is completely accurate for your readers. Let's go back and double-check your source (book, video) to be certain that it is correct.

Additional ideas for intermediate-grade students

- Encourage students to pause and reflect on new learning about the content and the process so far.

  Make a brief screen capture video to describe your process for learning. Think about how you created your question, searched for information, and made sense of what you read and viewed.

- Promote students to take pride in their work.

  Remember these projects will be shared with your families at open house. Think about how you want your work to be viewed by others. Correct spelling and grammar shows you have carefully edited your work so others are able to read your ideas.

- Guide students toward critical analysis.

  Let's look at who wrote this article and who publishes this website. Has the article been published recently? Is the author an authority? Is the publisher trying to sell us a product? Answers to these questions help us to evaluate the truthfulness and usefulness of this article.

Listen in as Karen describes how her students began taking on more active, self-directed roles as part of their inquiry experiences:

As my students became intrigued by elephants, they naturally wanted to learn more about them and study areas of interest. Because of the work that we did together, they internalized the inquiry process and sought out ways to study elephants that were important to them. For example, two students became captivated by how much elephants eat and tried to get a better understanding of what it meant for one elephant to consume as much as 100 people do in a day. They realized that to more fully comprehend this, they would have to know what elephants eat, so they began researching for the answer on their own. They decided to depict what they had discovered in a labeled illustration (see Figure 5.4). Two other students wanted to know more about the fingers at the end of trunks. They intensely studied photos, text, and other resources. They discovered that the fingers of African and Asian elephants are not alike, and took it upon themselves to explore the similarities and differences. The students were personally motivated to learn about these topics, and as a result, they independently acted on the knowledge they had gained. In the process, they became more focused and purposeful in their learning.

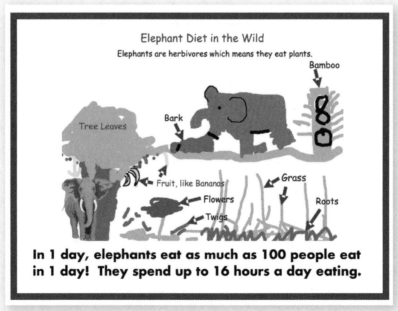

FIGURE 5.4 Student research on an elephant's diet

Pulling It All Together

Across Chapters 1–5, we've introduced several ideas designed to help you build a culture of inquiry and intentionally work toward PDI in ways that encourage turning knowledge into action and learning with intent. The PDI triangle (pictured in Figure 5.5) illustrates the overlapping layers of ideas to consider when implementing PDI practices into your classroom routine.

In the remaining chapters, we model some of the many ways we have seen elementary school teachers and media specialists intentionally teach toward a culture that values all four sets of PDI practices while paving the way for self-directed learners of any age to have ownership and agency in their learning. Each teacher in our book works in a different context and employs different ways of supporting learners with and without technology. However, across their classrooms, three questions and a subset of related questions outlined in Figure 5.5 can be used to frame their efforts in ways we believe can develop a culture of PDI over time:

- How do I cultivate inquiry in my classroom?
- How do I teach with intent?
- How do my students grow to learn with intent?

As we shared in Chapter 3, the beliefs, expectations, values, and routines that we promote as part of learning are important indicators of our classroom culture. Focused efforts on building the foundational mindsets for productive inquiry are crucial and ongoing. The bottom portion of the PDI triangle reminds us that flexible plans for how to use time, language, supports, and learning spaces can grow curiosity, ownership, and thoughtful reflection among learners of any age.

Carefully woven into these plans are engaging activities intentionally designed to build students' foundational understanding and deepen learning through challenging questions and regular feedback. This is what we mean by *teaching with intent*. It happens at all phases and stages of the inquiry process and looks different depending on each unique context and set of student needs. We've positioned teaching with intent on the left side of the PDI triangle to recognize the critical role that teachers play in deciding how much (or how little) instruction and support is provided as students navigate the messiness of inquiry-based learning. It is here where each teacher decides how to cultivate student voice and choice in ways that connect learners to the curriculum, to each other, and to the world

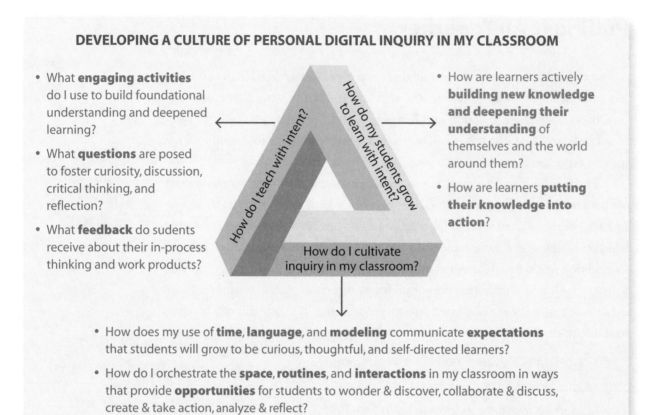

DEVELOPING A CULTURE OF PERSONAL DIGITAL INQUIRY IN MY CLASSROOM

- What **engaging activities** do I use to build foundational understanding and deepened learning?

- What **questions** are posed to foster curiosity, discussion, critical thinking, and reflection?

- What **feedback** do sudents receive about their in-process thinking and work products?

How do I teach with intent?

How do my students grow to learn with intent?

- How are learners actively **building new knowledge and deepening their understanding** of themselves and the world around them?

- How are learners **putting their knowledge into action**?

How do I cultivate inquiry in my classroom?

- How does my use of **time**, **language**, and **modeling** communicate **expectations** that students will grow to be curious, thoughtful, and self-directed learners?

- How do I orchestrate the **space**, **routines**, and **interactions** in my classroom in ways that provide **opportunities** for students to wonder & discover, collaborate & discuss, create & take action, analyze & reflect?

FIGURE 5.5 The personal digital inquiry triangle

around them. Chapter 8, in particular, offers many examples of what intentional teaching looks like in the context of PDI.

Questions on the right side of PDI triangle serve as a reminder that inquiry-based efforts are really geared toward moving students ever closer to becoming self-directed learners empowered to use their knowledge and turn it into action in ways that matter to them. We call this *learning with intent* and, however far away it may seem from our current reality, it always guides our thinking, planning, and reflection as part of the PDI design process.

Some days, as part of PDI, you will look around your classroom and see glimpses of children learning with intent. During those moments, it can be amazing to sit back and feel the excitement and passion in the room. Other days, things will not be quite as amazing, and you will stop to appreciate that inquiry is truly developmental (see Kuhn et al. 2000) and even poses challenges to middle school learners and beyond. Yet, we, as coauthors of this book, have seen firsthand the power of continuing to cultivate the dispositions and values of PDI as part of regular and meaningful opportunities for elementary-aged children to wonder and discover, collaborate and discuss, create and take action, and analyze and reflect. These are the powerful experiences that inspired us to write this book. We will have every hope that the classroom exemplars woven throughout the chapters help anchor the PDI framework in authentic experiences and inspire you to explore PDI in your own classroom.

One Step at a Time

At this point, you're probably thinking, wow, there's an awful lot that goes into planning for PDI in an elementary school classroom or media center. But, honestly, if you've been teaching for any amount of time, you realize there's a lot of planning that goes into any kind of teaching!

However, in case you are feeling a bit overwhelmed, we urge you to pause and appreciate that, if you've read this far, you may likely *wonder* how PDI plays out in other elementary school settings and hope to *discover* ideas you might adapt for your own use. If that's the case, you are right where you should be.

Your personal interests and willingness to learn more will fuel your own journey toward PDI. Much like how we started this book with a set of questions and encountered new ideas and many more questions along the way, each step of your journey will prompt more ideas and questions as well.

Your needs and interests may also inform your pathway through the chapters in this book. You might, for example, read each chapter in sequence, gradually moving through each layer of understanding about the core elements of PDI and how they play out in different contexts. You might also choose to skip right to the unit examples of PDI in action (see Chapters 7–9), and work backward to deepen your thinking about the principles informing these plans. In the spirit of personal inquiry, we encourage you to reflect on your interests and comfort level and create your own pathway through the ideas in this book. Whichever path you choose, hop on board and let's continue to explore PDI together.

Planning for Personal Digital Inquiry

Find additional ways to engage with these ideas in the online study guide for Chapter 6.

bit.ly/PDIstudyguide

Each day in the classroom or media center, you are faced with making a myriad of instructional decisions. Planning for PDI is no different. To describe this complex and multidimensional process, we break it down into a flexible series of practices. In reality, you may simultaneously consider many of the issues we describe, or consider them in a different order, or not at all, depending on your situation. Please know that planning for PDI is not a lockstep process, but we want to be thorough in our descriptions so that we meet our readers' varied learning needs.

A focus on the planning process stems from our realization that planning is the key for successful PDI to occur in the classroom. Cultivating skilled inquirers takes practice, time, and diligence. Although the planning process may be complex, it's not beyond reach. In fact, many dedicated teachers see their own professional learning across their career as a series of questions and a search for answers. These teachers know that each time an inquiry unit occurs in the classroom, both teachers and learners inch toward the goal of becoming a community of learners who can wonder and discover, collaborate and discuss, create and take action, and analyze and reflect.

They also know that intentional planning to teach the PDI process, although challenging and cyclical in nature, is a skill that they can master as teachers. As we were writing this book, the three of us had a pivotal conversation as we tried to understand this idea of planning for PDI.

Beth: So what does planning for PDI really look like in the classroom?

Julie: Well, there are lots of models of student inquiry and diagrams of the research process. But few of these models and diagrams visualize the intentional planning that takes place beforehand. We want this book to offer a rich description of this intentional planning process—but it's complex and not easy to explain because each teacher is unique and may approach the process in different ways. And of course, each group of learners is unique and shapes the inquiry experience as well.

Karen: When planning an inquiry study, I needed help to see where to more effectively direct my own teaching. Becoming aware of the elements of wonder and discover, collaborate and discuss, create and take action, and analyze and reflect helped me to better design and balance this inquiry work. Now I also look closely at relevant standards and the depth of knowledge. Our work together gave me an organizational framework that I didn't have before. Although there are many factors to consider when planning, having these guidelines makes it much easier.

Beth: But it's tricky to explain how you, Karen, or any teacher works through this planning process. We can begin by emphasizing that learning about teaching toward PDI is actually an inquiry process in itself. Teachers form their own questions that drive their search for information and the application of these ideas with their students. It's like inquiry within inquiry!

Julie: Yes, that's exactly how I think about PDI. I think a good next step is to describe the planning process, while helping teachers understand that it's a flexible, fluid, loose sequence, rather than a lockstep, rigid sequence. That way, the planning model reflects an approximation of what a teacher might do, without directing exactly what a teacher should do.

In light of this conversation, we propose a model for planning PDI that is designed to recognize the complexities, yet provide support for educators who want to move toward integrating PDI into their teaching. Our planning model is in line with the idea of backward design (McTighe and Wiggins 2012), where we start with the end in mind by identifying desired results and then creating plans for reaching these results.

A backward design process supports planning for PDI in at least three ways. First, it helps you to intentionally choose where to focus your teaching amid the range of wonderings and discoveries your students will make when given the opportunity to explore a topic. Second, sharing learning outcomes with students helps them to prioritize where to focus their learning efforts. Finally, this backward design process aligns with research that suggests the importance of first selecting learning outcomes and activity types before identifying technology tools (Harris and Hofer 2009). Activity types are what teachers and students do when engaged in a particular learning-related activity. In the context of PDI, activity types include opportunities for students to wonder and discover, collaborate and discuss, create and take action, and analyze and reflect as part of their inquiry experiences. Put simply, once you have identified a clear set of expectations for learning and teaching, you can use these expectations to design authentic opportunities for personal inquiry and *then* make purposeful choices about digital texts and tools (see the three green circles in Figure 6.1).

In our model, we encourage you to consider each element as a possible next step in your planning for PDI. Keep in mind that planning for PDI, just like the inquiry process itself, is reiterative, with one question leading to more. Thus, we've envisioned the process as an overlapping set of planning elements. At the core are three guiding questions (see the triangle in Figure 6.1):

- How do I teach with intent?
- How do my students grow to learn with intent?
- How do I cultivate inquiry in my classroom?

Simultaneously a teacher considers ways of setting expectations for teaching and learning, planning authentic learning experiences, and making purposeful choices about teaching and learning. Although this process may seem complex at first, with knowledge and practice, PDI planning can become another aspect of the many instructional decisions a teacher makes within a lesson, a day, and a week. From our own experiences and what teachers tell us, the PDI planning process involves moving back and forth between the elements, tweaking and revising plans and activities to respond to student needs and questions that arise. It's our goal, throughout this book, to make the planning process as straightforward as a complex process can be, by sharing lots of rich examples and the thought processes used by teachers to plan for these activities.

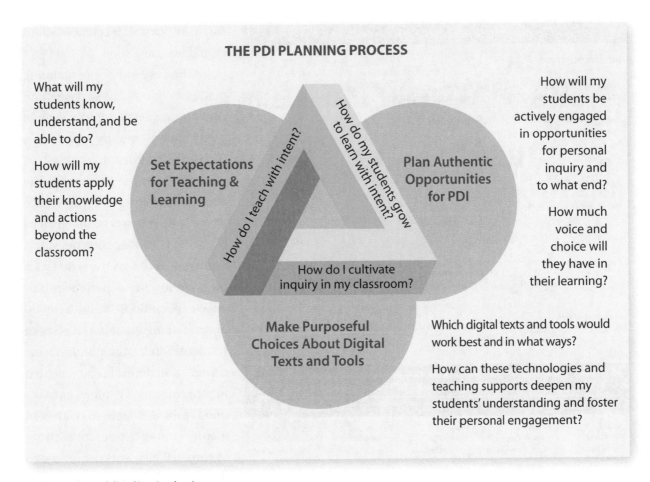

FIGURE 6.1 Personal digital inquiry planning process

Use the Personal Digital Inquiry Planning Guide to Organize Your Plans

In the true spirit of backward design, before we walk you through each part of the PDI process, we introduce you to PDI planning guide (see Figure 6.2), which can, ultimately, help you organize all of your plans in one location. This template can be used to succinctly summarize the key PDI opportunities you have planned and reflect on how they align with expected learning outcomes and relevant curriculum standards.

Overall, the three main sections of the planning guide are aligned with the three parts of the PDI planning process shown earlier in Figure 6.1: (1) set expectations for teaching and learning, (2) plan authentic opportunities for PDI, and

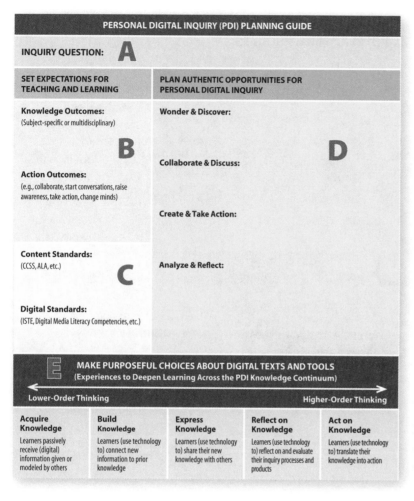

PERSONAL DIGITAL INQUIRY (PDI) PLANNING GUIDE

INQUIRY QUESTION: **A**

SET EXPECTATIONS FOR TEACHING AND LEARNING	**PLAN AUTHENTIC OPPORTUNITIES FOR PERSONAL DIGITAL INQUIRY**
Knowledge Outcomes: (Subject-specific or multidisciplinary) **B**	**Wonder & Discover:**
	D
	Collaborate & Discuss:
Action Outcomes: (e.g., collaborate, start conversations, raise awareness, take action, change minds)	
	Create & Take Action:
Content Standards: (CCSS, ALA, etc.) **C**	**Analyze & Reflect:**
Digital Standards: (ISTE, Digital Media Literacy Competencies, etc.)	

E   MAKE PURPOSEFUL CHOICES ABOUT DIGITAL TEXTS AND TOOLS
(Experiences to Deepen Learning Across the PDI Knowledge Continuum)

⟵ Lower-Order Thinking   Higher-Order Thinking ⟶

Acquire Knowledge	**Build Knowledge**	**Express Knowledge**	**Reflect on Knowledge**	**Act on Knowledge**
Learners passively receive (digital) information given or modeled by others	Learners (use technology to) connect new information to prior knowledge	Learners (use technology to) share their new knowledge with others	Learners (use technology to) reflect on and evaluate their inquiry processes and products	Learners (use technology to) translate their knowledge into action

FIGURE 6.2 Personal digital inquiry planning guide

(3) make purposeful choices about digital texts and tools.

The very top of the planning guide (section A) has space to note the central question that will guide your students' inquiry experiences for a particular length of time. On the left side of the planning guide, you can list key learning outcomes (section B); note space for curricular-based knowledge outcomes and action outcomes to ensure that your planned inquiry experiences balance expectations for both *knowing* and *doing*. Section C has space to identify relevant standards for content and digital literacy aligned to your learning outcomes, and section D provides space to synthesize planned opportunities for each set of core PDI elements connected to these outcomes. The bottom row (section E) offers a way to organize plans to maximize your use of digital texts and tools along a continuum of experiences most likely to foster deep understanding and personal engagement. See Appendix B for a full-page version of the personal digital inquiry planning guide.

As is the case with any of the templates we provide, this planning guide is not designed to constrain your thinking into a rigid sequence of steps. However, we have found the template offers a way to move back and forth between the three core ideas as part of a flexible plan.

For those of you planning your inquiry for the first time, you may be able to fit most of your initial plans on a single page. For those of you who are revisiting and revising plans from any inquiry you've tried previously, your plans might be more detailed. Either way, educators we have worked with explain the value of having the main gist of their plans encapsulated in such a planning guide. After the inquiry unit has ended, this format also makes it easy to share and exchange a summary of your accomplishments with other educators who can then adapt or build on work for their own purposes.

The remainder of this chapter walks you through each step of the planning process with examples to get you started. Then, in Chapters 7 and 9, you will find several examples of completed PDI planning guides to inspire your own reflections and conversations about what PDI can look like in your classroom.

1. SET EXPECTATIONS FOR LEARNING AND TEACHING

Reflect on Interesting Questions and General Expectations

Learning outcomes play a key role in plans for any PDI experience, but before jumping right in to identify learning outcomes, we encourage you to pause to consider your overall expectations for teaching and learning through PDI. These broad expectations touch on what you value about learning in general, rather than related to a specific unit or content area. Consider these as the big ideas about what you hope to accomplish on any given school day. Importantly, these expectations are also grounded in the unique interests, abilities, and needs of the students in your classroom. In this early phase of planning, we have found it helpful to consider the following questions:

- What issues, problems, or questions might be worth exploring with the learners I am working with this year?
- What do I want students to accomplish during and after their learning and how does this connect to my curriculum?
- What open-ended experiences are likely to prompt my students' curiosity and personal interests as an integral part of learning?
- What do I want to accomplish with my teaching to support the important work my students will do?

To get a sense of what this initial planning might look like, Karen reflects on her expectations in the early stages of a class inquiry into plants. Throughout the process, she intentionally weaves in ideas for how students will be active and engaged in real-world learning.

I will plan opportunities for my first graders to

- closely study the radishes they will plant in the garden, comparing and contrasting the four types of radishes;
- take care of the plants, taking turns to water and weed the garden;
- watch the garden change and record the growth;
- work in small groups to create signs, using creativity software, to display in the garden to show the different types of radishes;
- taste the harvest and create a healthy meals.

In Table 6.1, notice how Karen uses a series of "I want" statements organized into three sections to answer questions about general expectations. This practice helps solidify her values and expectations as a foundational element of the inquiry-based culture she hopes to cultivate in her classroom community. After considering relevant standards, she outlined some of her hopes for what she and her students would accomplish as part of their inquiry into plants. She thought carefully about what kinds of open-ended experiences would be likely to encourage students to wonder, explore, and discover new questions to guide their learning about this curriculum-based topic in personally relevant ways.

Karen is at the stage in her own PDI process where she's also seeking more depth and connections across her students' inquiries. So, at the bottom of Table 6.1, Karen explains how she expects the students' knowledge and independence to grow over the course of the year. If you are new to PDI, you may not yet be prepared to think reflectively across multiple topics and units. However, Karen's thinking can help form both a short-term and a longer-term vision for teaching with inquiry.

Identify an Estimated Timeline for Your Students' Inquiry

If you are new to designing inquiry-based experiences for children, you may wish to start by planning for one small project at a time. Consider a topic connected to the curriculum that generated an initial buzz in your classroom. Estimate how long you'd like your first project to be (for example, two days, two weeks, or two months), and then begin brainstorming about what students will learn and do as part of their inquiry experiences. When getting started, we find that teachers tend to have a specific time set aside for inquiry and plan for an activity that can be completed during that time. But as teachers and students are ready, inquiry may

TABLE 6.1

KAREN'S BROAD EXPECTATIONS FOR TEACHING AND LEARNING	
Curriculum Connections	**Teaching Supports**
• I want my curriculum to be content-rich, drawing upon the standards and the questions and experiences of my students. • I want my students to have many hands-on experiences to encourage their questions about important content (e.g., looking at different kinds of seeds, planting seeds in an outside garden, taking care of plants and watching the garden grow, exploring indoor plants that come from different places around the world, such as cactus plants from the desert and orchids from the rain forest).	• I want my students to be able to work independently as the year goes on, so I plan for ways to gradually release responsibility whenever possible. • I want to teach with depth and understanding, thoughtfully asking and answering questions, encouraging reflection and further questioning. • I want to support independent learning as well as collaborative learning. • I want to think carefully about how to best incorporate learning tools, including digital tools, to make teaching and learning more effective.

Connections Across the Year

• I want to design a cohesive year where learning builds as time goes on and instruction supports that building. I think our inquiry into plants can foster connections to our later inquiry studies of geography, pollination, and the chicken life cycle.

• I want to teach in a way that supports recognizing crosscutting concepts in line with the science standards. I want my students to understand and be able to articulate the similarities and differences across different systems (for instance, plant life cycle and animal life cycle).

move into a workshop time. An inquiry activity may expand to several sessions, with students picking up where they left off and connecting their learning from one session to the next, thus better matching their own pace of learning.

Identifying a focus and planning out a timeline gives flexible structure and serve as important early aspects of the planning process. Also consider how best to prepare students for the work ahead of them. For students who are less familiar with inquiry experiences, planning may involve designing a sequence of tasks to build skills over time. If you and your students have experience with inquiry, aim for more depth, rather than breadth by selecting thematically-based inquiry projects that play out over longer periods of time. Try combining seemingly separate themes under a common umbrella, then sequence units and related inquiry experiences to build knowledge in meaningful ways.

Planning to span learning across inquiry experiences may necessitate more up-front thinking. Connecting, combining, or resequencing themes can facilitate clearer connections and deepen children's understanding of key content across the year. The extra time spent planning for connections pays off when students have more depth of knowledge and can better understand how ideas are connected to each other.

Plan and Preserve Time in Your Daily and Yearlong Schedule

Making and preserving time for inquiry is an especially important part of the planning process. What we give time to shows what we value in our classroom culture. As you consider the range of possible inquiry experiences, a vital part of the PDI planning process is to intentionally make time in your schedule for students to ask questions, talk with others, creatively share new ideas, and reflect on the quality of their work.

Inquiry time may occur once a day, once a week, or in smaller time segments on a more flexible schedule. The time routines let children know that inquiry is a valuable part of the learning process. Many teachers tell us these regular opportunities for children to talk freely and reflect on their learning lead to new questions and increased motivation for learning more.

Whether you are new to inquiry or have loads of experience, it makes sense to take the time to periodically reflect on your own classroom context. Consider how you might intentionally build into your schedule small but regular blocks of time for inquiry. Think about what it would take to make inquiry time a reality for you and your students. While contemplating these same ideas for our own teaching, we compiled a list of key ideas to consider.

- **Curriculum Connections:** When and where during your day or week might you have opportunities to integrate connections between reading, writing, math, science, and social studies that might be relevant to a particular inquiry topic? Thematic connections can foster a deeper understanding by connecting school topics and real-world ideas. Inviting students to explore these topics for even thirty minutes once a week can spark initial conversation and questions that can naturally lead to further exploration down the road.

- **Scheduling Issues:** When are certain children most likely to get pulled out for special services, and how might you avoid scheduling PDI activities during these times so no child is left out? Are there ways to have specials or encores scheduled so that it gives longer amounts of classroom time for literacy blocks?

- **Consider Schedule Rotations:** Once you have identified a block of time during the school day, how many times during the week are feasible to save for PDI activities? If your school operates on a six- or seven-day cycle (as opposed to a five-day week), be sure to consider how these rotations will affect your timing each week.

- **Protect the Time:** After building this time into your schedule, remember to keep it a priority and to not let other activities interfere (as much as possible). Share the schedule with your students so they come to anticipate this special time together; soon, you will find they look forward to these opportunities and begin to make plans for how they can best use their time when it comes.

- **Access to Devices:** When would you and your students have access to digital devices (e.g., a laptop cart, a set of iPads), and is there a schedule for sharing these devices with others at your school? Negotiating a regular space on this schedule early in the school year helps projects run much more smoothly.

- **Peer-to-Peer Support:** Sometimes sharing devices with a partner teacher (even at a different grade level) creates an opportunity for one class of students to visit another class to provide peer-to-peer support or conversation around different dimensions of a similar topic.

- **Flexible Seating:** How can you use flexible seating to facilitate students' work in pairs or small groups during different parts of the school day? Are there tables that can be lowered so students can sit on the ground to more easily gather together instead of using chairs?

- **Positive Tone:** Woven through everyday instructional routines is an emphasis on building relationships. A trusted, caring adult can set the tone for the classroom interactions and model for students effective ways to communicate that promote learning. Because PDI often entails asking questions, collaborating, and sharing insights, it is imperative that students feel their contributions will be respected. Taking a few minutes to recognize extra effort, or notice positive interactions, can go a long way toward ensuring that children feel respected and safe in your classroom community.

Making and protecting time in your schedule, building personal relationships, and encouraging engagement provide the framework for envisioning a specific set of inquiry experiences as part of your curriculum.

Identify a Guiding Question

The starting point of any inquiry is a good question. This question guides you and your students along a clear path, fueled by diverse interests, but focused enough so that students do not become overwhelmed by the possibilities. We believe the key to effectively using essential questions is to teach students to be the ones who ask the questions. A teacher may provide an overarching question, which creates a space for focused learning, but within that space-learners are designing their own questions, making their own wonderings that guide the day-to-day PDI activities.

When a teacher designs a guiding question, it must be broad, yet specific enough to connect to the curriculum. Some examples of the types of questions used to guide the PDI experiences are described elsewhere in this book:

Grades K–2

- What is special about elephants?
- How do animals form communities, work together, and adapt to their environments?
- How is life different in Antarctica?

Grades 3–5

- What conditions create a tornado?
- How do animals survive in extreme environments?
- Who are the heroes and legends we admire, and why are they important to us?
- How have inventors turned their ideas into realities?

Want to know more about teaching children to ask questions? Check out the book *Essential Questions: Opening Doors to Student Understanding* (2013). Authors Jay McTighe and Grant Wiggins describe the ways essential questions can make the curriculum more accessible and deepen students' understandings.

Crafting a guiding question early in the PDI planning process helps to give the unit focus and provides guidance when teachers are designing instructional activities. Consider these characteristics when designing an essential question:

Broad and Openended. An essential question invites participation in the inquiry process. If the question is one that can be easily answered with a few words, little research, reading, and learning occurs.

Piques Learners' Interest. Upon an initial read of the question, learners of all ages should be encouraged to pause and wonder. When considering Karen's first-grade class inquiry to answer the question, "What makes elephants special?" (see Chapter 5), a learner may know facts about elephants but not be exactly sure what makes these giant creatures special. With Beth's question to fourth graders about "What conditions create a tornado?" (see Chapter 9), a learner may be curious why tornadoes are common in some parts of the United States and not in others. Essential questions often cause teachers to wonder along with their students.

Multiple Resources Needed. To fully answer an essential question, information will likely be harvested from more than one source. A thought-provoking essential question requires a rich collection of information that may include nonfiction books, websites, video clips, images, interviews, primary source materials, hands-on experiences, and reflection journals, just to name a few.

Additional Questions. An essential question often leads to more questions. Although it may or may not be possible to answer these additional questions during the PDI unit, learners can come to realize the power of questions that lead to more questions, which serves as the foundation of lifelong learning.

Although there are many nuances to consider, remember that generating an effective question hinges on genuine curiosity, which provides the starting point for inquiry.

Identify Relevant Standards

Educational standards can also guide the planning process toward PDI. For some teachers, standards drive their daily instruction. For others, standards serve as a broad overview, with the district curriculum providing a more specific guide. Whatever your situation, we imagine that at some level, standards steer the boat of effective instruction and can inform your design of specific learning outcomes.

Listed on the next page is a collection of national standards available to draw from when planning a PDI unit. Many professional organizations have integrated elements of inquiry, digital literacy, civic action, and higher levels of thinking into their standards. We encourage you to explore some of the standards discussed here and identify those that could be addressed as part of your inquiry plans.

NATIONAL STANDARDS FOR PLANNING A PDI UNIT

Common Core State Standards (CCSS) for Reading, Writing, and Math are organized around reading, writing, speaking and listening, and language with threads of inquiry implicitly woven throughout.	www.corestandards.org/	
Next Generation Science Standards (NGSS) are organized around a framework that emphasizes practices, crosscutting concepts, and core knowledge, all of which link to inquiry.	www.nextgenscience.org/	
College Career and Civic Life (C3) Framework for Social Studies State Standards suggests that inquiry is pivotal to effective instruction focused on preparing students to be informed decision makers in a democratic society by using questions to spark curiosity and deepen exploration needed to understand ideas in the real world.	www.socialstudies.org/c3	
Learning Targets in Digital and Media Literacy for Children in the Elementary Grades, a framework created by Renee Hobbs and David Cooper Moore, emphasizes five competencies as fundamental to how we learn and communicate today with digital media across all subject areas: the ability to access, analyze, compose, reflect, and take action in the world.	bit.ly/learningtargetsmedialit	
The American Association of School Librarians (AASL) Standards Framework for Learners, from the American Association of School Librarians, is closely aligned with PDI through the six shared foundations: inquire, include, collaborate, curate, explore, engage. The four domains of think, create, share, and grow provide the underpinnings to support this learning.	bit.ly/aaslstandardsframework	
International Society for Technology in Education (ISTE) Standards for Students promote inquiry by calling on students to be constructors of knowledge, designers of solutions, and communicators who are adept at using a variety of digital tools for various purposes.	bit.ly/ISTEstandardsforstudents	
International Society for Technology in Education (ISTE) Standards for Educators parallel the ISTE Standards for students by setting an expectation for educators to play seven key roles, all of which support inquiry: learner, leader, citizen, collaborator, designer, facilitator, and analyst.	bit.ly/ISTEstandardsforedu	

NATIONAL STANDARDS FOR PLANNING A PDI UNIT, *CONT.*		
P21's Framework for 21st Century Learning Standards give clear support for innovative teaching methods that bring together an inquiry approach, information literacy, higher-order thinking skills, and supportive technologies (i.e., devices, software, social networks) in relevant, real-world contexts.	bit.ly /p21learningframework	
Literacy for ICT: A Model for 21st Century Learning from K–12 are not educational standards, per se, but they are designed to represent a developmental continuum for digital literacy and relevant dispositions aligned with information communication technologies and content area learning.	bit.ly/literacywithICT	

Translate Broad Expectations into Learning Outcomes

Once you have a general sense of what you hope students will accomplish during their inquiry experience, and how they are informed by relevant standards, an important next step involves translating these ideas into clearly defined learning outcomes. It is true that students may move toward these common outcomes on different paths and have unique ways of demonstrating their learning. Nevertheless, clearly laying out these more fine-tuned expectations at the beginning of an inquiry unit will help you and your students stay focused on the end goals.

To identify learning outcomes, revisit the list of broad expectations that you brainstormed previously, and begin to refine your thinking, focusing more closely on the actual content of the PDI unit. The following questions may serve as a guide:

- What should students know, understand, and be able to do?
- What important ideas and core processes are worthy of understanding about this content or discipline?
- What will have lasting value beyond the classroom?

As you craft these learning outcomes, we encourage you to consider both knowledge outcomes and action outcomes. *Knowledge outcomes* are broad, general curriculum-based statements that describe what learners should know, understand, and be able to do at the end of a lesson, a project, or a unit. These are clearly articulated statements that define student learning, not a list of activities. Typically, these knowledge outcomes are directly linked to curriculum-based standards in one or more disciplines (e.g., literacy, language, math, science, social studies, art, music).

Inquiry-based knowledge outcomes, in particular, aim to move learners beyond acquiring and recalling knowledge to build, express, reflect on, and apply their knowledge in ways that inspire deeper understanding and active engagement as part of PDI. Later in this chapter, we'll explain more about these ideas.

Here are a few examples of knowledge outcomes from Karen's first-grade inquiry into what makes elephants special:

- Determine important ideas across multiple informational texts on a particular topic.
- Compare and contrast findings from multimedia resources.
- Use informational writing and drawing skills to synthesize key ideas around areas of personal interest.

Action outcomes are statements that focus on what learners do with their knowledge as active participants in and beyond the classroom. Action outcomes offer opportunities for students to take an active role in shaping decisions that affect their lives, individually and collectively. Thus, taking action requires that children are active with their new knowledge. In their book *Discovering Media Literacy: Teaching Digital Media and Popular Culture in Elementary School*, Renee Hobbs and David Cooper Moore outline ways that young children can use their knowledge and skills to "take action" (2013, 17) by:

- participating in a creative community;
- being aware of and sensitive to differences among people;
- making connections between current events, the community, and the self;
- generating ideas to improve a thing or an event;
- collaborating to solve a meaningful real-world problem.

The work of Stephanie Harvey and Harvey Daniels also calls on teachers to provide opportunities for children to ask questions, seek information, collaborate, and share. For example, in their book *Inquiry Circles in Action: Comprehension & Collaboration* (2009), the authors include reflection and advocacy as ways of taking action. This means that children might be encouraged, for example, to:

- demonstrate learning and understanding in a variety of ways,
- become teachers as they share their knowledge with others,
- reflect on their knowledge building or their cooperative process,

- consider changes in their own beliefs or behavior,

- take action through writing, speaking, community work, or advocacy. (232)

We like to think of action outcomes as ways to encourage young children to use their knowledge and skills to start conversations, raise awareness, and change minds in ways that help others. These might be friends, classmates, family members, people in their neighborhood, or other people connected with a particular issue or problem in the larger community and beyond.

At the simplest level, action outcomes might involve students collaborating on a project together, practicing how to integrate their individual ideas into a creative product. Then, students are invited to share their ideas by posting them on a hallway bulletin board to make public work that is rarely seen by others outside the classroom walls.

With elementary-aged children, action outcomes may initially be defined by a teacher who seeks to model action in developmentally appropriate ways. With models to draw on and guided practice, learners take more responsibility in choosing to represent and share their knowledge in more personally relevant and rewarding ways. When students are taught to take action, they develop a better appreciation of being connected not only to their school, but to their outside community as well.

Here are a few examples of action outcomes from Karen's first-grade plant inquiry:

- Share the garden and plant projects with kindergarten and fifth-grade buddy classes.

- Post plant projects on hallway bulletin board to share with school community.

- Plant more than needed to donate produce to local food bank to help others.

Planning for action outcomes intentionally creates space for learners to not only demonstrate their knowledge, but to use that knowledge to do something important about what matters to them. Notice in Figure 6.3 the pride, sense of community, and use of content-rich vocabulary captured in this first grader's reflection about what she learned by doing during their plant inquiry. Even

FIGURE 6.3 A first-grade reflection: "We planted a garden and we learned about plants. Then we planted an amaryllis and we watched it grow. Then with a paintbrush, we pollinated the amaryllis. I learned by doing!!!!!!!!!!!!"

for first graders, inquiry "starts with lived experience . . . where people actively shape their own learning as they work on real problems within their own communities" (Bruce and Bishop 2008, 704).

2. PLAN AUTHENTIC OPPORTUNITIES FOR PERSONAL DIGITAL INQUIRY

Once you have a clear vision of what you want students to know and be able to do, it's time for the part of the planning process where the real fun begins. It's time to envision ways to flexibly engage children as partners in learning as you guide them toward the learning outcomes. At this point in the planning process, you will begin to generate ideas for how your inquiry plans might integrate the core PDI practices that lead to knowledge building, knowledge expression, and personal action.

More specifically, we invite you to ask yourself what kinds of engaging experiences and teaching supports are likely to create intentional opportunities for your learners to wonder and discover, collaborate and discuss, create and take action, and analyze and reflect as part of their inquiry process. Think about ways to make learning hands-on or interactive. Consider activities that encourage learners to deepen their understanding through reading, writing, viewing, or doing.

If coming up with ideas for creating intentional learning opportunities is challenging for you, we invite you to try out the PDI questioning tool shown in Figure 6.4 and Appendix F. You will recognize the PDI elements in the circle design. Additionally you will see guiding questions to prompt the design of instructional activities that lead students to a deep understanding of the learning outcomes while gradually promoting engagement and self-direction in their learning.

Please note that this format and these questions are designed to inspire you to imagine flexible opportunities for student-directed inquiry in your classroom, rather than to constrain your thinking. In addition, your initial planning should not be limited to precisely when and how these opportunities will play out across the span of time you set aside for this project. Rather, we encourage you to first think broadly across your inquiry plans, jotting down brief thoughts about hands-on activities, print and digital resources, and teaching supports (e.g., discussion prompts, modeled lessons) you might include *somewhere* in your project. Often, this leads to the realization that some kinds of opportunities occur much more often than others. This may cause you to reimagine what learning can look like

PERSONAL DIGITAL INQUIRY QUESTIONING TOOL

Use this space and guiding questions to brainstorm initial ideas for how you might integrate opportunities for each set of PDI practices into your inquiry unit. Aim to create flexible ways for students to deepen their understanding of learning outcomes and incorporate their own voice and choice into how they engage with the ideas.

GUIDING QUESTIONS

How will learners analyze content to build their understanding of challenging information and how will they reflect on their choices and their learning at multiple points in their inquiry process?

How will learners engage with content and hands-on experiences to activate their wonderings and discover more about their inquiry topic?

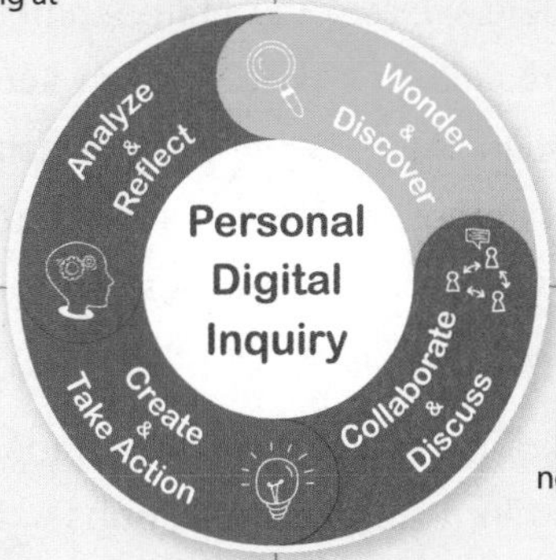

How will learners express their interests and new understandings through creative work designed to start conversations, raise awareness, take action, or change minds in their learning community or beyond?

How will learners collaboratively engage in joint conversations around shared interests to discuss interpretations, make connections, and negotiate differences in thinking?

Consider how digital texts and tools and other technologies may be used to support and/or facilitate each of these inquiry practices.

FIGURE 6.4 Personal digital inquiry questioning tool

in your classroom with planned opportunities for some of the missing elements. We have found the most productive plans include all four sets of practices as an integral part of the PDI experience. Chapter 6 gives examples of how Beth and Karen used this questioning tool to inform their planning of PDI.

Finally, try not to get too bogged down in thinking about technology applications at this point in your planning. Think more holistically about the kinds of inquiry experiences you envision learners having and how you might best support these activities. We find that thinking broadly at this point makes it easier to stay focused on key learning outcomes rather than on the bells and whistles of digital tools. You can find many concrete examples of teaching students how to productively engage with each core set of PDI practices in Chapter 8.

3. MAKE PURPOSEFUL CHOICES ABOUT DIGITAL AND NONDIGITAL TEXTS AND TOOLS

At this point in the planning process, an important question becomes, How can digital and nondigital resources be used to facilitate deeper thinking across the inquiry experience? Here, we seek to reframe thinking about technology. Instead of being a device for practicing skills, technology supports the different ways of combining digital texts and tools (see Figure 6.5) and instructional scaffolds for specific purposes.

This is an important point that bears repeating: technology supports PDI and not the other way around. Thus our definition of technology use becomes nested within the belief that planning for PDI is a cyclical and reflective process that entails

- envisioning new opportunities for learning and mapping these to curriculum standards (sections A, B, C, and D of the PDI planning guide in Figure 6.2),

- reflecting on how new ways of learning can foster deeper understanding and increased engagement (sections D and E of the PDI planning guide),

- integrating digital texts and tools to purposefully support understanding and expressing ideas from new learning (section E of the PDI planning guide).

DIGITAL TEXTS	DIGITAL TOOLS
Include photos, videos, multimodal and multilingual texts with text-to-speech capability for building knowledge, deepening understanding of key concepts, and increasing motivation with challenge and support	Enable teachers and students to organize, analyze, reflect, create, and share that new knowledge and ideas with others

FIGURE 6.5 Digital texts and tools work together to enhance and enrich core personal digital inquiry opportunities.

To facilitate this thinking, we created the PDI knowledge continuum (see Figure 6.6) as a tool for aligning instructional activities, both digital and nondigital, with the knowledge demands required to be successful. To us, this continuum

MAKE PURPOSEFUL CHOICES ABOUT DIGITAL TEXTS AND TOOLS
(Experiences to Deepen Learning Across the PDI Knowledge Continuum)

←——→

Lower-Order Thinking   Higher-Order Thinking

Acquire Knowledge	**Build Knowledge**	**Express Knowledge**	**Reflect on Knowledge**	**Act on Knowledge**
Learners passively receive (digital) information given or modeled by others	Learners (use technology to) connect new information to prior knowledge	Learners (use technology to) share their new knowledge with others	Learners (use technology to) reflect on and evaluate their inquiry processes and products	Learners (use technology to) translate their knowledge into action
Related outcomes When given access to ___, students will list, label, identify, define, arrange, match, quote, etc.	**Related outcomes** Learners will discuss, analyze question, interpret, connect, construct, etc.	**Related outcomes** Students will create ___ to argue defend, express, explain, synthesize, etc.	**Related outcomes** Students will reflect, revise, interpret, critique, compare analyze, categorize, conclude, etc.	**Related outcomes** Students will share with ___ to (raise awareness, teach others, start conversations, change minds) about ___.

FIGURE 6.6 Personal digital inquiry knowledge continuum

(which appears as section E of the planning guide) guides the most important part of the planning process because it brings together deeper thinking and technology use.

Within the PDI planning process, we encourage integrating learning outcomes that require both lower-order and higher-order thinking into planned inquiry experiences. As shown in the continuum in Figure 6.6, knowledge outcomes can range from students *acquiring* knowledge and using this knowledge to *build* their own ideas to students taking a more active role in *expressing, reflecting, or acting on* their new knowledge to meet various learning outcomes.

For example, accessing information about recycling from a child-friendly website is an effective use of technology that uses lower-order thinking to acquire knowledge. When we pair their viewing of this website with a second website and add discussion prompts for partners to compare ideas across the two sites, we get students more actively involved in building their knowledge. Our students' thinking and learning move to a higher level when we ask them to use the knowledge to create a video promoting recycling to be shared on the school website. After they share the video, students might reflect on the steps they took to create their video, explaining how they each contributed to the final product. And when they use a letter writing campaign to convince the local television station to use their information and video to create a public service announcement, the students are at the highest level, acting on knowledge.

Notice that the digital aspects of each knowledge outcome in the continuum are placed in parenthesis to remind you that technology use is optional, but not required, to deepen learning as part of inquiry. Later in this chapter we'll point you to purposeful uses of digital texts and tools designed to enhance your teaching and increase student engagement at each level of thinking.

Generate Inquiry Experiences and Related Outcomes Linked to Increasingly Higher Levels of Thinking

As you organize your inquiry plans along the PDI knowledge continuum, you may notice more experiences are sorted into some parts of the continuum and fewer in others. If so, we invite you to reimagine what learning can look like in your classroom by brainstorming ways for students to actively work at some of the higher levels. Here it naturally fits for students to have more agency in their learning—if given the opportunity. Once you have envisioned some of these other possibilities (in section E of the planning guide), you might modify your set of learning outcomes and PDI opportunities (sections A–D in the planning guide) to match your expectations of lower- and higher-order thinking across your inquiry plans. Planning in this way ensures that students have the chance not only to know and understand key concepts but also to transfer and use what they have learned to different disciplines and real-world contexts.

For guidance in crafting inquiry experiences and related outcomes linked to the levels of thinking in the PDI continuum, we have included a short (but definitely not exhaustive) list of specific verbs at the bottom of each cell in Figure 6.6. These example verbs are designed to help you generate learning outcomes and related experiences where students demonstrate increasingly higher levels of thinking and active engagement. Outcomes to *acquire* and *build* knowledge are completely acceptable, but aim to balance these with opportunities for learners to *express*, *reflect*, and *act on* knowledge—outcomes shown to foster students' deeper understanding and engagement with inquiry project ideas.

Blend Teacher- and Learner-Guided Experiences into Your Inquiry Instruction

As you begin to use the PDI knowledge continuum in your planning, it's important to also consider who is selecting and using the digital and nondigital resources and for what purposes. In Figure 6.7, we deliberately collapsed the five levels of knowledge outcomes along the continuum into two categories, teacher-guided and learner-guided, to call your attention to the value of both kinds of experiences as part of PDI.

Experiences at the beginning of a multiday inquiry unit or those planned as part of modeled or guided inquiry (as discussed in Chapter 2) are typically where students benefit most from more *teacher-guided* uses of technology for the purpose of acquiring and building knowledge (relatively lower-order thinking process shown in the two left columns of Figure 6.7). This is when, for example,

WHAT INFORMED OUR PERSONAL DIGITAL INQUIRY KNOWLEDGE CONTINUUM

In creating our PDI knowledge continuum, we intertwined information from the work of several respected educational leaders.

Bloom's Digital Taxonomy, developed by Andrew Churches (2009), highlights important knowledge goals linked with varied uses of technology.	bit.ly /bloomsdigitalt axonomy	
Depth of Knowledge (DOK) levels outlined by Norman Webb (2002) categorize tasks according to the complexity of thinking required to successfully complete them.	bit.ly /webbsdepthof knowledge	
Universal Design for Learning (UDL) guidelines, created by Anne Meyer, David Rose, and Dave Gordon (2014), encourage educators to select technologies that offer multiple ways for learners to access, engage with, and express information.	www.udlguide lines.cast.org	

In their book *Discovering Media Literacy*, Renee Hobbs and David Cooper Moore (2013) introduce ideas about how technology can support children's desire to use digital tools to create, reflect, and act on knowledge gained through inquiry. Many of these ideas are represented toward the right end of the PDI knowledge continuum.

teachers select texts and digital supports (e.g., media, text-to-speech tools) that enable different learners to access and *acquire important content knowledge* at their level to use later in the inquiry unit. Teachers may also organize digital resources in an online classroom learning space, such as Google Classroom. The resources can be paired with digital tools and thinking prompts that encourage learners to *build knowledge* by connecting, comparing, and synthesizing ideas. These more teacher-guided tasks are designed to intentionally support students' ability to access information and build an understanding of key concepts related to expected learning outcomes.

As inquiry progresses over the days, inquiry may become more learner-guided as students collaboratively discuss and analyze ideas they encounter. These experiences naturally stimulate a wide range of opportunities for learners to express, to

Teacher-Guided Uses of Digital Texts and Tools for Building Knowledge		Learner-Guided Uses of Digital Texts and Tools for Turning Knowledge into Action		
Acquire Knowledge	**Build Knowledge**	**Express Knowledge**	**Reflect on Knowledge**	**Act on Knowledge**
Teachers provide organized access to challenging information with • text-to-speech tools, • simulations, • videos, • multimodal texts and images. These digital resources enable learners to acquire important content information as a foundation for further learning.	Teachers introduce additional multimedia resources and pair with digital tools and thinking prompts that encourage learners to • connect ideas, • compare ideas, • synthesize ideas across multiple sources.	Learners use open-ended drawing tools, graphic organizers, digital apps, and presentation tools to • diversify how to express knowledge, • open up possibilities for collaboration.	Learners use writing, drawing, video, and screencasting tools to • document their thinking, • analyze and annotate texts, • compare and contrast concepts, • compare their inquiry processes and products over time.	Learners use social media and drawing, presentation, video, and open-ended creativity tools to • share, • comment, • replicate, • revise/remix, • collaborate, • advocate important ideas, • empower others.

FIGURE 6.7 Teacher-guided and learner-guided uses of digital texts and tools to promote PDI knowledge outcomes

reflect on, and to act on the knowledge they have gained. The increasing number of easy-to-use digital tools designed for children opens the door to increased opportunities for all learners to have a more active role in deciding how they might creatively express, reflect, and use (or act on) what they have learned.

For these reasons, we have grouped the three knowledge outcomes at the right end of the PDI continuum (express, reflect, and act on knowledge) as potentially more *learner-guided* inquiry experiences that inspire authentic opportunities for students to document what and how they are learning over the course of the inquiry unit (or across the year) while also taking more ownership by actively applying their knowledge in personally relevant ways. For example, learners can choose from a variety of open-ended digital texts and tools to represent and *express* their knowledge. At different points in their inquiry, they can use digital tools to document their ability to analyze texts and thoughtfully *reflect* on their learning. And, as described in the previous recycling example, students can use social media and a range of digital tools to create videos, write letters, and collaboratively share in ways that advocate for others—all ways of acting on their knowledge in personally empowering ways.

As discussed in Chapter 2, each opportunity for students to choose how they engage with digital resources to build, express, reflect, and act on the knowledge gained are tangible ways for teachers to intentionally weave in a gradual release of responsibility and differentiated supports. At the same time, teachers work to increase students' agency and engagement in their own learning. This is the heart and soul of PDI and the intentional teaching decisions that lead to learning with intent. In the next section, we offer additional strategies for how to select and use digital texts and tools for certain purposes.

Henry Jenkins, an expert in media literacy, writes about a number of skills that are linked together in ways that are similar to our PDI knowledge continuum. Jenkins argues that for learners to be able to fully participate in today's digital world, they need to be skilled *consumers* of knowledge created by others as well as creative producers of new knowledge for different audiences. To learn more, you can read the full report, *Confronting the Challenges of Participatory Culture: Media Education for the 21st Century.*

Confronting the
Challenges of
Participatory Culture
bit.ly/macfoundchallenges

Categorize Digital Texts and Tools According to Features That Support Inquiry

Identifying digital resources that match your purpose provides a strong rationale for how to use technology to support teaching and learning during PDI. Essentially, we are choosing technology tools based on the tools' ability to support the pillars of inquiry—deep thinking, knowledge building, idea creating, and information sharing. Once we begin thinking of technology use in this way, it becomes easier to identify the features that link various tools together. No longer do we need to fret if our favorite app is not available anymore or turns into a required paid subscription. Knowing the features you and your students liked best can help you find a new tool that serves the same purpose.

In our own inquiry instruction, we have found it helpful to organize technology tools into two overarching categories:

- Tools to enrich knowledge building during inquiry

- Tools to expand knowledge creation through expression, reflection, and action

Within each of these categories, we have included broad statements of purpose that can then be matched to specific types of technology tools that we describe in more detail (see Table 6.2 and the following descriptive list). Of course, the purposes of digital texts and tools can overlap and change during different phases of inquiry, and one tool can serve several purposes. For example, a graphic organizer tool is great for brainstorming ideas with the class, expressing early thinking about a topic. Later in the inquiry project, that same tool might be chosen by a student team to support the oral presentation of their project.

Similarly, a screencasting tool such as Screencastify or Jing might be used by the teacher to create a short video lesson about an important concept (e.g., teacher-guided activity to foster knowledge building) and, later in the inquiry process, students might create a screencast recording to express what they have learned so far, to reflect on what challenges they are still facing, or to create a public service announcement, for example, that allows them to turn their knowledge into action. The important point is that you try to balance your use of technology with both teacher-guided opportunities that enhance knowledge

TABLE 6.2

DIGITAL RESOURCES TO ENRICH KNOWLEDGE BUILDING AND EXPAND KNOWLEDGE CREATION	
Enrich Knowledge Building Primarily teacher-guided inquiry experiences	**Expand Knowledge Creation** Primarily learner-guided inquiry experiences
Digital Texts and Tools for Accessing Information and Building Knowledge • Assistive technology • Informational websites or portals for younger learners • Interactive lesson builders • Multimodal texts (videos, audios) • Online simulations • Search tools for younger learners • Teacher-created digital books • Teacher-created graphic organizers • Teacher-created quiz/review activities • Teacher-created screencasts • Teacher-created virtual reality experiences	*Tools for Expression* • Annotation tools • Brainstorming tools • Coding tools • Collaboration tools • Graphic organizer tools • Video discussion tools *Tools for Reflection* • Screencasting tools • Student portfolio tools • Video reflection/discussion tools *Tools for Creation and Taking Action* • Digital composition tools • Games and quiz creation tools • Graphics and image creators • Infographic tools • Multimedia presentation tools • Simulation creation tools • Virtual reality creation tools

building and learner-guided opportunities that promote creating and sharing that knowledge with others.

Next is an alphabetical listing and brief definition of the categories of digital resources we have found most useful in supporting inquiry.

- **Annotation tools** allow you to highlight, or otherwise mark up a document or resource without changing the original content. Tool features may also let users tag comments and share on social media or let multiple users annotate the same document at the same time.

- **Assistive technology tools** offer users alternative ways of accessing information and expressing their ideas to share with others. Features might include text-to-speech tools (that read text aloud from the screen), speech recognition tools (that change voice into text), or digital writing tools that predict word choices based on just a few letters or provide digital pictures to represent words or ideas.

- **Coding tools** give users hands-on ways to think logically and critically while solving problems. These tools help introduce younger learners to the basics of computer programming and robotics and may assist some students in designing creative ways of expressing or sharing what they learned.

- **Collaboration tools** support users with features to promote sharing and collaborating, giving and taking feedback, group note-taking and file annotation, and other forms of working with a partner or small group to creatively build and share knowledge together.

- **Digital composition tools** enable users to express their ideas by combining photographs, video, animation, sound, music, text, and often, narrative voice, into a single platform.

- **Graphic organizer tools** (or **brainstorming/mind mapping tools**) promote visual ways of organizing information that can help in problem solving, decision making, studying, planning research, brainstorming, and classifying ideas. Graphic organizers or mind maps can be used to create templates for thinking, note taking, representing, and sharing final products of inquiry.

- **Infographic tools** are used to create visual images such as charts or diagrams that represent information or data. Infographics are often used to present information quickly and clearly in visually appealing ways.

- **Information websites or portals for younger learners** are specially designed websites that integrate information created for children in a uniform way. These websites often bring together age-appropriate texts, pictures, games, and photographs into a searchable interface organized by theme, topics, subject area, or age group.

- **Interactive lesson builders** weave digital elements into instruction that enable users to engage with content in more active ways, such as stopping to ask or answer a question, choosing the pathway through a lesson, manipulating objects, expressing their vote, or giving feedback as part of the lesson.

- **Multimedia presentation tools** provide opportunities for children to create presentations that include animations, video, and/or audio (voiceover, background music, or sound clips) to share their ideas with an audience.

- **Multimodal texts** combine information from two or more systems including visual, audio, spatial, linguistic, and gestural systems. Informational websites that have multimodal texts enable learners to access and learn about information in multiple formats.

- **Search tools for younger learners** are specially designed search engines customized to meet the needs of elementary-aged children in terms of safety and age appropriateness.

- **Simulation tools** enable children to explore real-life situations and phenomena in a safe environment while having some control over the choices they make.

- **Screencasting tools** allow users to create a digital recording of all the action that happens on a computer screen and a person's narration about the action or their thinking. Teachers can create screencasts of customized minilessons about an inquiry topic or a short tutorial on how to use a certain digital tool. Students can create screencasts to document their conversations and evaluations of their work or use as a format for sharing their final inquiry products with others.

- **Social media tools** include any websites or applications that enable users to create and share content or to participate in social networking. For younger children, this might include viewing and commenting on age-appropriate blogs, sharing photos of collaborative projects in a private learning space, or getting homework help from experts on the Internet.

- **Student portfolio tools** help build a personal narrative of a student's growth in learning and achievement over time. Teachers, and optimally students themselves, can use these tools to privately or publicly add, annotate, and/or comment on work samples in just about any format imaginable—including audio, video, drawings, photos, and other kinds of archived documents— and then creatively organize these files to represent their learning over time.

- **Video reflection/discussion tools** prompt student discussion or reflection around specific topics or open-ended conversations. These simple tools enable students to record short videos of their thoughts and then invite others into a video dialogue by responding with their own feedback or ideas.

- **Virtual reality tools** typically use special headsets or other kinds of projections, in combination with a three-dimensional environment or image, to generate realistic images, sounds, or other sensations that simulate your physical presence in that environment. Virtual reality games for children allow them to explore places and phenomena they might not otherwise ever be able to experience.

Your school or district technology coordinator will likely know quite a bit about each of these categories and would be a good initial person to ask for support in matching your teaching purposes and inquiry needs with certain categories of digital texts and tools for your students. If you're not sure what questions to ask as you start your planning, the list of digital considerations in Appendix A may help you get started.

Expand Your Toolbox of Digital Resources

It's our goal in this book to focus on the purposes for using digital resources rather than getting bogged down in particular apps and programs. However, we also realize how important it is to explore the features of actual texts and tools while getting a sense of how educators use these to support the inquiry process. So, with the caveat that by the time this book appears in print, it is likely that some resources may no longer be available, we point you to several examples of digital texts and tools to satisfy your hunger for concrete examples to explore. The resources are sorted into digital texts to enrich knowledge building and digital tools to enhance knowledge expression and creation.

Digital Texts to Enrich Knowledge Building

One way to spark curiosity and support students' knowledge building during inquiry is to point them to informational websites focused on specific content areas or interdisciplinary topics. Here, we point you to a few of our favorite websites for younger learners.

Digital Texts to Enrich Knowledge Building in Each Discipline		
Little Explorers Picture Dictionary is part of the Enchanted Learning website. It contains over 2,500 illustrated dictionary entries that lead to useful images, diagrams, text descriptions, and translations into several different languages. Many terms lead to collections of digital resources around themes such as holidays, dinosaurs, geography, biomes, geology, and astronomy.	bit.ly /enchantedlear ningexplorers	
Wonderopolis, created by the National Center for Families Learning (NCFL) in 2010, is a collection of over 1,900 (and growing) daily wonders. Each wonder begins with a short video designed to draw learners in and is followed by an engaging text and thought-provoking activities about topics of interest to young children. Digital supports are also embedded into each text to reinforce key vocabulary and build comprehension skills.	www .wonderopolis .org/	

Math

Interactive Math Dictionary, created by educator Jenny Eather, contains over 950 interactive entries to bridge the gap for children who might benefit from multimedia exploration of simple and more complicated math concepts. Many entries allow students to manipulate objects, actively explore the properties of each concept, and check the accuracy of their manipulations.

bit.ly /jennyeather math

National Library of Virtual Manipulatives, from Utah State University, is a digital library containing Java applets and other math activities for children in grades K–5. Students can explore age-appropriate concepts around numbers and operations, algebra, geometry, measurement, data analysis, and probability.

bit.ly /libraryvirtualma nipulatives

Science

Journey North for Kids, created by Annenberg Learner, provides local tracking data about seasonal changes around the globe through pictures, stories, slideshows, and more. Teaching tools, observation handouts, and questioning strategies to inspire close observation as children track the annual migration journeys of monarch butterflies, robins, hummingbirds, tulips, eagles, whooping cranes, or gray whales.

bit.ly /journeynor thforkids

National Geographic Animals provides a kid-friendly space to explore photos, facts, games, and videos about all kinds of animals.

bit.ly /natgeoanimalsf orkids

OLogy is a science museum for young children created by the American Museum of Natural History. Photos, descriptions, videos, and interactive activities are designed to spark readers' interests about fourteen different areas of study, such as anthropology, archaeology, paleontology, and zoology.

bit.ly /OLogyScience

Social Studies

Utah Education Network (UEN) offers a large collection of videos and interactive texts linked to social studies topics, including geography, environment, US history and government, and ancient civilizations.

bit.ly /utahednetwork SS

Newsela provides both free and subscription-based access to daily news about current events geared toward elementary school–age learners. The website also offers text sets around topics of inquiry and a unique system for adjusting the reading level of each text to match the varied needs and ability levels of young readers.

www.newsela .com

The range of visual and multimedia texts available on the Internet enables teachers to easily customize the use of media to meet the needs and interests of learners. Pics4Learning (www.pics.tech4learning.com), for example, is a free, curated image library with copyright-friendly photos and illustrations in educational categories such as animals, countries, food, space, and geography. If you want to add a little mystery and some inferencing skills to the conversation, you might begin by showing only a piece of an image and asking students to guess what the image is using evidence from the image provided (see Coiro 2015). This gives students an authentic opportunity to orally express their thinking while using picture cues as a first step toward later using evidence in writing to support their reasoning.

To extend this idea even further, JigZone (jigzone.com) is an online gallery of digital jigsaw puzzles appropriate for all ages, with puzzle sizes from 6 to 247 pieces. The gallery features a large collection of themed categories such as art, animals, flowers, holidays, ocean life, transportation, or travel for puzzles that can spark curiosity related to many elementary-level curricular themes. You can upload your own photos to turn into puzzles and ask students to solve the puzzles to begin a reading activity. You can also send a puzzle postcard to student email accounts or embed the puzzles into your own classroom website or blog.

As we've discussed throughout the book, video is also a powerful form of teaching that fosters curiosity. For example, SchoolTube (www.schooltube.com) is a safe video-searching resource for students and teachers. You can search for age-appropriate tutorials created by other classroom teachers or explore a growing collection of student-created videos about topics of inquiry. Take time to explore some of these digital resources with your grade-level colleagues and consider how you might use them to spark initial conversations with students about topics they are reading.

> You can find more instructional ideas for using digital resources to enrich knowledge building in Julie Coiro's article "The Magic of Wondering: Building Understanding Through Online Inquiry" in *The Reading Teacher* (2015).

Digital Tools to Enhance Knowledge Expression and Creation

In addition to diverse collections of digital texts, there are several high-quality compilations of digital tools worthy of exploration to spark new ways of thinking about technology use as part of learning and inquiry. Here are three of our favorites.

Bloomin' Apps is Kathy Schrock's collection of digital tools aligned with Bloom's Revised Taxonomy, including the categories of remembering, understanding, applying, analyzing, evaluating, and creating.	bit.ly /BloominApp	
Allan Carrington's **Padagogy Wheel** helps educators to think systematically about integrating technology into instruction, based on the belief that pedagogy should be the foundation that guides decisions about the use of educational digital tools. The Padagogy Wheel shows the link between Bloom's Taxonomy (create, remember/understand, apply, analyze, evaluate) and elements of the SAMR model (substitution, augmentation, modification, redefinition) for integrating technology into teaching.	bit.ly /teachthoughtp adagogywheel	
The **Technology Integration Matrix (TIM)** (with videos), developed by the Florida Center for Instructional Technology, links various ways to use technology to enhance learning. Across the left side of the matrix are five characteristics of meaningful learning environments: active, collaborative, constructive, authentic, and goal-directed, and across the top of the matrix are the five levels of technology integration: entry, adoption, adaptation, infusion, transformation. Each cell of the matrix describes the combination of two elements through written text, video lesson examples, and links to teaching resources.	bit.ly /technologyinte grationmatrix	

We certainly appreciate how difficult it is to keep up with all of the digital resources that come and go over the course of a school year. We encourage you to also explore and discuss tools and texts with colleagues, whether at your school, through social media, or at conferences and workshops. With technology, there is more than any one person can know, but collectively we can build a strong knowledge base about tools and texts that support PDI.

PART II

Integrating **Personal Digital Inquiry** into Teaching and Learning

The inquiry units and lessons featured in Part II offer tangible examples of how teachers across the grade levels are using the PDI planning guide and underlying principles of the PDI framework to purposefully embed higher-level thinking and technology use into inquiry. In sharing these examples, we realize that every teacher and their context are unique. We hope these examples inspire you to decide what works best for you and your students as you strive for a balance of teacher-guided and learner-guided experiences with and without technology to support your vision of PDI in your classroom.

7

Personal Digital Inquiry Planning in Action

In this chapter, we will illustrate what PDI planning looks like in action by providing examples of two units. In each example, Beth and Karen articulate their thinking while moving through the flexible sequence for planning PDI outlined in Chapter 6: setting expectations for learning and teaching, planning authentic opportunities for PDI, and making purposeful choices about digital texts and tools.

Each example begins with a completed PDI planning guide, and in the narratives that follow, Beth and Karen explain some of their reasoning behind the design choices they made before and during the implementation of their inquiry study. They also include additional notes about how they may have made different decisions under other circumstances, how their thinking evolved over time, or other pieces of advice about the process. We hope this close, inside look at their thinking will help you formulate your emerging plan for PDI as well.

Find additional ways to engage with these ideas in the online study guide for Chapter 7.

bit.ly/PDIstudyguide

Personal Digital Inquiry in Fourth Grade

Setting the Context

In my role as a media specialist, I (Beth) had the opportunity to teach a daily fourth-grade reading group of eleven students. Although identified as skilled readers, some of the students had never read an entire children's novel and all had limited experience with the inquiry process. Most children at the school came from families living in poverty. Many efforts were being made to mitigate the effects by building a strong and positive school culture, including teaching students about perseverance, stamina, and goal setting.

The children had already begun reading the novel *Maniac Magee* by Jerry Spinelli (1989), which is the story of a boy who becomes a legend by bringing people together in a town where people with racial differences never cross the line from one side of the town to the other. Stories such as this can teach students about others who have faced challenges in their lives and pushed on to inspire many. As we started reading, I began to realize that a study of heroes and legends seemed like a natural extension of the novel as a way to identify role models while also promoting tolerance, understanding, and acceptance—hopefully leading to a better appreciation of each other and the power of positivity. The inquiry question that guided our study was: *Who are the heroes and legends we admire and why are they important to us?*

The district language arts curriculum, based on the state standards and the Common Core State Standards (CCSS), provided one guide for planning our inquiry, along with the state Curricular Standards for Library/Information and Technology Education. By drawing on standards in both language arts and library/information, I hoped to increase students' ability to access and comprehend information—two overlapping processes that are integral to successful inquiry.

The experiences I planned were also designed to align with the fourth-grade teachers who followed standards from the district course and grade-level English Language Arts (ELA) standards. For our inquiry into heroes and legends, I followed these same standards but added the American Association of School Libraries *Standards Framework for Learners* (2018). Since the unit included a research component, it seemed important to also include these standards. Most teachers do not realize standards exist for a school media curriculum. I believe it's important to bring together the two areas of ELA and school media, because many key elements overlap and

---

Notice how Beth works to foster a culture of inquiry in her library by stepping back to acknowledge her students' prior experiences and then intentionally designing a realistic starting place for using novels as a way to teach life lessons and inspire their curiosity.

support each other. You can find the key standards aligned to our inquiry at the end of the completed PDI planning guide in Table 7.1 and a brief listing of standards below the learning outcomes in the left column.

While reading the novel, early on we had a discussion about overall reading goals and several questions that guided our reading and thinking as students worked to construct meaning from the novel (see Figure 7.1). We also discussed present-day and historical heroes and legends, which intrigued the children and linked to my hopes to engage them in identifying role models who could shape their own thinking. At this point, more concrete planning for extended opportunities to wonder, discuss, analyze, and take action started to take hold. The right side of the PDI planning guide outlines the key opportunities I planned aligned to each set of core PDI practices; I explain how I used the PDI questioning tool to further guide my thinking about these opportunities in the next section. The bottom of the guide

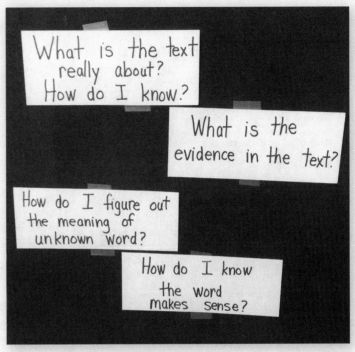

FIGURE 7.1 Overall goals and questions to guide our reading of the novel *Maniac Magee*

helped me plan for learning experiences and the use of digital texts and tools that fostered personal engagement, knowledge building, and knowledge creation.

After completing the novel, we moved from reading fiction to exploring nonfiction to capitalize on their interest and connect more explicitly to our schoolwide goals. Combining fiction and nonfiction texts also gave students the opportunity to deepen their understanding, to make personal connections, and continue to build reading and viewing comprehension strategies alongside some new digital inquiry practices. The students were still relatively new to inquiry, with this being only the second inquiry project we had worked on together, so a modeled/structured inquiry process seemed to best meet their learning needs.

Next, I share my thinking and planning more explicitly—first, by highlighting some of the key expectations for teaching and learning in my context, and second, by explaining some of the particular scaffolds I put into place to support and encourage my students throughout the inquiry process.

TABLE 7.1

PERSONAL DIGITAL INQUIRY (PDI) PLANNING GUIDE
Heroes and Legends (Grade 4): Created by Beth Dobler, Topeka, KS

INQUIRY QUESTION: Who are the heroes and legends we admire, and why are they important to us?

SET EXPECTATIONS FOR TEACHING AND LEARNING	PLAN AUTHENTIC OPPORTUNITIES FOR PERSONAL DIGITAL INQUIRY

SET EXPECTATIONS FOR TEACHING AND LEARNING

Knowledge Outcomes:

Students will ...

- identify role models who inspire and shape thinking,
- increase their ability to access and comprehend information, presented as text, video, and image,
- compare and contrast fiction and nonfiction about a similar topic,
- recognize ways to organize information into a cohesive form,
- identify and use a process for paraphrasing.

Action Outcomes:

Students will ...

- determine important details from text, video, and image sources,
- record information on various note-taking forms (numbered list, two-column notes, concept web),
- reflect on their learning throughout the inquiry process,
- create a one-page poster presenting information,
- orally share information and poster with younger students.

Content Standards:
- Topeka Public Schools
- District English
- Language Arts Standards

Digital Standards:
- District Technology Standards
- American Association of School Librarians Standards Framework for Learners
- Digital Media Literacy Competencies

(See next page of table for details.)

PLAN AUTHENTIC OPPORTUNITIES FOR PERSONAL DIGITAL INQUIRY

Wonder & Discover:
- Draw from fiction to serve as inspiration to consider our own heroes and legends.
- Provide background information by defining the terms *hero* and *legend* and presenting modern-day examples of each. Brainstorm additional heroes and legends, discuss, recording on Venn diagram.
- Select a hero or legend for further study.

Collaborate & Discuss:
- Discuss reading goals and guiding questions for comprehension.
- Model and discuss ways to determine important details from various sources (print article or book, video, image) and to layer this information for developing a deeper understanding.

Create & Take Action:
- Utilize a classroom digital space to access digital resources for the project.
- Develop paraphrasing skills by utilizing a four-step process: read, close (book or screen), think, and write.
- Create a one-pager to synthesize information from notes. Include hero/legend's name, four admirable qualities, an image, web link, quote, noteworthy actions, and reason for your interest.
- Present one-pagers to younger students.

Analyze & Reflect:
- Analyze information and use a variety of note-taking formats to record important details.
- Reflect on the process of analyzing, note taking, and creating through a stretch journal. Create at least four entries.

TABLE 7.1 (*continued*)

MAKE PURPOSEFUL CHOICES ABOUT DIGITAL TEXTS AND TOOLS				
(Experiences to Deepen Learning Across the PDI Knowledge Continuum)				
Lower-Order Thinking				**Higher-Order Thinking**
Acquire Knowledge	**Build Knowledge**	**Express Knowledge**	**Reflect on Knowledge**	**Act on Knowledge**
Teacher curates print and digital resources for each hero/legend. Digital resources are shared with students in class digital space (Google Classroom) for easy access.	Teacher models the process of reading or viewing and identifying important details within a text, a video, and an image.	Each student creates a one-pager with words, symbols, and images to describe their hero or legend. An online source for information is cited.	Learners reflect on the process of analyzing resources and summarizing information on a note-taking form by journaling on a digital document shared with the teacher.	The students' one-pagers provide the framework for an oral presentation to second graders.

Standards

Topeka Public Schools District Fourth-Grade Language Arts Course/Grade-Level Standards (www.tpscurriculum.net/standards/standards.cfm)

Reading—Informational

LA.04.RI.7: Interpret information presented visually, orally, or quantitatively (e.g. in charts, graphs, diagrams, timelines, animations, or interactive elements on Web pages) and explain how the information contributes to an understanding of the text in which it appears.

LA.04.RI.10: By the end of the year, read and comprehend informational texts, including history/social studies, science, and technical texts, in grades 4–5 text complexity band proficiently, with scaffolding as needed at the high end range.

Writing

LA.04.W.5: With guidance and support from peers and adults, develop and strengthen writing as needed by planning, revising, and editing.

Digital Media Literacy Competencies
(bit.ly/learningtargetsmedialit)

Access: Develop skills for identifying important information from multimedia sources.

Analyze: Create layers of information accessed from multimedia sources.

Speaking and Listening

LA.04.SL.1: Engage effectively in a range of collaborative discussion (one-on-one, in groups, and teacher led) with diverse partners on grade 4 topics and texts, building on others' ideas and expressing their own clearly.

Technology

4.3.C: Validate and evaluate the new information based on previous experience and knowledge

4.3.E: Find similar ideas from multiple sources.

AASL Standards Framework for Learners
(www.standards.aasl.org/wp-content/uploads/2017/11/AASL-Standards-Framework-for-Learners-pamphlet.pdf)

- Learners participate in an ongoing inquiry-based process by engaging in sustained inquiry.

- Learners gather information appropriate to the task by organizing information by priority, topic, or other systematic scheme.

- Learners select and organize information for a variety of audiences by integrating and depicting in a conceptual knowledge network their understanding gained from resources.

KEY EXPECTATIONS FOR TEACHING AND LEARNING

Before embarking on the unit, I gave much thought to several intentional instructional decisions that could guide our work all the way through the unit. I had lots of ideas, but wanted to funnel these into a cohesive plan. The PDI questioning tool supported this process (Figure 7.2). By sharing my decisions and a rationale for these up front, I hope

PERSONAL DIGITAL INQUIRY QUESTIONING TOOL

Use this space and guiding questions to brainstorm initial ideas for how you might integrate opportunities for each set of PDI practices into your inquiry unit. Aim to create flexible ways for students to deepen their understanding of learning outcomes and incorporate their own voice and choice into how they engage with the ideas.

GUIDING QUESTIONS: Who are the the heroes and legends we admire, and why are they important to us?

How will learners analyze content to build their understanding of challenging information, and how will they reflect on their choices and their learning at multiple points in their inquiry process?

Students will analyze nonfiction texts, including a book or website article, a video, and an image to describe a hero or legend. Journaling will prompt students to reflect on their learning process.

How will learners engage with content and hands-on experiences to activate their wonderings and discover more about their inquiry topic?

Students will use a fiction text to prompt wondering about real-life heroes and legends, to be explored by reading and viewing nonfiction books, online texts, and media.

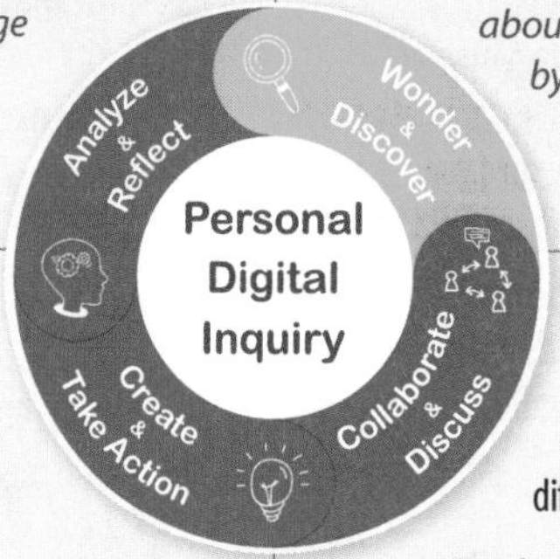

How will learners express their interests and new understandings through creative work designed to start conversations, raise awareness, take action, or change minds in their learning community or beyond?

Students will create a visual summary (one-pager) and share hero and legend information with younger students to inspire their own wondering.

How will learners collaboratively engage in joining conversations around shared interests to discuss interpretations, make connections, and negotiate differences in thinking?

Students will collectively create criteria for the differences between a hero and a legend, along with suggesting possible heroes and legends for further study. Within the group discussion, students will justify the inclusion or exclusion of a person who does not meet our hero or legend criteria.

Consider how digital texts and tools and other technologies may be used to support and/or facilitate each of these inquiry practices.

1. To focus attention on using technology to access information, include digital images, websites, and videos as sources of information to prompt rich analysis and discussion.
2. Have students share their reflections on a shared digital document to help keep their materials neat and organized and give them practice with their typing skills.

FIGURE 7.2 Beth's completed version of the PDI questioning tool

to convey the deep thought, and at times inner struggles, I faced during the planning process. As a teacher new to inquiry, I didn't (and still don't) have all the answers, but I continually work on moving toward the type of teacher I want to become.

DEVELOPING DEEPER UNDERSTANDING

When I first planned the unit, I paired fiction and nonfiction texts together so readers could build or fill in gaps in prior knowledge and spark curiosity. In addition, we focused on layering information from print, video, and images to deepen understanding. The combination of *Maniac Magee* and the study of factual information about an actual hero or legend gave students the opportunity to deepen their understanding, while also building reading and viewing comprehension and digital inquiry skills.

Across these examples of teaching and learning goals, notice how Beth aligns her plans with specific aspects of the school's curriculum and knowledge she has about explicit supports her students might benefit from to be successful in their inquiry experiences.

FOCUSING ON VOCABULARY, COMPREHENSION, AND WRITING

Our reading of fiction and nonfiction texts provided inspiration for questions, research, and writing (see Figure 7.3). Note taking, a strategy emphasized schoolwide, teaches skills for organizing information. Various structured note-taking frameworks can serve as scaffolds for learners, so I decided to teach three note-taking structures during this unit, as a way to develop key vocabulary, practice comprehension strategies, and promote writing.

FIGURE 7.3 Creating a one-page summary of key information

HONING IN ON IDENTIFYING IMPORTANT INFORMATION

Data from our district reading assessments revealed fourth graders' struggles with identifying important information when reading both fiction and nonfiction texts. My experiences with teaching reading also support this assertion, as I have observed students taking notes and copying down just about everything they read. Knowing how to pick out what is important is challenging. Essentially, a reader must decide what to store in memory and what to let go. I set the goal for this unit to provide lots of modeling and thinking aloud as I worked through this process with various texts, and to give guided, then independent activities for students to practice this skill.

DEVELOPING MULTIMODAL LITERACY SKILLS

Our school is rich with technology, as the fourth graders each have an iPad and Chromebook. The devices are most often used for skills practice and taking assessments. I wanted to move students beyond these uses and focus on using technology to access information, so I included digital images, websites, and videos as sources of information, in addition to books. The use of print and digital resources supports the concept of layering information to deepen learning. In this way, the technology supports our learning, rather than driving our learning.

To keep our unit manageable, I located the print and digital resources for the students' research. I found the books in the library, and I searched for the images, websites, and videos I thought would be most beneficial for students to use to learn about their heroes and legends, and I made the links to these available in our digital learning space. Although I recognize the value of students searching for information online, I chose not to teach these skills in this unit. I wanted the emphasis to be on identifying important ideas and organizing information, so students could focus and learn how to do these well. Preparing students to locate truthful and useful resources online includes the teaching of Web literacy skills, which would be integrated into our next unit.

CHOOSING PURPOSEFUL USES OF TECHNOLOGY

There were times during our heroes and legends unit where I chose to use or not use technology for certain reasons. Using technology to access resources opened up the possibilities. I could find high-quality, age-appropriate videos through our school library database and useful images through a Creative Commons search. Finding websites the students could easily read and understand was a bit trickier, but again, I had lots of possibilities on the Web. Sharing web links in our classroom's digital space let students easily get to the links. Another use of technology included the students' reflections written on a shared document. I could read and respond to their reflections at any point in the inquiry process—no lost papers or messy handwriting. Plus the students seemed to enjoy typing rather than handwriting their thoughts, which I could tell by their positive reactions during reflection time.

Several structures for organizing notes are integrated into the unit, and I chose to have students make notes on paper. Paraphrasing is a challenging task at best, but when going from digital to digital, the temptation to cut and paste is very high. When using paper, there is still the tendency for many to copy word for word. To mitigate this, I used a think-aloud to model my own paraphrasing, emphasizing the process: read, close (book or screen), think, write. I also created an anchor chart as a reminder and then continued to monitor students as they worked.

EMBEDDING REFLECTION THROUGHOUT INQUIRY

At one point in my teaching career, I had highly valued reflection for my students, but I had unknowingly moved away from this practice. Based on my professional reading, I decided now was the time for reflection to return. Because the students and I were fairly new to PDI, I felt that waiting until the end of the unit to reflect would not be the best decision. At that point in the process, most students are eager to be finished with the project or rushing to meet a deadline; they are definitely not in a good place to think deeply and learn more. Plus, I was hoping that the students' reflections would reveal ways I could make small adjustments in the midst of the unit. So I planned to embed shorter reflection points after each layer of information activity, and then I could check on these shared documents along the way.

SCAFFOLDS AND RESOURCES TO SUPPORT PERSONAL DIGITAL INQUIRY IN THE MEDIA CENTER

Now that you know what informed my planning and design decisions, this next section outlines some of the explicit teaching practices and informational texts (print and digital) I used to support my students as they learned more about their selected heroes and sought to teach others about their new insights. We began our inquiry by reflecting on ways that Maniac Magee might be characterized as a hero or legend. Then I shared definitions of a hero and a legend, and we discussed the differences and similarities. Next I displayed a slideshow with photos and orally shared information about people who would be considered heroes and legends today, including Cezar Chavez, Malala Yousafzai, Martin Luther King Jr., and Rosa Parks. I began here, rather than asking for examples from students first, because I wanted to pose new possibilities for students to consider for wondering and discovering. After my presentation, the students were invited to share their suggestions for particular heroes or legends. Together we organized our list into categories, and each student selected a hero or legend to get to know (see Figure 7.4).

Next, I located a book, image, website, and video about each student's hero or legend and uploaded these onto a table in a Google Doc that students could access in our Google Classroom.

The resources I selected for students provided a range of modalities for accessing information—books, images, websites, and videos provided rich opportunities for

Notice how Beth designed opportunities to reflect on past experiences and explicitly teach students how to analyze information sources to inform their ability to wonder and then discover new ideas about their selected hero or legend. In addition, efforts to use technology to find information on the Internet are aligned with the PDI knowledge continuum as a way to help students to access and build knowledge.

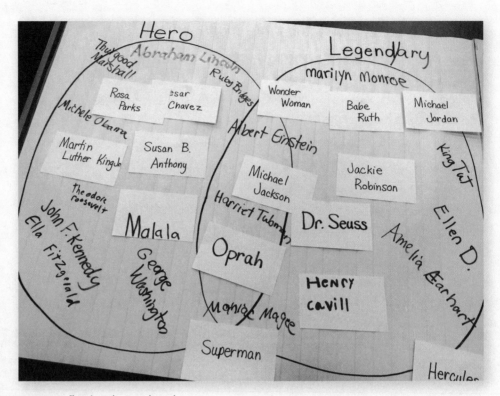

FIGURE 7.4 Choosing a hero or a legend

reading, viewing, and analyzing information. For written texts, I selected books and website articles with each student's reading abilities in mind. For images, I looked for photos with background details to add to the students' understanding about their hero or legend. For videos, I selected clips with factual information about the person's life, rather than speculation or rumors, which provided an opportunity to introduce the idea of critical evaluation skills and the need to be diligent when checking on online sources of information.

Students used three forms of structured note-taking tools to record and organize important information as they analyzed resources: a two-column note format (for books and images), a concept web format (for collecting website ideas), and a numbered list (for noting details from a video). For each type of resource, I modeled how to find and record information using my own legend, Amelia Earhart. I began by thinking aloud as I comprehended the information, pointing out times when I found details and times when I made inferences. Next, I summarized and made notes on the structured note-taking form (for examples, see Figures 7.5 and 7.6). To help me get into the habit of thinking aloud, I began by using prompts such as these:

Malala Yousafzai

born
1. July, 12, 1997

2. In Mingora, Pakistain

3. She Recived Noble peace
   prize.

4. Got Shot Oct, 9, 2012

5. Children's Activist, Womens Rights
   Activist.

6. Had Really Bad brain
   Damage.

7. The youngest person to Recive
   A Noble Prize

8. She wrote a book called
   "I AM MALALA".

9. Lives in birmingham, England.

10. She's 19 years old
    Right NOW

FIGURE 7.5 Numbered list for note taking

Two-Column Notes

Your name Salvador Date 3/8/17

Hero or Legend:

Title of the Text:

Main Idea	Details
Who? Who is the hero or legend?	Malala Yousafzai
What? What did this person do to become a hero or legend?	Malala fought So young Girls can go to School.
Where? Where was this person born, where did the person grow up, live?	Mingora, Pakistan She lives in Birmingham, England
When? When was this person born, when did the person die (if not alive), when did this person do the things that made him/her a hero or legend?	Malala was born in Mingora, Pakistan. And malala fought So young Girls to go to School.
Why? Why should we learn about this person?	She was brave enough To go to School Even though She wasn't Supposed to.

FIGURE 7.6 Structured note-taking form

- First I will _____, because _____. Next I will _____, because _____.

- I am doing this because _____.

- Notice how I _____.

- I decided not to write _____, because _____.

- I am thinking about what to do/write next.

Thinking aloud is, in itself, a type of reflecting on our own thought processes. As with all good reflection, we must first be aware of our thoughts and actions. It's tough to reflect if one is working on autopilot. So when looking for a place to begin to teach reflection, I begin here, at my own awareness of what I am thinking and doing. As I model my own reflections, I hope students begin to see that my awareness is actually a pretty natural process. Once I move away from the prompts, then I can more easily analyze what I am doing and share this with others—just as I hope students will soon be doing more independently or with a partner.

Thinking aloud is a great way to support students as part of modeled inquiry. Here Beth models how to read, summarize, analyze, and reflect as part of the inquiry process; with time, she expects that students will engage in these practices more independently.

For this set of inquiry experiences, I also added the element of formative reflection, or built-in opportunities for reflection during the process, rather than waiting until the end, when learners might typically reflect on a final product. After reading or viewing each text or video and making notes individually or with a partner, we paused to talk about what we learned and our process for learning. To facilitate their thinking, learners were asked to reflect on what they had done and learned, recording these ideas in a stretch journal, or a place to stretch their thinking through writing (see Table 7.2).

The journals were available as an online document in our digital classroom space. Learners were asked to record their reflections three times, one for each resource/note-making activity. My purpose was to encourage students to: (1) think deeply about their own thinking and learning; (2) slow down the inquiry process to emphasize the importance of thinking. I have seen learners want to quickly bypass the process of reflection, so they can rush on to create the project. Reflecting during the inquiry process gives learners a clear message: we are here to learn.

These formative reflections also helped to know if students understood what we were doing and why we were doing it. It also gave students an opportunity to publicly record and add their own voices about what inquiry looks like. This proved to be an effective way to introduce routines that foster feelings of agency

TABLE 7.2

STRETCH JOURNAL			
	What did we do?	**How did we do it?**	**How will I use it in the real world?**
Genessis	We made a bulleted list.	We watched a video and stopped to write down important stuff.	We will use it for making lists of homework (etc.).
Annalise	We wrote a list.	We went through the video once, and then we went through it again and looked for info.	I can make a list when I go to the store for groceries or do chores at home.
Keelie	We made a bulleted list.	We watched a video and we put facts but, not in a complete sentence.	I can use it for shopping or any list.
Norma	We numbered a list.	We watched a video. We put ten things important things on the paper.	In college I will have to write down lots of important stuff.

and self-efficacy as students come to realize that each of us has something to contribute to the learning that takes place in our classroom community.

For this inquiry project, I also built in time for student discussion: when students were independently seeking and recording information about their hero and legend and working on their culminating activity (see the next section). I knew that the students had little experience with working independently on a project over the course of several days, and I wanted to keep them focused on learning and creating their project. At the end of each class session for five days in a row, we paused a few minutes early for check-in partners to meet and discuss their progress so far. I provided a specific prompt to get each discussion started, but students soon took charge by giving feedback, making suggestions, asking questions, and holding each other accountable for meeting deadlines. During work time, if a student had a question and I was busy, the check-in partner became the next resource. A happy side effect of the check-in partners was the sense of community that developed when students knew someone else could and would support their efforts.

The culminating activity for our heroes and legends inquiry was to create a one-page poster on 11-by-17-inch construction paper and share it with a class of second graders during an oral presentation (see Figure 7.7). The poster included the following elements:

- an image of the person and the person's name
- adjectives describing the person (two on each side around the outside edge)
- an inspiring quote from the person
- a statement of what the person did to become a hero or a legend
- a hand-drawn image to symbolize the person
- instructions to complete this statement: I believe we should learn about [insert person] because …
- the URL for the website used to locate the information

I made the decision to create the project on paper rather than screen to align with the fourth-grade curriculum and meet similar grade-level expectations. A one-pager is a way of organizing information that follows a particular format, and teaching this format is a schoolwide expectation. In addition, the structured format provided a scaffold for the students who had limited experiences with creating projects. A digital project may have provided a similar structure, but again, because of our time constraints, it was more important for me to focus on the process of creating a project than having to also teach how to also use the digital tool. Once

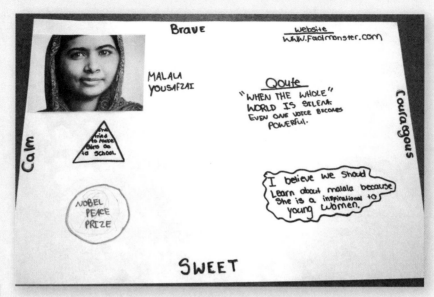

FIGURE 7.7 One-page poster for organizing and presenting information

Notice how Beth designs opportunities for students to create and take action by increasing awareness among their peers, while also providing several scaffolds so students are successful in their efforts. She uses rubrics to introduce students to important language and clear expectations and to show how to accept feedback from others—carefully building foundational skills that will enable her to gradually remove these supports in future inquiry projects.

the students experienced the inquiry process itself, then in our next unit we would add the additional layer of using a digital tool.

The one-page poster was then used as a guide for giving an oral presentation to younger students. A speaking rubric had been developed for use in our school district, emphasizing ideas and content, language, organization, delivery, and visual aids. Prior to the presentation, we discussed each element of the rubric and what each element looks like at the beginning, developing, advanced, and proficient levels. During my explanations, I demonstrated what a person might do at each level.

Reflections and Next Steps

Excitement and pride were evident in the students as they shared their projects with others. Their sense of accomplishment was contagious, and I smile to myself when thinking about how each student learned and grew during this inquiry unit. Although I couldn't say the students accomplished the objectives with mastery, they are certainly on the path toward this goal by growing in these areas:

- identifying important information in multimedia sources
- organizing information in a note-taking format
- reflecting on their learning alone and with a check-in partner
- summarizing their learning by creating a project
- sharing their learning with others

As with any unit, there are elements I wish had gone a bit differently. Getting important information from an image and video proved more challenging than doing so from text. The students struggled to see the image as a source of information and viewed the video as entertainment. Much modeling and guided practice was needed. Even though we focused on paraphrasing, this skill continues to be a challenge. Many times students have heard the phrase "Put it in your own words" but without a clear explanation or modeling of the process. It likely will take several more explicit lessons before it becomes second nature.

Overall, the inquiry unit taught me much about my own teaching and my students as learners and guided me into our next inquiry unit. I set out to have formative reflection be an important part of the unit for myself and for the students. This was the students' first attempt at reflecting, and if I were to do this again, I would spend more time helping students consider their thought processes more deeply, so they can begin to understand how they learn. Questions to guide discussions in a subsequent unit might include: How did you decide what is "important stuff"? Why did we view the video more than once? Why didn't we use complete sentences on our numbered list? I believe reflection, for both teachers and students, becomes richer with practice.

Personal Digital Inquiry in First Grade

Setting the Context

For several years, I have been exploring different ways to teach my class of first graders about plants, trying to figure out the best timing, sequence, and combination of activities, all while wondering how to start incorporating new standards. There are many possibilities to consider, and it is a challenge. My curriculum thinking starts with looking at the layout of the whole year and what tools I have available. For example, sometimes we have access to an outside garden, while other years I need to teach with seeds indoors. My plans are also influenced by what digital tools will be available and when they will be ready to use; it is about making the most of what I have that particular year.

A few years ago, our first-grade team made the decision to study plants at the beginning of school and, when we could, have a fall, instead of a spring, garden. The inquiry question that guided our study was: *How and why do flowering plants make seeds?* Studying about plants from the start would provide a solid foundation for future inquiries and meant that students could connect their learning about plants to other studies throughout the year, like geography in the winter, flowers in the winter/early spring, and chicks in late spring. We also changed what was planted in the garden to better incorporate the Next Generation Science Standards, by studying four varieties of the same kind of plant to learn about inheritance and the variation of traits. I organized my thinking about this study, including planned PDI opportunities and related standards, by using the PDI planning guide (see Table 7.3).

Socially, the garden also became a common focal point for my new class, helping students get to know one another at the beginning of the year (see Figure 7.8). The students planted seeds together, made garden signs, created journals, and took turns taking care of the plants while studying how they grew (see Figures 7.9 and 7.10).

FIGURE 7.8 Students examining a butterfly in our radish garden

FIGURE 7.9 First graders collaborate to make a journal page describing the variety of radishes using Wixie.

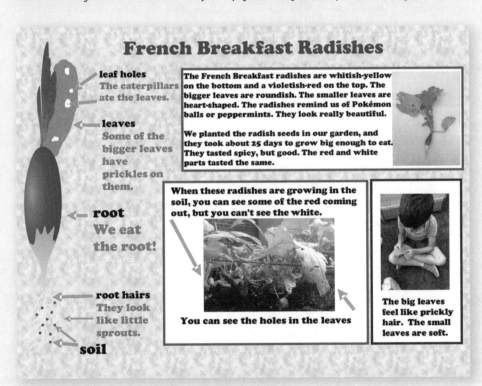

FIGURE 7.10 Journal page about radishes created by students

TABLE 7.3

PERSONAL DIGITAL INQUIRY (PDI) PLANNING GUIDE
Flowering Plants (Grade 1): Created by Karen Pelekis, Scarsdale, NY

INQUIRY QUESTION: How and why do flowering plants make seeds?

SET EXPECTATIONS FOR TEACHING AND LEARNING	PLAN AUTHENTIC OPPORTUNITIES FOR PERSONAL DIGITAL INQUIRY

Knowledge Outcomes:

Students will ...

- understand the parts of the plant and their functions and how they work together,
- find that the same kind of plant can vary,
- learn about the parts of the flower and role of pollination in seed production,
- study relationship between flowers and bees,
- discover ways flowering plants reproduce,
- study seed dispersal,
- learn about biomimicry and use this to pollinate a flower to produce seeds,
- study informational text,
- record observations and reflections,
- measure plant growth over time,
- compare and contrast plants and animals,
- practice using digital tools.

Action Outcomes:

Students will ...

- learn to collaborate with a partner,
- understand value of asking questions,
- respect the responses of others,
- belong to a community of learners,
- share in planting and caring for plants,
- communicate information with others,
- create a project to teach others.

Content Standards:

- Next Generation Science Standards
- Common Core State Standards

Digital Standards:

- Digital Media Literacy Competencies

(See next page of table for details.)

Wonder & Discover:

- Examine different varieties of amaryllis plants; plant amaryllis bulbs and observe changes as they grow and flower; study the parts of the flower, including with a magnifying glass.
- Examine ways pollination occurs in nature; generate questions about pollination.
- Explore ways to transfer pollen; find the best ways to transfer pollen and create a hand pollinator.
- Wonder about results of pollinating some amaryllis flowers but not others.
- Observe changes as the seeds develop; study seeds.

Collaborate & Discuss:

- Discuss different varieties of amaryllis plants; talk about changes to the amaryllis as it grows; collaborate to learn about the parts of the flower.
- Collaborate in small groups to measure the amaryllis.
- Discuss the videos on hand pollinating and various pollination methods; discuss how being able to hand-pollinate flowers might be useful to solve problems in different situations.
- Collaborate to find answers to questions about pollination, and decide on questions to ask an expert.
- Work with others to record findings and reflections in plant journals.

Create & Take Action:

- Take notes; compose journal entries; draw interactive diagrams; videotape and screencast to record student observations, questions, new understandings, and reflections, as well as document changes to the amaryllis plant as it grows, flowers, and forms seeds.
- Measure the amaryllis plant to create an actual-size picture of the plant for the journals.
- Hand-pollinate an amaryllis plant using the chosen methods.
- Create questions to interview a plant expert or beekeeper.
- Create a class project to teach others; share new understandings with buddy classes and parents.

Analyze & Reflect:

- Analyze the amaryllis plant and its parts at various stages of maturity.
- Reflect on observations through discussion, writing, and drawing.
- Articulate and record (digitally and nondigitally) student understanding of the parts and functions of flowers and how seeds are formed.
- Reflect on the role of pollinators and their importance; evaluate the effectiveness of different methods of hand pollinating.
- Analyze connections between plant life and other areas of study such as sunlight, the seasons, geography, and animal life cycles.

TABLE 7.3 (continued)

← MAKE PURPOSEFUL CHOICES ABOUT DIGITAL TEXTS AND TOOLS →

(Experiences to Deepen Learning Across the PDI Knowledge Continuum)

Lower-Order Thinking   **Higher-Order Thinking**

Acquire Knowledge	Build Knowledge	Express Knowledge	Reflect on Knowledge	Act on Knowledge
Teacher shows online resources, including videos, for students to learn background information on flowers and pollination. Teacher or students take photos of the amaryllis plant and their work to record the project and have materials for students to use when writing in their journals.	Students research flowers and pollination using books, videos, and online resources (including PebbleGo) to build their knowledge of plants and study vocabulary.	Each student creates a flower journal complete with photographs, as well as digital and handwritten illustrations. They use screencasting to share information they have learned, and they record pictures and videos on Seesaw.	Collaborative pairs evaluate the content of their plant and flower journals, looking at accuracy, detail, layout, and clarity, and make changes to words or drawings/photos as needed. They reflect on their understandings of plants, sunlight, seasons, flowers, and pollination to make connections.	Students share their pollination journals with others. They interview a plant expert or bee expert. They create a slideshow to share with kindergarten buddy class, fifth-grade buddy class, and parents to teach others and answer questions about pollination and flowering plants.

Standards

Next Generation Science Standards

www.nextgenscience.org/search-standards

From Molecules to Organisms: Structures and Processes:

NGSS.1-LS1-1 Use materials to design a solution to a human problem by mimicking how plants and/or animals use their external parts to help them survive, grow, and meet their needs.

NGSS.1-LS1-2 Read texts and use media to determine patterns in behavior of parents and offspring that help offspring survive.

Heredity: Inheritance and the Variation of Traits:

NGSS.1-LS3-1 Make observations to construct an evidence-based account that young plants and animals are like, but not exactly like, their parents.

Common Core State Standards (CCSS) in English Language Arts

CCSS Reading

CCSS.ELA-LITERACY.RI.1.3 Describe the connection between two individuals, events, ideas, or pieces of information in a text.

CCSS.ELA-LITERACY.RI.1.4 Ask and answer questions to help determine or clarify the meaning of words and phrases in a text.

CCSS.ELA-LITERACY.RI.1.5 Know and use various text features to locate key facts or information in a text.

CCSS.ELA-LITERACY.RI.1.6 Distinguish between information provided by pictures or other illustrations and information provided by the words in a text.

CCSS.ELA-LITERACY.RI.1.7 Use the illustrations and details in a text to describe its key ideas.

CCSS.ELA-LITERACY.RI.1.10 With prompting and support, read informational texts appropriately complex for grade 1.

CCSS Writing

CCSS.ELA-LITERACY.W.1.2 Write informative/explanatory texts in which they name a topic, supply some facts about the topic, and provide some sense of closure.

CCSS.ELA-LITERACY.W.1.5 With guidance and support from adults, focus on a topic, respond to questions and suggestions from peers, and add details to strengthen writing as needed.

CCSS.ELA-LITERACY.W.1.6 With guidance and support from adults, use a variety of digital tools to produce and publish writing, including in collaboration with peers.

CCSS.ELA-LITERACY.W.1.7 Participate in shared research and writing projects.

CCSS.ELA-LITERACY.W.1.8 With guidance and support from adults, recall information from experiences or gather information from provided sources to answer a question.

CCSS Speaking & Listening

CCSS.ELA-LITERACY.SL.1.1 Participate in collaborative conversations with diverse partners about *grade 1 topics and texts* with peers and adults in small and larger groups.

CCSS.ELA-LITERACY.SL.1.1.A Follow agreed-upon rules for discussions (e.g., listening to others with care, speaking one at a time about the topics and texts under discussion).

CCSS.ELA-LITERACY.SL.1.1.B Build on others' talk in conversations by responding to the comments of others through multiple exchanges.

CCSS.ELA-LITERACY.SL.1.1.C Ask questions to clear up any confusion about the topics and texts under discussion.

CCSS.ELA-LITERACY.SL.1.2 Ask and answer questions about key details in a text read aloud or information presented orally or through other media.

CCSS.ELA-LITERACY.SL.1.3 Ask and answer questions about what a speaker says in order to gather additional information or clarify something that is not understood.

CCSS.ELA-LITERACY.SL.1.4 Describe people, places, things, and events with relevant details, expressing ideas and feelings clearly.

CCSS.ELA-LITERACY.SL.1.5 Add drawings or other visual displays to descriptions when appropriate to clarify ideas, thoughts, and feelings.

Digital Media Literacy Competencies

- Analyze: Compare and contrast resources
- Create: Brainstorm and generate ideas; compose creatively using language and image; work collaboratively.

KEY EXPECTATIONS FOR TEACHING AND LEARNING

Having engaged in several inquiry experiences with her first graders in previous years, Karen now seeks to improve the sequencing of these experiences across the school year. In this way, her planning shifts to supporting students in building foundational knowledge that can be leveraged in the next unit to further deepen learning through inquiry.

Notice how Karen intentionally plans journal activities that document students' abilities to analyze and reflect on key content. In turn, these reflection activities informed students' knowledge building and facilitated their stronger connections between inquiry experiences across the school year.

By November, having spent the fall studying our garden plants, my students knew about the parts of plants, the function of each part, and how these parts work together to help plants live. Through their hands-on garden experiences, students had also learned about what plants need to grow and how to care for them. Together, we had compared and contrasted the four different types of radishes and enjoyed eating the harvest.

By letting some plants continue to grow so they would produce flowers and seeds, a few radish plants shot up, became much taller, and developed small flowers on top. My students were amazed and carefully observed these changes. They recorded their discoveries using the Seesaw app on their iPads, captioning their photos with statements like, "You will see the bud peeking out from the leaves." Although there was not enough time for the radishes to develop pods containing seeds, the students were surprised that radish plants could produce flowers, and they started to better understand how plants need to have ways to make seeds so they can make new plants. We also had a plant expert visit our class and share actual radish pods so the children could see what the pods did look like. All of these experiences prepared them for their study of flowers and pollination.

While planning for our flowering plant inquiry, I decided to start with the PDI questioning tool that Julie had introduced me to, in order to brainstorm ideas and clarify my thinking. I tried to make sure that I incorporated all of the important elements of inquiry into my planning. Organizing my thinking with these questions in mind and seeing my responses in the quadrants helped me balance my ideas. I typically start with opportunities to wonder and discover and work around clockwise. The completed PDI questioning tool shows the variety of activities and learning I planned for this unit (Figure 7.11). To encourage student agency, I included opportunities for students to explore related questions of personal interest. As we continued our study of flowers into the winter, I continued to make teaching decisions to intentionally spark deeper learning and more connections as we examined the process of pollination.

RECORDING WONDERINGS, QUESTIONS, DISCUSSIONS, AND REFLECTIONS

To help students process and remember their thinking, I find that having a written record of their work is an important component of an inquiry study. Depending on the unit, these recordings can be digital or nondigital, but we usually have a combination of the two. For this study, my students created pollination journals to record their

PDI QUESTIONING TOOL

Use this space and guiding questions to brainstorm initial ideas for how you might integrate opportunities for each set of PDI practices into your inquiry unit. Aim to create flexible ways for students to deepen their understanding of learning outcomes and incorporate their own voice and choice into how they engage with the ideas.

GUIDING QUESTIONS: Why and how do plants make seeds?

How will learners analyze content to build their understanding of challenging information, and how will they reflect on their choices and their learning at multiple points in their inquiry process?

> *Students will carefully analyze the plant and its parts at various stages of maturity and reflect on their observations through discussion, writing, and drawing.*

How will learners engage with content and hands-on experiences to activate their wonderings and discover more about their inquiry topic?

> *Students will use the parts of a flower, watch the plants as it grows and matures, closely study the pollen, pollinate the plant, observe changes to the plant, watch how seeds develop, study seeds.*

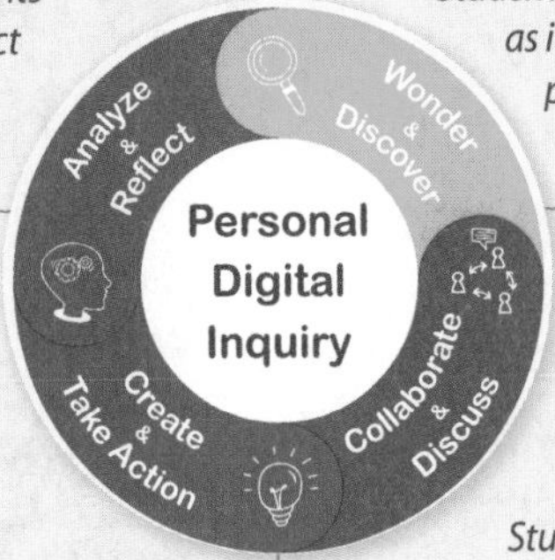

How will learners express their interests and new understandings through creative work designed to start conversations, raise awareness, take action, or change minds in their learning community or beyond?

> *Students will keep a detailed journal of their study, including writing pieces, drawings, and photographs. Small groups will work together to measure amaryllis plant and create actual size picture for journals, by cutting out and assembling the parts. They will share their new understandings with their buddy classes and parents.*

How will learners collaboratively engage in joining conversations around shared interests to discuss interpretations, make connections, and negotiate differences in thinking?

> *Students will discuss changes in the plant as it grows, talk about parts of the plant, discuss the video on hand pollinating, collaborate in small groups to measure the plant, and create an actual size picture for journals, generate questions about pollinations, and collaborate to find answers and record questions in journals.*

Consider how digital texts and tools and other technologies may be used to support and/or facilitate each of these inquiry practices.

1. Research videos on hand pollination to learn more about topics.
2. Find best ways to have students record questions and answers in individual journals.
3. Explore collaboration possibilities using Seesaw on iPad.

FIGURE 7.11 Karen's completed version of the PDI questioning tool

observations, questions, and thinking. Each student had a journal, but students worked on projects together with other students, in pairs or small groups (see Figure 7.12).

I made their printed journals out of 12-by-18-inch pieces of construction paper folded in half and tied at the spine with long pieces of raffia. At the centerfold, I inserted an extra long sheet of construction paper, double the width of the other pages (12 by 36 inches), and folded them in on each side creating one large sheet when opened up. In this centerfold, there was space for a life-size picture of an amaryllis plant (see Figure 7.16).

Notice how the inquiry experiences in Karen's classroom move flexibly across overlapping PDI elements. Her carefully designed journal templates support students as part of guided inquiry, while students naturally move in and out of opportunities to wonder, discuss, reflect, and explore more as they collaboratively document and share their work with others.

I created journal page templates on the computer, with headings, lines to write in, and places for illustrations. All students had their own page to write on, and, then, they pasted their completed pages into their journals as the unit progressed. In this way, I had some flexibility in what went into the book, in case we wanted to add or take away some of their writing pieces for the finished book. We took many photographs of the plant to include in the book as well. Their collection of journal pages demonstrated many of the learning outcomes I had outlined for students and also depicted some of their unique discoveries made along the way (see Figures 7.13 through 7.17 for a collection of pages from amaryllis journals).

FIGURE 7.12 Students study the amaryllis plant through illustration.

CHOOSING PURPOSEFUL USES OF TECHNOLOGY

When I decided to create this study, I was not sure about the best way to pollinate the amaryllis plant, so I did some research for ideas. I found a helpful YouTube video called "How to Pollinate an Amaryllis Flower" (MrBrownThumb 2013). When it came time to teach the unit, I shared this video with my students as well.

The first year I did this study with the students we took a lot of photographs of the amaryllis to incorporate into their journals. The second year our class had full access to an iPad cart, so I found ways to enrich this study using this technology. When we studied the garden earlier in the year students used the Seesaw app on their iPads to take photographs of the radishes and create audio recordings describing their labeled plant illustrations. In this unit about flowers and pollination, we used the app to photograph the amaryllis and video record students talking about their findings. Prior to the taping, students wrote down notes to help them

"How to Pollinate an Amaryllis Flower"
bit.ly/pollinateamaryllis

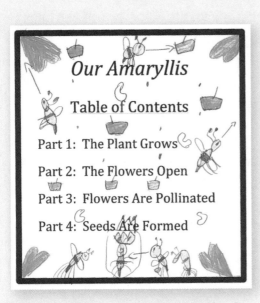

FIGURE 7.13 Table of contents, depicting the bee "dance" that bees use to tell others where to find nectar

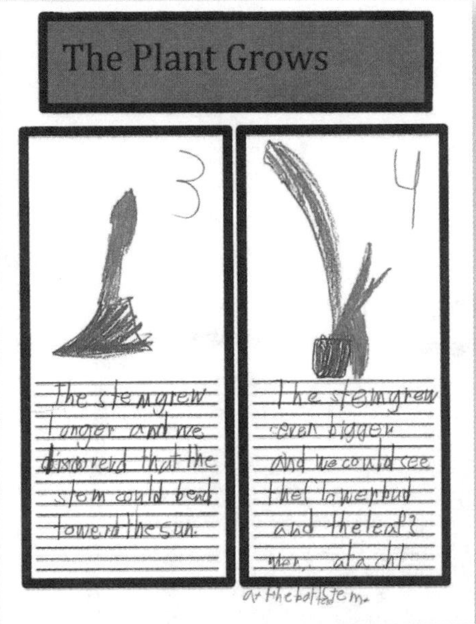

FIGURE 7.14 "The stem grew longer and we discovered that the stem could bend toward the sun."

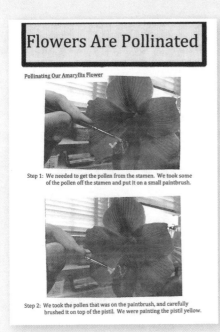

FIGURE 7.15 Shared writing about hand pollination with photographs

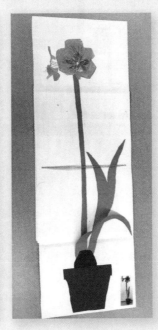

FIGURE 7.16 After measuring all the parts of the plant, the students created templates to construct life-size amaryllis plants in the centerfolds of their journals that opened up.

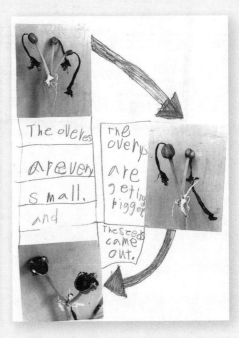

FIGURE 7.17 Labeled photographs showing changes in the plant as the seeds developed

remember what they wanted to share with others. They also worked in small groups to discuss what they had learned, and this became another record that could be shared with classmates. In addition, I used their recordings as an assessment that informed later instruction to clarify some misunderstandings that students had.

SO MANY FOLLOW-UP QUESTIONS

After hand-pollinating the flower and observing the seeds that developed, students were more connected to their learning because of the role they played in the pollination process. They kept saying that they felt like bees as they pollinated the flowers (Figure 7.18). Influenced by these experiences, when we discussed pollinators in nature, the class became fascinated with bees. Their interest launched a follow-up guided inquiry bee study, filled with much collaboration and discussion.

We took out additional books from the library. I ordered multiple copies of two nonfiction books (*National Geographic Readers: Bees* by Laura Marsh [2016] and *It's a Good Thing There Are Bees* by Lisa M. Harrington [2014]), and I pointed students to an online site, PebbleGo, that gave them access to age-appropriate information on bees. The students studied these resources individually, in pairs, in small groups, or as a whole class.

Pollinating Our Amaryllis

FIGURE 7.18 Student writes a journal entry about hand-pollinating a flower by using the paintbrush, writing, "It was so fun I felt like a bee."

Students were intrigued with the close-up photos of honeybees, especially seeing how the pollen clung to the bees' bodies or inside the pollen baskets on the bees' legs. They wanted to know and discuss how the bees were able to get the pollen into the baskets, how they knew where to find nectar, and how much nectar the bees had to collect to make honey. What were the jobs of the bees in the hive? How do they make hives? What are the roles of the worker bees, queen bees, and the drones? Students were surprised to learn about solitary bees, and together, they tried to understand how a bee could live on its own. They were also enamored with the parts of a bee. How can they fly with four wings? Why do they have five eyes, and what do these eyes do? What do bees really see, and how is that different than how we see? The discussion, questions, and answers continued to grow. Students recorded their questions, drew detailed illustrations, and talked together about their discoveries.

Integrating Outside Resources to Support Personal Digital Inquiry in the Classroom

COLLABORATING WITH THE SCHOOL LIBRARY MEDIA SPECIALIST

Many of their questions could be answered by the classroom resources, and students enjoyed helping each other find and learn new things. Other questions were too difficult to answer and required doing research with higher-level resources and adult assistance. As a result, I looked beyond the classroom and sought help from our school library media specialist so the students could continue their inquiry work.

Because students were more eager to find answers to particular questions, I grouped them by common interest. These groups included three students who wanted to study about how bees fly; several students who sought more detailed information about how bees see; and another small group that wanted to learn more specifically about how solitary bees live on their own. As I met with each group, I listened to the students and helped when necessary to clarify their ideas. I asked them to record their questions in their pollination journal page, leaving space for an answer. With the resources from our school library and the help of our supportive library media specialist, Carole Phillips, we worked with the students to answer their questions by simplifying challenging texts and other online resources.

INTERVIEWING A LOCAL EXPERT

Some of the questions deserved richer answers than we could find in books and videos. It was time for someone with more knowledge to guide them. Over the years, it has been very beneficial for students to listen to and interview experts. With some research, it is possible to find excellent local authorities on a range of subjects, and if not local, experts who live farther away are often willing to meet through videoconferencing.

After a bit of investigating, I learned about a local nature center with a beekeeper who regularly speaks with student groups about pollination. I invited him to come to our class as an expert to share his experiences and answer questions. He carefully described the pertinent artifacts that he brought in, such as beekeeper equipment, beehive drawers, honeycomb, and honey. We were able to use our time with him to answer questions that the class had collaborated on in advance. He even presented a detailed slideshow that included a higher-level explanation on how bees see.

Notice how Karen's purposeful selection of appropriate and compelling digital and nondigital texts further guided wondering and discovering as students naturally generated additional questions for study as part of their knowledge-building experiences.

Our class visitor offered information that only people with expertise in a field have, such as bees have good days and bad days! Having an expert answer their thoughtful questions, and being able to follow up on their questions with interesting conversation, was validating and empowering for my first graders. For me, that day was the highlight of our school year. My students worked together as a team to prepare for and enjoy our visit from the expert. Because they had learned so much together, we also grew as a community through our collective study.

CELEBRATING OUR LEARNING

Notice how Karen taps into the expertise of individuals in her community, intentionally planning opportunities designed to foster students' real-world connections to people and ideas outside the walls of her classroom, while also enabling them to create and take action in developmentally appropriate ways.

As a culminating activity, all of the students worked together on a book to record, remember, and present their new knowledge and understanding of important bee information. Anytime we create a group project to share with others, I make the contributions of each child relatively equal. To simplify this project, I had each student create one favorite fact page on paper that we combined to make into a book. The class insisted on adding a page at the end of the book to take action and let others know how important it is to help save the bees.

After scanning each of their pictures into the copy machine, I used the digital tool Wixie to combine all of the scanned pictures together into a slideshow, and I typed in the text of their words on each page (see Figure 7.19). Wixie also enabled me to easily add music to their show and turn it into a movie. The students discussed

Honeybees have baskets for the pollen on their legs.

We need to take care of the bees! The number of bees in the world is going down. We have to help bees so they can make honey for us and pollinate flowers. We can help by planting flowers that they like.

FIGURE 7.19 Class-created book about bees

what they learned with their kindergarten buddies, fifth-grade buddies, and parents. Through their hard work together, they had become the experts.

Reflections and Next Steps

This inquiry study showed me how important it is for young children to have the opportunity to explore and collaborate over time. Gradually building their learning through the year, and giving them the chance to notice and ponder ideas that intrigued them, had clearly made a difference. Thinking back, I believe it all started with the fall garden study, which helped my students realize that their observations and questions really mattered (see Figure 7.20).

In looking at the unit in terms of PDI opportunities, it was interesting for me to see how each of the elements contributed to a comprehensive experience. Changes to our plants happened gradually, and letting the students encounter them in real time, like feeling the pollen, hand-pollinating the flower, and watching how the plant changed as the seeds grew inside, made it possible for them to better understand these concepts. As one student stated about our amaryllis, "It's cool that you don't even notice that it's growing, but it is." It made for a more effective way for students to wonder and discover.

FIGURE 7.20 Students captivated by an ant climbing up a plant stem

Giving students the chance to discuss ideas and work with others, whether peers or outside experts, made a positive difference as well. As one child wrote, "When we work with a partner it is easier for us because they help us when we do not know something." Keeping a journal, and taking action by sharing their new understandings with others, assisted students in remembering what they had learned and solidified their thinking. Finally, through analyzing and reflecting, students were able to form deeper understandings and connections, including across units of study. For example, in a written reflection, a student compared a chick using an egg tooth to hatch out of an egg to a seed being able to get out of the plant because "the ovaries get bigger and then they burst so the seed gets out," and this way the chick and seed can "both get out" of the egg or plant (see Figure 7.21).

All the work that my students did together through reading, writing, drawing, photographing, observing, and researching elevated their questions and conversations. Natural collaborations took place based on common interests, and students learned from one another. The ongoing nature of our work provided regular opportunities for my first graders to reinforce their learning, deliberate their ideas, refine their questions, discover shared interests with peers, and make connections across curriculum areas. Clearly, they were making personal connections that mattered to them.

Students also took their learning with them. For example, during their free time, some students formed a bee group and constructed hives out of paper; others wrote stories about amaryllis flowers. One child created cards for home asking for a family garden; another wanted a magnifying glass for a birthday present. Outside of school, students discovered information that pertained to our topics that they heard on the news, and they would share it with the class (like how some bees were making blue honey); we would follow up together to get the full story (the bees were eating from containers of candy waste) (National Geographic 2012).

As for next steps, I will definitely place more emphasis on bees when we study flowers and pollination again. In the meantime, I also found a few mentor texts to further develop this study. In the book *Turn This Book into a Beehive! And 19 Other Experiments and Activities That Explore the Amazing World of Bees*, author Laura Brunelle (2018) has several bee activities that I would like to include, such as showing why bee wings make a buzzing sound. Mostly though, over the next few years, there will be numerous changes to the science we teach in first grade, as we work to find the best ways to fully incorporate the Next Generation Science Standards. I will also continue to integrate curriculum around inquiry purposefully throughout the school year in the most cohesive way I can.

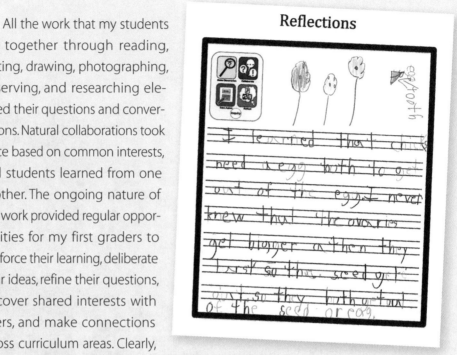

FIGURE 7.21 First grader's reflection comparing chicks hatching out of eggs to seeds bursting out of ovaries

Notice the depth of learning and student engagement that resulted from Karen's intentional weaving of the four core sets of PDI elements in a purposeful sequence of inquiry experiences across the school year. And her students leave first grade with the confidence and skills to pursue their own interests in the future.

Colorful Honey National Geographic Slideshow
bit.ly/coloredhoney

Intentional Practices to Foster Personal Digital Inquiry

In this chapter, you will learn

* strategies for weaving intentional teaching practices into your implementation of PDI while aiming toward flexible teaching and authentic learning

* how to enrich each set of PDI opportunities with experiences designed to model aspects of inquiry, scaffold knowledge building, and enhance students' ability to monitor and reflect on their learning throughout the inquiry process

Find additional ways to engage with these ideas in the online study guide for Chapter 8.

bit.ly/PDIstudyguide

You might remember in Chapter 5 we introduced the idea of teaching with intent. Now that you know more about preparing the learning environment for PDI and you've seen two examples of PDI in action, it's time to return to the idea and dig a bit deeper. In a nutshell, our goal with PDI is to prepare learners to ask, search, understand, share, and put ideas into action. Whether you teach kindergarten or fifth grade, arriving at this goal begins with identifying meaningful learning targets that connect to children's personal interests and then making intentional instructional decisions that guide students through the inquiry process.

We have described intentional teaching as making purposeful instructional decisions around these three components:

Engaging activities are designed to intentionally build foundational understanding and then to deepen learning with student-driven inquiry.

Thoughtful questioning is designed to intentionally foster wondering, analysis, and collaborative discussions.

Meaningful feedback is designed to intentionally encourage reflection about their processes and products and provide guidance for next steps.

In this chapter, we focus on intentional teaching practices connected to the core elements of PDI:

- wonder & discover
- collaborate & discuss
- create & take action
- analyze & reflect

For each element, we identify specific instructional activities from our own teaching or ones we have gleaned from our colleagues in various settings. These teaching friends have helped us to recognize four common overarching types of instructional activities that cut across grade levels: modeling, building knowledge and deepening learning, scaffolding, and monitoring and giving feedback. For each element of the PDI model, we hope to give you a glimpse of inquiry in action and inspire you to possibly try out or adapt these activities to make them your own. Before proceeding to these useful instructional activities, we would like to briefly remind you of two key concepts: authenticity and flexibility.

KEEPING AUTHENTICITY AND FLEXIBILITY AT THE FOREFRONT

We want to reiterate the importance of creating *authentic* learning experiences where students ask their own questions and discover the answers to questions that are interesting and meaningful to them. In the perfect world, PDI would always be, well . . . personal. But we also recognize there are times when district expectations, curriculum maps, or scope and sequences may infringe a bit on this personalness. At times, the teacher may select the topic or focus of what students will study. But during these times, students should be given the opportunity to enter the inquiry from different points by generating a question to ask experts or discovering their own fun fact related to the topic. Whenever possible, students can do follow-up research, learning at their own speeds and levels, on questions that are personally significant to them.

An aspect of PDI that either causes excitement or dread among teachers is the *flexible* nature of the inquiry process. A teacher doesn't always know where students' interests and questions will take a lesson or a project. There is no pre-made lesson plan or script to guide a teacher. Students will need time to explore and learn at their own pace to encourage growth. There are moments when the teacher takes the lead and guides students through inquiry and moments when the teacher stands back and lets children's curiosity grow and develop. It's during these less-directed moments that students may take more initiative in their own learning. Through gradually releasing responsibility, we prepare students for that time in their future when they will ask their own questions and seek their own answers.

Throughout this book, we have presented the four core elements of PDI in a circle format, which is meant to depict the circular flow of inquiry. But it's difficult to depict a complex process, such as inquiry, in a two-dimensional model on paper or on screen. During the inquiry process, a learner may analyze before asking questions or reflect amid a collaborative discussion, and taking action might lead to wondering. The idea here is that authentic PDI entails merging the PDI elements in various combinations and various orders, depending on the interests of learners, the influence of the curriculum, and a host of other factors unique to each teacher and group of learners. Never would we want teachers to think that the PDI model entails following the elements in lockstep order, one at a time, for a certain time period. This would be an inauthentic, rigid way of representing a learning process that should be personal, flexible, and authentic.

TEACHING HOW TO WONDER & DISCOVER

Curiosity drives each of us to know or learn more. A sense of inquisitiveness leads us to wonder and discover, both of which work together and complement each other. Wondering means asking questions, conducting research, and exploring possibilities, which correlates to learners seeking answers, making connections, and satisfying curiosities. The processes of wondering and discovering as part of inquiry form a continuous, interdependent dynamic. This chapter section seeks to bring to light the ways teachers can model, build background and deepen learning, scaffold, and monitor wondering and discovery.

Wondering and discovery...

- drive inquiry
- build on natural curiosity
- intensify engagement
- enhance observations
- increase awareness
- invite richer questioning
- encourage making connections
- enrich vocabulary
- support understanding higher-level concepts
- foster confidence
- compel students to read and write
- promote independent research
- lead to innovation

FIGURE 8.1 A student wonders about the flowers on a bean plant

Model for Wonder & Discover

Modeling and thinking aloud are key to fostering wondering and discovery because each gives students a window into our thought processes. Why is this important? Because, although curiosity may come naturally to humans, asking questions in a school setting may not. "Thinking in questions" (Rothstein and Santana 2011) is a mental skill, involving a thinking process that we cannot easily pass on to our students without explaining how we do it ourselves. Explaining how *you* activate wondering is not the same as explaining how *to* activate wondering. It's most helpful if you are talking aloud about the thinking you do as you sense your own curiosity and putting this curiosity into words by generating questions. To do this effectively, we, as teachers, must become aware of our own thought processes. This can be easier said than done. Because, as adults, we have so much experience with wondering and discovering, it's easy to move through the process without this important aware-ness. We must slow down our thinking, be mindful of our thoughts, and share these in a way that scaffolds students until they are able to activate their passion for wondering and discovery on their own.

Through our modeling, we can teach concepts and vocabulary along the way. Engaged students are like sponges, and they will begin to use our words, ask questions in the way that we do, and show a similar passion that we display for discovering information. In Karen's first-grade classroom, students are encouraged to use content vocabulary learned from modeled inquiry lessons. It takes time and practice for students to be able to use the vocabulary and ideas from teacher modeling. Shared writing helps students learn how to write their own individual pieces. In Figure 8.2, a page from a student's polli-nation journal, previously discussed in Chapter 7, includes a seed from the amaryllis plant the class hand-pollinated, along with a photo of the seed and the seed pods it came from. To the right is the class shared writing piece about pollinating some

FIGURE 8.2 A page from a student's pollination journal

of the amaryllis flowers. Below that the student describes in her own words what happened: "The amaryllis grew seeds. The seeds grew and grew because we polli-nating [*sic*] it. One flower we cut the stamen and the pistil so it didn't grow seeds."

First Karen modeled the vocabulary (i.e., *pollination*, *stamen*, *pistil*) in her instruction, and then students integrated these key words into their writing. Karen sparked engagement by creating a culture of inquiry, intentionally setting up opportunities, texts, routines, and scaffolds that piqued students' interest, nurtured curiosity, and valued different perspectives. Our goal is to lead students from modeling to guided practice and then to independent practice.

For younger students, Karen also used slightly different words to represent the key elements of PDI, framing the process with vocabulary that made sense to her first graders and pairing the elements with graphics that encouraged conver-sation around critical practices she modeled, particularly at the beginning of the school year. This classroom poster (see Figure 8.3) intentionally modeled ways of talking about what they were doing, and children referred to it often to reflect on

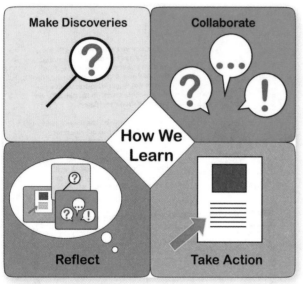

ART: NICHOLAS BLACKWOOD

FIGURE 8.3 A child-friendly graphic to help young learners understand personal digital inquiry

their own discoveries and how they connected to the bigger picture of inquiry in action.

For both full inquiry units and single inquiry lessons, it's critical to intentionally plan to model wondering by thinking aloud about the way your own experience prompts questions and the fact that discovering answers often leads to more questions. Students must also be given opportunities to ask their own questions, whether individually or shared with a group, because "when you ask your own questions, you are basically challenging yourself" (Rothstein and Santana 2011, 43). Expecting students to ask their own questions gives value to their curiosity. Teaching students, especially young students, to ask meaningful questions is no small task. You will need to model, model, and model more. But when students are asking meaningful questions, you can design instruction based on children's curiosity, which promotes motivation and engagement.

Build Background and Deepen Learning for Wonder & Discover

Although questions may reveal what we do not know, they can also give a glimpse of what we do know, or at least what we think we know. Before asking students to verbalize their wonderings and set off on discovery, build their background knowledge through books, discussions, real objects, videos, field trips, guest speakers, simulation activities, and real-world experiences. You will likely find the students' questions reach higher levels of sophistication when they have background knowledge and vocabulary that lets them better connect what they know to what is yet to be learned.

For example, when Karen's first graders were studying geography, they gathered books on the continents from the library and did preliminary research on PebbleGo. After they had researched, studied, and gained a solid background of information, the students asked higher-level questions that they couldn't find answers to in their initial resources. They sought out additional books from the library and online resources, and they had people who had lived in other places around the world come and share information.

As students share their wonderings aloud or through writing, be observant for gaps in their background knowledge, misinformation, or misuse of vocabulary. Effective questions that can solidly lead students through the inquiry process rely on students knowing accurate information, even if it's at a simplistic level. For example, Beth worked with a third-grade teacher to teach an inquiry unit about animals from extreme environments. One student wondered why a bobcat would live in the desert where it is hot all of the time. He did not realize that at night the desert can become quite chilly, and the bobcat's thick fur lets him adapt to the changing temperatures.

The best questions for an inquiry project are the ones that cannot be answered easily, such as, What is the difference between a landfill and a dump? If a question is too simple, and the answer located easily and quickly, then the inquiry process becomes a surface-level activity. Good questions are not too narrow, not too broad, but just right (Dobler and Eagleton 2015). Near the beginning of an inquiry project, you may notice that students are asking general questions, possibly testing the waters to see what you expect or possibly because their sparse background knowledge and understanding of vocabulary keep them at this general level. But as students gather more information through background knowledge-building activities, their thinking broadens, their vocabulary refines, and their questions become more complex.

During Beth's fourth-grade tornado inquiry, one of the first lessons invited students to ask questions about tornadoes. Their questions included ones like, Why do we have tornadoes and how do tornadoes form? After gathering information through reading a website and viewing a video, the group returned to asking additional questions. With facts and descriptive language now in their repertoire, the questions became more specific: How does the EF scale measure the strength of a tornado, and what is the difference between a tornado and a strong wind storm? It was easy to see how deeper prior knowledge leads to more specific and thoughtful questions.

Giving students an opportunity to brainstorm and record questions, whether as a group or an individual, lets students begin to see that their ideas are valued. They can also learn more about the breadth and depth of curiosity by listening to others. Early on, pausing in this process to judge or answer questions sometimes will slow down or even halt the question-asking process by getting students off track. We have also found that referring to these questions, and addressing them at a later time when students are better able to understand the answers, is critical.

An important goal of PDI, besides asking good questions, is the construction and deepening of knowledge. Hands-on activities can do just that, as well as inspiring rich questions and developing vocabulary. In studying about pollination, most of the first graders in Karen's class had heard of but did not have a good understanding of pollen, the structure of a flower, or the concept of pollination, even with excellent books and videos. Karen knew her students would benefit from seeing pollen, as well as the process of hand-pollinating a flower. So, as is more fully discussed in Chapter 7, the students planted an amaryllis bulb that grew in a pot in their classroom and documented the changes in a pollination journal.

In watching an amaryllis plant grow and hand-pollinating the flower, students gained a deeper appreciation for the parts of a flower and the role of the pollinators. Watching the ovaries grow over time, and eventually seeing the seeds inside, made it possible to better comprehend an abstract concept. This helped students to make connections later in the year, especially between fertilized and unfertilized eggs, when studying the chicken life cycle. It also resulted in the class becoming intrigued with learning more about pollinators, which sparked an inquiry study on bees. Thus the learning continued.

Scaffold for Wonder & Discover

Thinking more deeply about ideas can occur when a teacher provides a gentle nudge toward more independence, as students are ready. The old adage never do for students what they can do for themselves must be coupled with being on the lookout for what students are ready for next, then providing just the right amount of scaffolding to get students on their way.

Scaffolds for wonder & discover support learners as they ask their own questions or are inspired by questions developed with classmates or the teacher. Statement and question stems, such as "I wonder about . . ."; "What happens if . . . ?"; "Why does . . . ?" can guide students toward deeper thinking and wondering. Third graders in Elena Valencia's class were able to ask lots of questions, but their questions mostly remained at the surface, focusing on *what* rather than *why* or *how*. Elena's goal was to encourage deeper questions, which in turn would encourage deeper thinking.

To scaffold this learning, Elena identified a text set on Newsela.com entitled "Happy Chinese New Year" that aligned with the social studies curriculum. Before having the students dive into the text set, students were asked to consider what they knew about the Chinese New Year and what they wondered about and then to write a question on a shared document. This process of intentionally building background knowledge and setting a purpose for reading creates a model for what Elena hopes students will be able to do on their own by the end of the school year.

Next, students explored the text set, selecting two of the four articles to read. Then students considered what they wondered now that they had more information, and each wrote another question on the shared document. Pairs compared and contrasted the two sets of questions. Elena reflected with the class about the supports in place during this activity. In this way, she helped students recognize the scaffold and what would occur next as they began to work more on their own.

Although open inquiry gives children the chance to develop questions based on their interests, a more structured inquiry activity scaffolds the inquiry process for students by sparking their interest in topics selected by the teacher, whether related to the curriculum or to real-world or civic engagement. Allison Preston's second graders were posed with a real-life challenge. The school had recently been remodeled and an outdoor courtyard was created. The second-grade class had been selected to design the layout and select the plants for the courtyard.

Working in small groups, the students looked for information on two websites provided by Allison, one related to landscaping and the other related to wildflowers native to the area. Each group's goal was to identify ten flowers, trees, or shrubs that could grow in the courtyard and record their information on a chart. The second graders were given parameters for their wondering, which let them experience the inquiry process within a supported situation.

In another classroom, fourth-grade teacher Tyler Gill also provided scaffolding for wonder & discover by teaching his students to think in questions. First students were asked to respond to these questions using an online poll:

1. What do you want to learn?

2. How do you want to learn it (i.e., watch a video, learn from the teacher, read a book, do an experiment)?

3. How can you prove to me what you learned?

The students' responses led to individual, small-group, and whole-class inquiry projects during the next quarter of the school year. When one student asked why the sun shines yellow and the moon looks white, Tyler pointed her to an online collection of science resources he created for the class. Tyler believes the biggest challenge his students face with inquiry is "finding relevant, important, information in a timely manner," so he scaffolds by making collections of age-appropriate online resources available to students in their classroom space on the school's learning management system, so learners can ask and begin to answer their own questions.

Monitor and Give Feedback for Wonder & Discover

Learners enjoy knowing, and deserve to know, of their progress throughout a unit of study. Intentionally monitoring and providing feedback lets students realize that we see each one as an individual learner whose questions and ideas are valued. Interest and engagement can grow, and new learning connections can form. Feedback for wondering and discovering may be informal—a smile, a thumbs-up, or a targeted comment recognizing or guiding a student toward the learning goal. More formal feedback, such as using a rubric or giving a letter grade, likely occurs later in the project, when students create a product to demonstrate their learning, as we see in Jeremy Guski's fifth-grade class.

The project began with Jeremy's students discovering what it would be like to go back in time as part of an interdisciplinary immigration study. From February to April, each student created a fictional, but historically accurate, person and wrote a detailed journal of the immigration experience, including the reasons for leaving the home country, the trip to the United States, and assimilation to a new home. Throughout this part of the project, Jeremy provided individual feedback through periodic responses to students' journal entries.

After reading, researching, and writing about the topic for about a month and a half, the students were ready to use what they learned to become part of this experience, with the help of digital tools. Each student selected an old photograph that included people and a location that matched the story of the character from the journal. Using a green screen and Photoshop, each student dressed up in a period outfit and found a way to be incorporated into the old photo. Jeremy created a rubric to give students feedback about their work, including their descriptions of the image and their use of technology.

Elsewhere, kindergarten teacher Deb Krisanda intentionally used feedback as students were learning new content about nature. Deb gave her students the time, information, and hands-on experiences they needed to explore the world around them. She provided multiple opportunities throughout the year for students to wonder and discover. Her students were encouraged to notice and explore by taking nature walks around the school. Concepts such as the harvest and the farm-to-table movement were explained. In the winter, her students observed the bird feeder outside their classroom and watched an amaryllis plant grow and flower. In the spring, kindergartners documented the changes to the bulbs they had planted in the fall.

As children wrote and drew the information, Deb provided feedback. Deb has found that her students are more engaged when the class talks about what they see. Experiences are supported through conversations that activate and create rich background knowledge, monitor students' understandings, and correct misconceptions and fill in gaps as needed. Students knew, from hearing Deb's continual feedback, that asking deeper-level questions was valued in this classroom.

Wondering and discovery can occur naturally if the conditions are right. But in the frenetic pace of the classroom, a thoughtful teacher often needs to intentionally create the learning situations that foster these processes by modeling, building background knowledge, scaffolding, and monitoring. With curiosity being the bedrock of inquiry, we simply can't leave its spark and growth to chance.

TEACHING HOW TO COLLABORATE & DISCUSS

Learning is social and part of a mutually constructive process that involves face-to-face talking, listening, and consensus building. When learners seek answers to essential questions, talk through information, and solve problems together, they essentially create new knowledge for themselves and each other. New understandings are also realized when learners use technology to interact with experts in the field or collaborate with teammates to share information and ideas. This is not the knowledge gained from memorization, listening to teacher lectures, or completing paper-and-pencil tasks. This kind of knowledge develops from a learner's active engagement, critical thinking, and flexible problem solving.

Intentionally creating collaboration opportunities offers students the chance to engage in joint conversations around shared interests, discuss interpretations, make connections, and negotiate differences in their thinking. Importantly, collaboration involves more than just cooperation and compromise. Ultimately, collaboration means collectively working toward a single goal, and synthesizing the ideas of everyone involved to come up with an idea that's greater than what you would have produced by yourself.

Collaboration and discussion . . .

- teach communication skills
- make abstract ideas concrete
- get ideas out on the table
- increase awareness of other viewpoints
- promote more question asking
- build vocabulary
- develop trust and friendship
- promote listening, connecting, and building on ideas
- encourage appreciation of others' strengths and challenges
- develop skills to advocate for a viewpoint
- foster depth of understanding
- build confidence

Some teachers structure teams as a way to facilitate students learning together, deepening understanding, delving into more multidimensional topics and issues, and supporting each other's learning. Although this may sound like a tall order for young learners, think of it as a process of working toward a goal. Each work session may not be perfect, and often, when learning new skills, it's two steps forward and one step back. But the skills needed to effectively support each other as a team of learners are important life skills and definitely worth the time. Consider what it's like to work on a team as a teacher. You must navigate personalities, be articulate in your own ideas, and find ways to support the group as a whole. By preparing students to learn and solve problems as a team, you are preparing them for learning opportunities now and well into their future.

Teachers who have witnessed the engagement of a team discussing a topic the members care about or the magic of a small group working together to design a project that reflects students' learning know that these are awesome sights to behold. Our challenge, as authors of this book, is to share examples that come as close to giving you a bird's-eye view of this process as possible. So, in this next section, you will find descriptions of intentional instructional activities from various grade levels that center around ways teachers can model, build background knowledge and deepen learning, scaffold, and monitor children's progress as they collaborate and discuss their questions and newly learned ideas.

Model for Collaborate & Discuss

We know when teaching a new concept to children one explanation is not enough, especially when it comes to being able to effectively collaborate and discuss. Every conversation is unique, and for a team to work together, each team member must have a toolbox of strategies to draw from when communicating with the group. Our goal is to support students as they fill their toolbox with techniques for active listening, along with informing, elaborating, and persuading. On some days, with some groups, the use of these tools will come easily; with others it will be like a hike up a mountainside with a forty-pound backpack, wearing flip-flops. A teacher's continual modeling and thinking aloud is a critical key to success. If PDI is new, the importance of teacher modeling is more obvious, but just because it's February and the students have been working on teams all year, it doesn't mean they won't continue to need teacher modeling and support.

For example, in an inquiry study of animals from extreme environments, students were first shown a slideshow of various animals from the desert and the Arctic, along with a bit of factual information about each animal. Next, each student identified three animals of interest. From these, students were matched to a partner with a similar interest. Then Beth, as the library media specialist, modeled the types of things she could say to a partner to explain what she was curious about or why she was interested in her selected animal, a camel. Next, students were asked to participate in a structured conversation. First, each one explained to their partner why the animal was chosen. Each partner was given three minutes to talk, with the teacher keeping time. After each partner had a turn, the pairs were given three more minutes each to talk about what they hoped to learn during the project (see Figure 8.4).

Modeling is key to passing on knowledge and experiences, but we don't want to linger at modeling too long. Moving students on to guided practice gives the opportunity to begin applying what has been learned from high-quality modeling.

FIGURE 8.4 Listening and speaking skills develop through inquiry group work.

Build Background and Deepen Learning for Collaborate & Discuss

The building of background knowledge is like a spiral; expertise builds over time, by gathering information from varied resources and sharing our ideas with others through writing, talking, and creating (see Figure 8.5). As background knowledge grows, an idea noticed in a resource may become a talking point for discussion, and newfound knowledge leads learners to develop the language to talk with more depth. Through discussion, learners develop a more complex understanding of concepts and ask more in-depth questions—possibly ones we can't even answer, which leads to a continued learning. In this way, opportunities to collaborate and discuss lead to a spiral of learning, and the new knowledge that stays with students because their minds helped to create it.

FIGURE 8.5 Students work together to deepen understanding.

At times, students know more about a topic than they realize. It just takes the right questions or information to prompt their thinking. This can be trickier for the teacher, though, who does not know much about the subject. In Karen's class, students wrote informational books on a topic of their choice. One child chose snowboarding and knew a lot about it but could not think of what else to write. Karen did not know much about the subject, so she searched online for snowboarding images. Once she looked them over to make sure that all of them were appropriate, she shared them with the student, who then began describing the different types of snowboards in great detail. Because of the images, Karen was able to ask better questions and engage this child in a deeper discussion. In turn, her first grader excitedly started writing down many thoughts. Because of experiences like this, visual images are now a tool Karen regularly uses to prompt thinking. Projecting a collection of images for the whole class to see makes it possible to have other students contribute information and ask questions as well, creating a richer conversation.

Screencasting, or making a video recording of a computer display screen, is a digital tool that can lead to deeper learning. While working on a project, or after it's completed, ask students to use a screencasting tool to record their description of their creation process. Students could prepare a script or talk informally about what they have learned. Some popular screencasting tools include Screencastify, Jing, and Screencast-O-Matic. Examples of talking prompts to follow:

- Describe the process for creating the project.
- Explain the biggest challenge the team faced.
- Tell us how the team solved a problem.
- Describe a new idea you learned.

A screencast lets students describe what they know and show their level of understanding verbally, which for younger children is typically at a higher level than they can write. Others, such as classmates or families, can then view the screencast as another conversation starter to help them gain a sense of the new learning.

Scaffold for Collaborate & Discuss

Creating an environment and activities where knowledge creation can flourish includes the use of scaffolds, or tools and strategies, to guide students' learning. For example, a structured note-taking form can facilitate learning as part of collaborative discussions. First, the teacher explains and models the note taking and then asks students to turn and talk to a teammate and explain the types of information to look for and record. Then, students are set to work, and the note-taking form guides that work and the students' thinking. Prompts on the form could request a summary of information and then a response to the question: Now that you know this, what does it mean? Support the development of communication skills by giving students opportunities for structured conversations with talking prompts to focus their conversation and ease back on the scaffolds as students develop their skills.

Also, teach students how to summarize and make connections based on what is read and viewed. Give reading and viewing activities a built-in structure, with prompts if needed, so that students pause and discuss along the way. This is the point where collaborate & discuss meet up with analyze & reflect. Although the discussion may focus on lower-level information, through access and recall, when the whole group comes back together, revisit the ideas. The teacher's role is important here, as you gauge the quality of conversations and intentionally select other examples or resources to talk about to continually spiral toward deeper understanding.

Technology tools may also provide scaffolding. Allison Preston, a second-grade teacher, uses text-to-speech tools to make text more accessible to her young readers, some of whom are reading below grade level or are not yet reading independently. At a collaboration station, a team may use technology to view a teacher-created digital presentation that includes images and pronunciation of unfamiliar words for nonreaders or English language learners. Presenting information in a variety of ways allows all students to have more exposure to text and concepts.

When researching, learners can also make notes in a variety of ways. A graphic organizer could serve as a format or scaffold, and learners can add details in words and/or sketches. During a fifth-grade science unit, an A to Z chart was created for the study of solids, liquids, and gases. Learners wrote, drew, or labeled an example for each letter of the alphabet. Within the same team, students responded in the way that matched their abilities, but they also learned by talking with and observing others.

To support small groups of learners as they collaborate on inquiry projects, Gracy Baker, a fourth-grade teacher, created a digital space in Google Classroom for each group. The students asked questions and responded to each other within a shared online document. Gracy used the online tool Today'sMeet for the students to have an online discussion about an informational text connected to their project. These digital conversations supported students' building of background knowledge and vocabulary, especially for those with limited prior knowledge of the topic. An additional benefit of the online discussion was the sense of anonymity that freed students to more easily express their ideas. One shy student who rarely spoke up in class eagerly contributed comments to an online discussion, finding it easier to type than to talk—although Gracy recognizes both are important.

Monitor and Give Feedback for Collaborate & Discuss

Monitoring student progress and giving feedback during collaborative discussions are key to guiding students toward the next level of learning. When students know what they are doing well and what they need to work on, a plan of action can be formed. By observing how groups are interacting and producing, Karen is able to better assess her students compared with solely focusing on the quality of their learning products. The group of four students in Figure 8.6, for example, illustrates students' ability to successfully discuss their ideas and share responsibilities for their project. The group reached this point after receiving teacher feedback about discussing what students wanted to include in their poster and learning how to take turns at the computer.

Observations of team interactions and the products they create provide evidence of the ways students apply their new knowledge and whether more practice is needed. Ask yourself:

- Are these conversations and collaborations actually being productive and deepening understanding?

- Who needs more modeling?

- Who might be able to have a bit more freedom?

- What kinds of texts and activities might you design next to keep the conversation going?

A teacher can weave feedback into the design of PDI, so that students have an understanding of their learning progress along the way and can improve the quality of their work. Feedback can make the most difference to students when it's specific to their task and moves away from praise and toward specific suggestions and tips.

The practices of collaborating and discussing pose challenges to teachers of students at all ages, since it's difficult to know if students are contributing equally to the inquiry process. There is no easy way to gauge exactly how much individual students give to or gain from a project. A teacher must be observant during collaborative activities and seek feedback from team members. Keep an eye on the goal—to deepen learning—and realize that working together can definitely be a way to do so when a teacher intentionally prepares students for a collaborative learning situation.

FIGURE 8.6 A discussion of ideas and shared responsibilities

TEACHING HOW TO CREATE & TAKE ACTION

When students create and take action, we often see excited, engaged, and motivated learners. We love seeing this! But we know some teachers may shy away from projects because they can be messy, noisy, and a bit unstructured. Keep in mind, the goal of inquiry-based learning is to develop engaged citizens, with an integrated focus on fostering individual growth, democratic participation, and social change (Coiro 2015). In this section, we will share instructional activities that make creating and taking action seem like a natural and doable part of the inquiry process.

When students have opportunities to express their interests and create new knowledge, they are participating, or taking part in their learning. Daniel Pink (2009), in his book *Drive*, reminds us that through participation, learners of all ages assert their autonomy and ownership of learning; in turn, their inquiries become more personal and engaging. When learners are engaged, they want to learn more, thus the cycle of participation continues.

Some believe participation to be the ultimate goal in learning (Casey 2013). Learners come to realize their roles, or identities, in the school community as readers, writers, learners, friends, and helpers. Having students work with experts or get involved in the real practices of different fields helps them understand different possibilities for their future as they take on and play with roles such as scientists, writers, and engineers. In this way, students are not just expressing new knowledge but are also beginning to learn the social significance of their actions by sharing their learning, teaching others, and taking action in their school community or beyond (see Figure 8.7).

Civic action is also considered a form of participation. When students investigate personally meaningful problems within their community, they often want to make positive changes or build awareness for others. Creating with digital tools becomes an easy way to turn one's knowledge into action because of the multiple audiences these technologies can reach. Whether it's sharing a blog post about the class recycling project or creating a digital poster advertising the student-organized used book drive, digital tools let students get the word out to a broad audience. As part of this process, students need to consider how their messages will be understood by others and be prepared to learn from the feedback they might receive.

Creating and taking action . . .

- activates new understandings
- inspires conversations
- leads to community engagement
- promotes imagination and creativity
- prompts multimodal presentation
- facilitates deeper knowledge
- encourages collaboration
- applies knowledge
- deepens and solidifies understanding
- increases personal engagement
- teaches others
- encourages self-reflection
- raises awareness
- shapes decisions and changes minds
- transforms thinking

FIGURE 8.7 An older student takes action by teaching a younger student

Model for Create & Take Action

Creating a project or taking action in the community requires two things: the ability to think logically through the inquiry process and a hefty dose of persistence. For students who have been fed a steady diet of brief instructional activities, it may take modeling and practice to develop the sustained attention needed to successfully create and take action. Even for a mini-inquiry project, like the one described next, it helps for a teacher to model the focused attention needed to seek answers to questions and to see this as valuable learning.

For example, one week in late September, media specialist Ann Au began the day in the media center with a chorus of crickets. Although typically nocturnal, their chirps lasted throughout the day, echoing from their newfound home behind the book cases. Every time a new class entered the media center, the students "discovered" the noisy insects. After a day or two, Ann decided to go with the students' interests and do a mini-inquiry activity about crickets. One particular group of second graders had a limitless supply of questions about

"How Do Crickets Talk"
article on
Wonderopolis website
bit.ly/cricketstalk

the creatures, including the all-important question, How do crickets make their chirping sound? This question led to a class reading of *Crickwing* by Janelle Cannon (2005) and the article, "How do Crickets Talk?" on the Wonderopolis website.

The next time these students returned, they were incredibly disappointed to learn that the crickets were no longer in the media center (thanks to a resourceful custodian). During the immersive cricket class, Ann had the opportunity to model many aspects of PDI, based on a shared experience that inspired students.

In several sections of this book, we have written about the importance of modeling and thinking aloud. But here, when it comes to putting the pieces together to create a project, we want to especially focus on the idea of a mentor and apprentice relationship. As the mentor, you coach learners by providing:

1. modeling—demonstration and think-alouds

2. scaffolding—verbal or visual supports or hints

3. fading—a thoughtful removal of support

Throughout this process, the coach evaluates progress, diagnoses problems, provides support, and gives encouragement and feedback (Collins, Brown, and Holum 1991), all with the goal of moving learners toward independence. Begin by designing your own creative project, modeling and thinking aloud about the strategies you use, including asking a thoughtful question, locating information, making sense of words and images, thinking about your audience, and creating a concrete way to share your new knowledge. Note where you use certain scaffolds throughout the process and how this support fades during your work.

For example, in a third-grade library unit about inventions that changed our lives, Tracy Austin chose the microwave and modeled the process of reading or viewing resources, deciding on important information, making notes, and then finally creating a digital slideshow presentation. Through thinking aloud, Tracy described how she made decisions about the creation of a title slide, which text and images to include on the additional slides, and why she selected a particular background template to support her content. Frequently, she paused to reflect on an option and why she chose not to include it, with the intent of helping students understand her reasoning. Letting learners in on the thought processes of an experienced person enables novices to both see and hear the process of creation. Modeling also shows experienced learners the possibilities for thinking in new or different ways.

When students see and hear you work through this process—when they see you make the process and your thinking visible—they have a better idea of what to expect and where to focus their attention in their own creative design. Modeling strategic knowledge, or being able to use concepts and processes to solve problems or complete tasks, teaches students to take control of their learning and move to deeper levels of understanding.

Build Background and Deepen Learning for Create & Take Action

Although creating may already be a part of your instruction, now is the time to make sure projects connect standards to deeper learning, focus on questions and choices, and emphasize learning over glitz. When adding the take action element to inquiry, keep in mind it can be as simple as leading a dog and cat toy drive for a local animal shelter or sharing information about animal adoption rates with families through an online newsletter. Learners feel empowered when they believe their learning changes the world in a positive way. Enthusiasm and interest are first steps toward deeper learning.

Visual literacy skills and strategies for using digital tools are important for building the background learners need to create projects that effectively convey their ideas. Creating the project—making the timeline, or designing the digital slideshow—is often where students want to begin in the inquiry process, even before they have gathered relevant information. We encourage students to deepen their knowledge and discuss their findings with others to add more substance and detail to their creative projects. Inquiry should focus on learning from the process, not just the completion of a project.

When Deb Krisanda's kindergarten class raised butterflies, the students observed and drew each stage of the life cycle. The students had the opportunity to closely examine the tiny caterpillars in their classroom to watch carefully as they grew. Students drew illustrations at various points of development to observe and document the changes taking place (see Figure 8.8). By looking closely at the caterpillars with magnifying glasses, it was easier to understand how the caterpillars moved, notice the pattern of their stripes, and see their features. As a result, students felt more connected to their learning and were more motivated to draw and create. Each student's drawings were then put together as an individual book to bring home.

FIGURE 8.8 A student can gain awareness and share new knowledge with their work.

Deepening learning entails making information our own, which can be one of the most formidable tasks for young children—or even for older students and adults. The temptation to copy or cut and paste is real, possibly because putting information into your own words is a challenging mental process of transforming ideas, and we may not have clearly taught this process; plus, cutting and pasting is just so easy! Teach students, beginning at kindergarten, the importance of giving credit for a person's ideas and creations. Instilling this concept will take lots of modeling and practice.

Younger children will need direction in locating the author or creator, which the teacher can provide during whole-class inquiry projects. Look to your school library media specialist or community public librarian to share tips on citing sources as well. As students become more independent, teach them a simple format for listing author and title of a work, along with the website address (URL) if available. Teaching about citing work could be embedded into a unit on digital citizenship, such as the one created by Common Sense Education (n.d.), which focuses on "empowering your students to make safe, smart, and ethical decisions online." These skills enable and empower students to have more voice and choice as they learn to be savvy consumers and producers of digital information.

In his blended fourth-grade classroom, Tyler Gill encourages students to create by turning their personal inquiry questions into research projects. Students learn, from the media specialist Christina Brunfield, how to put information into their own words and give credit for sources. In both the media center and the classroom, students use a four-square note-making process. Information is organized into four categories with a heading in each box of two notebook pages divided in half, as spaces for recording information found online. Since students tend to click often and fast, they may have difficulty remembering the location of information, and thus struggle to cite their sources. Teacher modeling demonstrates how to slow down the online reading process, to mentally notice where they find information, and to record the website title and URL for later use.

In their collaborative planning and teaching, Christina and Tyler deepen students' knowledge about creating a project; they teach ways to be a responsible researcher by explaining why and how to cite sources, first by using print materials. Students are given three books about a topic, and they create a project that includes the three cited sources. Students' practice with recording where they found information using print sources hopefully transfers to doing so with online resources, too.

Scaffold for Create & Take Action

If creating and taking action is new to your inquiry teaching, we recommend starting small. Rather than sending students off to work independently on a PDI project, you can provide scaffolding by working together to create a joint learning product. Begin as a whole class to formulate an inquiry question and gather information. Then have students work individually, in pairs, or in small groups to create one piece of the whole product. Each child, for example, could make a page for a class book or design one section of a class timeline. Creating a project together gives students a model of the learning and creation process, while also creating a sense of identity as a part of the group.

For example, Karen's class was interested in sharing what they had learned about the chicken life cycle on the bulletin board outside their classroom, shown in Figure 8.9. They decided to show the changes inside the fertilized egg, by having a flap picture that opened up. The eggs were cut from a template, and on the outside, they glued the day of development. Each child, randomly chosen, drew on the inside of one of the eggs. To make it more fair, the class had students who got the first three eggs, with less to draw, help the students for days 18, 19, and 20. Day 21 showed a photo of one of their chicks that hatched. This interactive display meant students enjoyed peering inside the eggs to see the changes in growth.

With more experience, students can turn their work into multiple products that take on different formats, sometimes led by the teacher or sometimes with more open-ended and flexible structures designed to increase student agency in the inquiry process. Recall our discussion at the end of Chapter 2 about how to slowly introduce more opportunities for voice, choice, and agency into your PDI plans. In this context, when students are ready to work in small groups with less teacher control, consider beginning by having each student take on a role, such as fact checker, illustrator, or note taker. These roles prepare students for the myriad of roles they will be expected to take on when working independently or on a team.

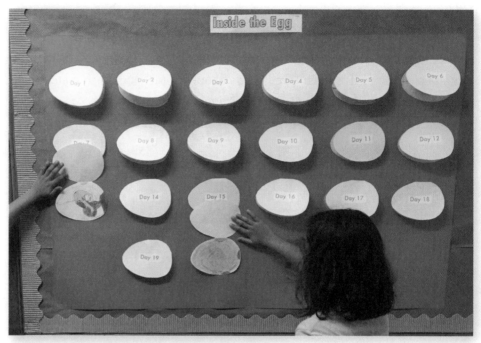

FIGURE 8.9 Class bulletin board display of changes inside the egg

With each creation experience, learners become better prepared for that grad-ual release of responsibility, moving toward working more independently or on a team to create a project or plan a community action event. An important part of this process is being able to make informed decisions about the role technology plays in project creation. Early on, these decisions may be made by the teacher and influenced by our own comfort level, consistency of Internet access, and devices, software, or app availability. As learners build their background knowledge, we hope to shift some of this responsibility to learners, having them choose a digital tool that best meets their learning needs, as we first described in Chapter 6.

Second-grade teacher Allison Preston and her students work together to select digital tools that enable each learner to successfully get their ideas across at their own level of learning. For example, her prolific second-grade writers chose to create their projects using a blog, but her students who were nonread-ers chose to show what they knew by using an app that lets them draw and label, such as Seesaw.

Although Allison prefers the Popplet app for creating a visual project, some learners prefer the PicCollage app, which serves a similar purpose. Either way, the students have access to instruction, in the form of anchor charts, about strategies for working independently with technology (see Figure 8.10). Student experts are identified to provide assistance to others when Allison is busy teaching other students.

Since each students' skill level with digital tools is unique, it can be quite challenging for a teacher, as the lone adult in the room, to meet the needs of all students. Relying on the motto "everyone learns from everyone," strive to draw upon the expertise within your classroom. Identify students who know how to use specific digital tools and designate these students as experts or assistant teachers. Encourage others to seek out the experts for help before asking the teacher. We have found that digital tool experts are not always the academically top-performing students in the class, so being identified as an expert lets each student shine in his or her own right. Teach individuals or pairs of students to design and run a learning station, where they teach others about a digital tool by:

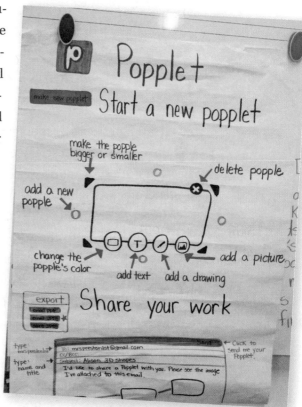

FIGURE 8.10 Anchor chart for using the Popplet app

1. demonstrating its use

2. providing an opportunity for exploration

3. supporting the creation of a practice sample

Half of the students can serve as teachers at the stations while others visit stations and learn new skills; then the roles can switch. Similarly, we've had occasions where older students visit classrooms of younger students for thirty to forty minutes and pair up to teach the younger students features of a tool they've used previously. This promotes student-directed learning (and teaching) and frees up the teacher to learn alongside young digital tool experts.

Teach learners the skills they will need for various aspects of the PDI process during a practice session or during a more structured, scaffolded time. This helps learners build the knowledge and confidence they will need to be successful in the future with longer, more involved, and less structured projects.

Monitor and Give Feedback for Create & Take Action

As learners develop the skills to move toward independence in their inquiry, whether working alone or on a team, our role as the teacher shifts to that of coach or supporter. Monitoring progress and giving feedback are powerful instructional components. Our efforts should match those of the learners, as our teaching becomes more targeted to specific learner needs determined by monitoring the following:

- understanding of key concepts
- ability to use digital tools to deepen learning
- collaboration skills
- pace of project work

Progress can be monitored through the use of informal tools completed by the teacher and/or students, such as a project timeline, narrative self-reflection, rating scale, or rubric. Feedback can be shared through teacher or peer conferences or written, typed, or spoken comments. Teach students, whether self-reflecting or sharing with others, to be specific and kind in their feedback.

One of Ann Au's priorities is to teach students to be independent researchers, as a way to prepare them for the type of work she knows they will do in middle school. When researching the essential question, *How did early Americans defy the odds?* Ann created a project timeline check-in system, where she began the work time with a checklist and quick oral report from students on their work goal for the day. The work time ended with a five-minute wrap-up where students wrote on a sticky note what they accomplished during that session and posted these on a bulletin board with a column for each day. Every few days students wrote an entry in their inquiry log, reflecting on their progress. These entries were staggered so Ann could read and reply to a few entries each day. From these, the oral reports, and her own observations, Ann monitored student progress and used the information to guide her feedback.

Monitoring learning during and after a project also entails checking with students to make sure they remember the purpose of the project and its connection to their learning goals. Kindergarten teacher Deb Krisanda harvested produce from the school garden and brought it to a local soup kitchen. Inspired by those actions, Karen's first graders made plans to donate a portion of their fall harvest to those in need. Both teachers worked to make sure their students understood the connection between their study of plants and then growing, harvesting, and sharing the vegetables with others. In this way, students better understand how to take action from an early age.

Karen hopes that getting students involved in giving to their community will make them more likely to try it on their own or with their families, making the process of turning knowledge into action less teacher driven and more authentic, as time goes on. Teachers can engage with the community to help learners monitor their learning and recognize what they have accomplished by using an online or paper questionnaire or looking over comments on a blog post or slideshow uploaded to the Web. With digital projects shared on the Internet, the potential for receiving feedback grows tremendously, but it also brings more opportunities for criticism. If negative feedback is shared, talk this over with students and help them learn from the experience.

In preparation for a visit from children's author Angela Cervantes, fifth-grade teachers read aloud the children's novel *Gaby, Lost and Found* (2015). In the story, Gaby and her friends volunteer at an animal shelter. Media specialist Liz Martinez extended the story into their library class by teaching information literacy skills to the fifth graders during a modeled inquiry project about dogs and cats. One team's inquiry explored the work done by an animal shelter. Liz and the students contacted the local animal shelter to check on adoption needs, and all of the students created posters advertising the pets available for adoption, similar to what Gaby did in the novel. The students drew pictures of the pets and wrote facts, based on their research, and the posters were given to the shelter to be displayed in the community.

The students were so enthusiastic about the project that they wanted to do more to help the pets. With Liz's support, the students developed a schoolwide campaign to collect gently used pet accessories (i.e., rubber toys, blankets, leashes, collars) to donate to the shelter. At the end of the yearlong project, the animal shelter director posted photos of the students on the shelter website, recognizing the class as the shelter's volunteer of the month.

Feedback, whether from a teacher, a peer, or a cyber-audience, can be a powerful learning tool. It can validate our identity as a learner and community member and can lead to lasting and profound learning. To truly realize the impact of PDI, all students need opportunities to express their interests and new understandings through creative work designed to start conversations, raise awareness, take action, or change minds in their learning community or beyond.

TEACHING HOW TO ANALYZE & REFLECT

When it comes to PDI, analysis entails a detailed examination of a text, an artifact, or an experience to determine the essential pieces and how they fit together into a whole. For children, this means taking time to notice important features and structures in the texts, images, and objects they are examining and intentionally thinking and talking about connections. Four key ideas guide our intentional teaching of analysis and reflection.

- **Close Reading** Zooming in to identify key ideas and the author's purpose and then zooming out to articulate how these insights connect to other texts, authors, and experiences (Fisher and Frey 2012).

- **Critical Thinking** Moving back and forth between the details and the big ideas to construct meaning, while deciding what information is important to include and discarding the rest (Cornett 2010), depending on your purpose.

- **Critical Evaluation** Determining the usefulness and truthfulness of information becomes even more important when using digital texts to ensure students are drawing on high-quality information (see upcoming information on page 175 about the WWWDOT framework for an instructional example of critical evaluation for elementary-aged students).

- **Critical Literacy** Thinking beyond the information on the page or screen and critically analyzing the author's message by questioning, examining, and even disputing the ideas, rather than accepting information at face value (Bukowiecki and Correia 2010; McLoughlin and DeVoogd 2004).

Intentionally planned discussions around texts and experiences give children "new ways of talking and thinking . . . to make informed critical decisions" in their everyday lives (Vasquez 2010, 36). Preparing students for this challenging mental work begins with intentional teaching decisions in the same four areas we focus on throughout this chapter: modeling, building background knowledge and deepening understanding, scaffolding, and monitoring and giving feedback.

Analysis and reflection...

- encourages deliberate and purposeful thinking
- promotes noticing important details
- leads to positive feelings about accomplishments
- strengthens ability to respond to challenges
- reveals hidden thinking processes
- provides tangible feedback
- invites multiple perspectives
- promotes positive, constructive growth
- fosters independent problem solving
- encourages work across multiple texts
- builds deeper understanding
- enriches connections across lines of inquiry
- makes learning stick
- encourages thinking about ways a project becomes personally meaningful
- informs and guides further inquiry

Model for Analyze & Reflect

Thinking critically about a text may be challenging for children, especially readers who are inexperienced or struggle with decoding and understanding the words and concepts. Begin by intentionally modeling ways of thinking so that all students benefit from learning to think deeply about concepts they want and need to learn. During a lesson, when viewing a text, image, or video, think aloud as you identify important details. Explain why and how you look beyond the surface. Thinking aloud can be tricky at first—we have noticed teachers (including ourselves) tend to explain *what* we are doing, but not *why* or *how* we are doing it. Effective thinking aloud means slowing down our own thinking and even dramatizing a bit, by adding details we may not have thought of during our own adult processing but we know would be helpful to less experienced learners.

Karen had her students work in pairs to closely read and analyze books about chickens. To prepare students for this activity, Karen did a think-aloud of her own close reading. She modeled the use of sticky notes to mark pages with an exclamation point (!) for an item of interest and then explained how she identifies it as an item of interest. Karen marked a question mark (?) on a sticky note when she did not understand or wondered about something and then wrote her questions on a note, all the while describing her thinking. Although the text was not challenging for Karen, she imagined the types of questions her students may create and attempted to mimic these during her own thinking aloud. Next, she invited students to select a text to read and mark their own interesting ideas and questions. Then partners discussed their questions and comments with one another, including a think-aloud about the process they used to decide what to mark and how to mark it.

Other times, Karen models how and why, to get into the habit of analyzing and reflecting on the process and thinking throughout the steps taken to complete a project. For example, she draws attention to things that work well and others that would work better with a different plan, and she discusses how sharing these kinds of reflections can help others when trying something new. She also helps students find connections in their thinking. For example, in Figure 8.11, when a student was writing about learning about the amaryllis, it came out as these observations: "I did not know that amaryllis seeds feel like seaweed. The pollen felt like powder. The amaryllis stem felt smooth." Karen encouraged the student to discover a common element in the responses, and the student eventually wrote: "I learn how it feels."

As children access mixed media in magazines, in newspapers, on television, and on the Internet, other factors become part of how we define critical reading. Parents and teachers need to work together to teach children how to recognize quality resources as well as how to recognize certain danger signs. Resources including the Common Sense K–12 Digital Citizenship Curriculum (Common Sense Education, n.d.) and Google's Be Internet Awesome Program (Google, n.d.) provide many activities and interactive games designed to model and then let students practice what it means to read and think critically in a digital world.

One important skill for young children is the ability to recognize the difference between information created to inform readers and information designed

FIGURE 8.11 First graders make connections in their reflections

The Common Sense K–12 Digital Citizenship Curriculum
bit.ly/commonsensedigital

Google's Be Internet Awesome Program
bit.ly/BeInternet AwesomeGoogle

to persuade readers or sell something (including a certain point of view); this is a more nuanced version of understanding the difference between fact and opinion. You can start these conversations by bringing several magazines and newspapers to your guided reading group to explore with students. Take a few minutes to model what you notice as you move between an article and an advertisement in one source. Then pass out the other texts to give children practice first identifying articles and advertisements, and second, talking through what is the same and different in each.

You can also model how to locate advertisements embedded within otherwise "safe" informational websites. For example, Funbrain (www.funbrain.com) features a wide range of educational games worth exploring with children. However, advertisements are splashed around the border of the activity and pop-up boxes sometimes appear. These may potentially distract children from their assigned activity, but these also serve as important opportunities for critical reading instruction. This website can be displayed on one computer using a projector, while the teacher facilitates discussion about which links lead to an educational game and which links lead elsewhere. Children can practice predicting and verifying their predictions.

Other websites embed commercial messages in more subtle ways, by including their logo on all the pages or by featuring free Web-based games or related links centered only around products that they sell. Some examples of these include American Girls, Lego, and Scholastic—websites children are likely to encounter in school anyway. Take time to explore these sites in large- or small-group guided discussions, sharing thoughts about why certain toys or books are featured on the website, how the ".com" in each URL can help to identify commercial sites, and what it even means to be a commercial website. These are important first steps toward helping young children think more critically about media and information.

Build Background and Deepen Learning for Analyze & Reflect

Analysis and reflection are at the heart of building background and deepening learning. It's when we dig deeper that we go beyond the surface, or what we already know, to reach new depths of understanding. This is challenging mental work! And it's not the work that is held off until all students have mastered foundational skills. Students who struggle with one aspect of learning can still analyze and reflect based on their experiences. PDI is not just for students who finish their work more quickly or those identified as more proficient in reading. Every student can analyze more closely, although some may require more scaffolding than others (see the next section). Because all students benefit from opportunities to think deeply about ideas, multimedia may provide more accessible "texts" for exploring ideas in a way that lets everyone participate. When viewing an image or video, ask these questions and discuss responses together.

- Who is in the image or video and who is missing?
- Whose voices are heard or discounted?
- What does the author want you to think?
- What would an alternative image or video look like?

Spend time helping students understand the biases brought by the creator or publisher and how these influence the message being shared. Compare and contrast various texts to help students begin to analyze messages themselves. Encourage students to draw from their background knowledge to support their analysis and conclusions.

Karen's first-grade students built up their background knowledge about chicks through hands-on activities, read-alouds, and online resources, gathering enough information to notice, appreciate, and reflect on specific details and ask more thoughtful questions. They studied photos, illustrations, and diagrams with interest. Partners had engaging discussions and enjoyed learning new information or raising new inquiries. Students pondered about how hens turn the eggs, asking, "How does the mother hen flip the eggs without breaking them?" Students stretched their understanding of the concept of a chick's egg tooth, a projection on the top the beak to help it break the shell when it hatches, wondering whether a snake also has an egg tooth. Partners then shared their findings with the rest of the class and researched answers to the questions asked. Some students became so intrigued with their new knowledge that they chose that topic to be the subject for a later poster project. The process of analyzing texts deepens students' learning and more questions emerge.

When locating information on the Internet, it's not enough just to identify what is important. Knowing the truthfulness of information on a website is critical. A quick Internet search reveals lots of instructional resources for teaching students about critical evaluation of information found on the Web, including Kathy Schrock's Guide to Everything at www.schrockguide.net/critical-evaluation.html.

Kathy Schrock's Guide
to Everything
bit.ly/SchrockGuideEverything

One specific tool, the WWWDOT framework (Zhang, Duke, and Jimenez 2011) guides students toward critical evaluation of online information by considering six factors:

- Who wrote this and what credentials do they have?
- Why was it written?
- When was it written?
- Does it help meet my needs?
- Organization of the site.
- To-do list for the future.

© 2011 International Reading Association

Media specialist David White taught a fourth- and fifth-grade combined class about critical evaluation through a website comparison activity. Prior to the lesson, David identified three websites about animal habitats and copied the website links into an online learning space for easy access for students. He began the lesson by explaining that he found three websites for their animal habitat project, but one was a fake website.

During the lesson, he taught students how to find the fake website. Using the WWWDOT list of factors and an example website, he thought aloud while searching for and answering each of the six questions. Then he asked students to work in teams to follow the same process with each of the three websites, recording their responses on a digitally shared document. The fake or bogus website, Dog Island at http://www.thedogisland.com, looked real at first glance, and the students were stumped, but he encouraged them to dig deeper and they eventually discovered clues and identified the fake website. David emphasized that these six factors can help them evaluate the quality of any website.

Scaffold for Analyze & Reflect

Analysis and reflection, although listed last in this section of the book, by no means occurs only at the end of the inquiry process. Come to think of it, there really is no end to the inquiry process, because analyzing and reflecting often lead to more questions, thus continuing the circle of inquiry. Throughout the process, learners analyze what they see, hear, and experience to fit this new information with what they already know. Learners can continually reflect on their process of learning the new knowledge gained, whether it's near the beginning, middle, or end of a project. But the high-level thinking it takes to analyze and reflect may not come easily for our students, even ones who seem skilled at other aspects of PDI. Certainly modeling is an important element in effective inquiry teaching, and scaffolding ranks right up there as an equally valuable way to lead students to the type of deep thinking that makes for lasting learning.

Karen provided scaffolding to encourage deep thinking among her first graders as they viewed a video of a mother elephant instructing her baby on how to move a rock. The students watched it together at the SMART Board, first just to observe, the second time slowly with pauses and rewinds to examine the parts, and a third time to make additional connections.

Through this process of analysis, students learned how to synthesize new material with what they had previously learned. With each view of the video, they noticed more about the strength, purpose, agility, and usefulness of an elephant's trunk and began to recognize the elephants' personalities. The students connected and empathized with the timid baby elephant, who was reluctant to take on the difficult task of moving the rock and needed multiple tries to take the risk. With partners, they discussed the deep mother-child bond, and the lengths the mother elephant went to teach her baby. Many students marveled while watching the mother elephant kneel down to become eye-level with the baby, to model how to move the rock to support the baby's efforts. The entire class applauded the baby's successes, and analyzed why the mother needed to teach her child and the importance of learning this skill in the wild. The collaborative discussion (reflecting after) showed how much the students learned, and the video served as a valuable tool as a means of reflecting on student understanding.

Another example of scaffolding for analysis comes from Elizabeth Gonzalez, who teaches a series of critical literacy lessons to help her fourth- and fifth-grade English language learners understand bias in informational text. Students are taught that all informational text contains some bias. Elizabeth explains that it's impossible for an author to write a news article or a website, or create an infographic, without some of his or her own views seeping in, even if it's on a small level. Simply by choosing to share one piece of information over another, bias is present, because different authors would likely make a different decision about what to include and what to leave out based on their own experiences and beliefs.

YouTube video of a mother elephant instructing her baby on how to move a rock.
bit.ly/elephantyoutube

Students begin to understand that their job as readers is to learn to recognize an author's choices and biases so they can better understand the author's message and carefully consider what may be missing from an article. Elizabeth teaches her students to ask themselves the following questions when reading an article on the children's news websites Dogo News at www.dogonews.com and Newsela at www.newsela.com:

- What is the main idea of the article?

- What are two or three supporting details?

- What is an important idea related to this article that the author does not include?

- What do you wish the author had told you?

- Why might the author have left this idea out?

Identifying bias can be challenging for children, especially for those who are learning English. Often a vocabulary lesson occurs before or within the lesson on bias, and at first, much scaffolding was needed for Elizabeth's students to answer the five questions. But with practice, her students begin thinking like detectives, looking for clues within the article, and considering what is missing as a way to create a deeper understanding of the author's message.

Some may think of reflecting as the easier of the two elements, possibly because a reflection stems from one's own experiences. But in our work with students, we have found that high-quality reflection—the intense look at our own understanding or performance—does not come naturally for everyone. Scaffolding the reflection process, which begins with our own thinking aloud, sets students up for success in creating that honest look at themselves. Various tools, digital and nondigital (see Table 8.1), can support reflection. Whether writing on a sticky note, making a voice recording linked to an image, or posting an item with comments to a digital portfolio, these tools can help to build the writing, speaking, and thinking skills needed to prepare a deep and meaningful reflection.

Providing scaffolding for creating projects and taking action lets learners ease into PDI. Learners come to realize they don't have to be experts from the start, and there is support if they have difficulty. Scaffolding PDI also lets teachers new to inquiry ease into different ways to structure learning or become accustomed to the use of new digital tools. Remember the tortoise and hare fable: slow and steady wins the race.

TABLE 8.1

REFLECTION TOOLS WITH AND WITHOUT DIGITAL DEVICES	
Reflection Tools	**Reflection Tools Using Digital Devices**
Reflective Journal—This provides open-ended opportunities to explore ideas, feelings, and attitudes about a product or the process and could be written as a class or individually.	A reflective blog might be posted online with comments enabled or not.
Prompted Reflective Writing—Prompts or questions guide the thinking and written responses from students; drawing could be a part of a response, especially for younger students.	Writing could be done on a digital shared document, giving others the opportunity to read and give feedback to the reflection.
Reflective Survey—Ask students reflection-prompting questions and provide a limited number of possible responses to circle and a space to include written comments.	Create a digital survey (i.e., Google Forms, SurveyMonkey) with possible responses and a space to type comments.
Reflective Portfolio—A collection of student work is created, with prompts or questions to encourage students to analyze their learning over time, between projects, and within a single project.	A digital portfolio app, such as Seesaw, could be used to collect links to or images of student projects. Reflection comments could be added by students and feedback by classmates and invited guests (families).

Monitor and Give Feedback for Analyze & Reflect

When students are analyzing resources and reflecting on their learning, help from a supportive teacher remains important. In fact, this may be the time when we can best meet the individual learning needs of our students by checking on their progress and giving pinpointed feedback to each learner.

Assessment, an everyday part of teaching, entails reading, listening, and observing students during the process of learning. The details we glean during this process guide our teaching moment by moment. "When we reflect on evidence of students' learning and understanding, we revise and reshape our subsequent instruction" (Harvey and Daniels 2015, 319). Our goal is to understand what our students have not yet learned, to gauge the quality of our teaching, and to determine what to teach next. In addition, assessment should reinforce our expectations, such as the idea that an inquiry project should contain substance rather than flash.

One challenge teachers face is recognizing individual learning and effort within a group setting. Learners of all ages deserve to know that the quality of their learning, at some level, is being determined on its own merit. We have all had one of those group work experiences where a team member did not give as much effort as the others. We can assess analysis and reflection skills with individual accountability in mind (see Figure 8.12).

Students want to believe their efforts won't be discounted based on the lesser efforts of another. At the same time, when students are working as a team, we want them to collaborate and support each other. A balance must be struck between individual accountability and group cohesiveness. Solutions must be embedded within the culture of the classroom, not seen as a quick fix. We have included suggestions that can support the building of a classroom culture that values both the individual and the team.

FIGURE 8.12 Striving for individual accountability within group projects can keep students focused on doing their best.

- Have students create a teamwork plan, mapping out and recording each group member's responsibilities. Periodically check in with the group (monitor) to determine if group members are doing their fair share. Record this information on a checklist or through anecdotal notes.

- Build in several checkpoints (monitor) during the unit. Specify to students what they should have completed by the checkpoint, and then conference with individuals or groups to see the evidence of their thinking and work and to hear the verbal explanation of their knowledge building. Use a rubric to indicate each student's progress.

- As a class, hold a debriefing after a work session, where students specifically share an idea they have learned (reflect). Record students' comments on a poster or digital grid. Making thinking public triggers students to put their thoughts into words, as well as raises the students' awareness of the type of thinking expected for an inquiry project. Refer to the grid when assessing student progress.

- Use technology to capture student thinking. Digital tools that let students record themselves discussing their learning (i.e., Flipgrid, Seesaw, Explain Everything) can be a part of a digital portfolio or collection of ideas and work that not only includes the final product but also captures evidence of the process of learning. When viewing these, use a checklist or record anecdotal notes to assess progress.

- When students collaborate on a written project, have students record their work in a different color or font. When it's time to evaluate the project, grade this part of the students' work separately using a rubric or scoring guide.

Hopefully we have expressed the message loud and clear that reflecting on our learning is important, but we also believe in the value of reflecting on reflecting, which entails thinking about the ways we think about our learning. When modeling our own reflections, we can pause and point out what we notice about our own thoughts. A teacher might say, "I am not happy with my buffalo habitat project. I included low rolling hills, but left out the tall grass prairie and I couldn't find a good image of a buffalo in the prairie habitat. I didn't have time to make the slides look very good, like with a cool background. Now when I think about this reflection, I see that I can easily find things about my project that I don't like, but I didn't say anything that is good. A lot of times I feel like my work is not as good as I want it to be." Young children will need lots of modeling and practice to reflect on their reflection, but this type of thinking helps to make children of all ages more aware of their own learning.

The challenging mental work involved in analysis and reflection is what keeps learners sharp and engaged. Keeping these two core practices in the forefront of young researchers' minds leads to the difference between PDI and merely creating a project about a topic. We want to go for the deep thinking and lasting learning that make our time and efforts worthwhile.

Our goal in Chapter 8 has been to share explanations and lots of instructional examples so you can begin to envision how to support and encourage PDI in various contexts and grade levels. These details will help you create a vision that begins to fit with your context, and it begins with a thought. Chapter 9 gives us a chance to explore PDI instructional units with more depth, so we can zoom in and examine how the pieces can begin to fit together.

9

Implementing Personal Digital Inquiry— Stories from the Field

In this chapter, you will hear from three teachers who planned and implemented PDI units. Each example includes

* information about what motivated each PDI unit

* detailed descriptions of the teaching and learning expectations

* insights about the design of PDI practices and use of digital texts and tools

* samples of student work

* reflections and next steps

* completed PDI planning guides

Find additional ways to engage with these ideas in the online study guide for Chapter 9.

bit.ly/PDIstudyguide

Personal Digital Inquiry in Kindergarten— Animals and Habitats

In my first years as a kindergarten teacher in Foster, Rhode Island, I (Ari) quickly realized that our school did not have a specific English language arts curriculum in kindergarten to support the development of the Common Core State Standards while also allowing for students to explore digital inquiry practices. Often, I found myself trying to create my own curriculum to meet my students' needs. I spent much of my time collaborating with colleagues and searching online resources such as Teachers Pay Teachers and Pinterest. During this time, my school also provided me with high-quality professional development on differentiated instruction and personalized learning. With this new knowledge, I became confident that the activities I created or found were able to meet the diverse needs of my students. However, the activities lacked cohesion. I struggled to challenge my young learners to use rich vocabulary, ask questions, and learn through exploration. So much of the learning that was happening in my classroom was led by me, not my students.

At the end of my second year, my principal approached me and one other kindergarten teacher to see if we were interested in trying out a new kindergarten curriculum called Focus on K2 (Boston Public Schools 2014). The curriculum, jointly created by teachers, researchers, and curriculum consultants in Boston Public Schools in collaboration with their Department of Early Childhood, is made publicly available for others to use in their schools. Activities in the curriculum encourage children to explore, ask questions, work together, think critically, make choices, and use their imaginations to solve problems while also developing essential literacy and numeracy skills. These opportunities align closely with the underlying principles and core elements of PDI, which is why I was asked to share some of my experiences in this book.

Generally, the yearlong curriculum is made up of four in-depth units that focus on themes relevant to the lives of young children; these include Our Community, Animals and Habitats, Construction, and Our Earth. "Each theme builds on the concepts and skills learned in previous themes allowing children to deepen their understanding and apply these skills and concepts with creativity and innovation" (6). In addition to more (and some less) traditional reading, writing, and math activities in our daily schedule, ninety minutes of each day were devoted to students engaged in center activities focused on these themes.

In my class, students could choose between six centers: art studio, writing and drawing, imagination station, library, blocks, and STEM. These center activities involved hands-on experiences with concrete materials in which students could interact with the world, ask questions, and seek answers to these questions. Importantly, multiple copies of the texts we were reading at other parts of the day were circulated around these centers. Vocabulary cards with key concepts connected to the texts were also added to the mix of materials at many of the centers.

Another common element across all four units was to make sure there was ample opportunity for students to regularly reflect on their learning and revise their work. I used a "Thinking and Feedback Protocol" to guide my students' reflections around five processes: looking, noticing, listening, wondering, and making suggestions for revision. Early on in the year, individual posters of a thinking process and a related image were used to prompt thinking and conversation; once students were familiar with each process, they worked with a partner to reflect and give feedback using all five processes in the protocol. At the end of center time each day, students had fifteen minutes to share out with the whole class about their work and what they were learning along the way.

Thinking About the Possibilities

I selected the second unit in our year to share here because it's an example of how to start small at the beginning of the year. Among the eighteen kindergartners in my classroom, there was a wide range of ability levels and access to prior experiences. A few students had attended preschool, but most had not. Some students came as beginning readers, and others had never before held a book. Because of this wide range of ability levels and the district's high expectations for what students would need to accomplish by the end of the year, I was mostly concerned about students reaching the end-of-year reading benchmark with a new inquiry-based curriculum. Before this year, our instruction in guided reading groups was having a positive impact on students' reading scores, so we were nervous about making a lot of changes to our curriculum. In addition, the new focus on deeper vocabulary knowledge was not something we had stressed previously in our teaching. Despite our anxiety about whether or not we would be successful, we jumped in headfirst, excited about the possibilities.

We began our study of animals and habitats in October, following the first six-week unit devoted to learning about our community. The inquiry question that guided our study was: *How do animals form communities, work together, and use and adapt to their environments?* You can find the complete PDI planning guide in Table 9.1.

Incorporating many of the recommended practices for building a culture of inquiry (see Chapter 3), our community unit focused on what it means for students to be a citizen in their own classroom. That first unit helped establish routines and expectations, and students began building relationships, learning how to collaborate with their peers, and gaining confidence in how to independently access materials in our classroom.

Children were encouraged, for example, to initiate their own writing projects by using photos, name labels, books in the classroom library, personal experiences, and materials in the writing center for inspiration (see Figure 9.1). These flexible opportunities for self-directed learning and choice making helped set the stage for deeper inquiry in future units.

TABLE 9.1

PERSONAL DIGITAL INQUIRY (PDI) PLANNING GUIDE FOR ANIMALS AND HABITATS UNIT
Animals and Habitats (Grade K): Created by Arielle Orefice, Foster, RI

INQUIRY QUESTION: How do animals form communities, work together, and use and adapt to their environments?

SET EXPECTATIONS FOR TEACHING AND LEARNING	PLAN AUTHENTIC OPPORTUNITIES FOR PERSONAL DIGITAL INQUIRY

SET EXPECTATIONS FOR TEACHING AND LEARNING

Knowledge Outcomes:

Students will . . .

- show how animals are part of interdependent communities that are affected by, and adapt to, the environment that surrounds them,
- differentiate between factual and fictional information in terms of purpose and text structure,
- describe how authors and illustrators convey meaning through text and images,
- develop a deeper understanding of key vocabulary concepts related to animals and their habitats and use words spontaneously,
- conduct research about an animal of their choice using print and digital resources.

Action Outcomes:

Students will . . .

- record information learned about animals and their habitats and compile into a class book,
- collaboratively transform a house/school area to a woodland,
- construct habitats using information gleaned from research.

Content Standards:

- Common Core State Standards (CCSS)
- Department of Defense Education Activity (DODEA) Social Studies Standards
- Next Generation Science Standards (NGSS)

Digital Standards:

- Digital Media Literacy Competencies

(See next page of table for details.)

PLAN AUTHENTIC OPPORTUNITIES FOR PERSONAL DIGITAL INQUIRY

Wonder & Discover:

- Generate questions about animals and their habitats using K-W-L Plus charts.
- Explore print and digital resources, including books, photographs, and videos.
- Discover new insights, and research to learn more deeply about chosen area of interest.

Collaborate & Discuss:

- Work with partners and/or in small groups to dissect owl pellets.
- Discuss and compare features of fictional and factual text; react to readings.
- Talk about author's craft, purpose, and intended audience.
- Use academic vocabulary to label animal habitat structures, collaborate with others, and describe their experiences and insights.

Create & Take Action:

- Reference and use photographs, books, digital resources, and personal experiences to construct and share informational texts and physical structures that depict the life cycles and habitats of wolves, owls, salmon, and frogs.

Analyze & Reflect:

- Observe teacher models of how to differentiate fact from fiction, choose a topic, and conduct research.
- Use graphic organizers, read-alouds, journaling activities, and hands-on small-group activities to analyze and summarize texts, models, and previous experiences.
- Use conversations, writing, drawing, and digital recording tools to reflect on new insights at multiple points in their inquiries.

TABLE 9.1 *(continued)*

MAKE PURPOSEFUL CHOICES ABOUT DIGITAL TEXTS AND TOOLS (Experiences to Deepen Learning Across the PDI Knowledge Continuum)				
← Lower-Order Thinking				Higher-Order Thinking →
Acquire Knowledge	**Build Knowledge**	**Express Knowledge**	**Reflect on Knowledge**	**Act on Knowledge**
Teacher curates diverse collection of print and digital resources that grows alongside student interests and shares with learners via classroom library and a digital environment called Blendspace.	Teacher encourages examination of fiction and nonfiction resources in print and digital formats; prompts dialogue; and facilitates active experiences around concepts and use of new vocabulary.	Learners work individually, in pairs, or in small groups to construct habitats, create nonfiction books, and sort and record features of a collection of fiction or nonfiction books.	Learners use dialogue, journaling, audio and video recording to reflect on their learning and creation process as well as what's depicted in their products.	Learners collaboratively apply their building, drawing, writing, and speaking skills and their new knowledge by connecting to science and literacy content in ways that matter to them.

Educational Standards:

- **CCSS.** All ELA standards in the areas of Reading Literature, Reading Informational Text, Foundational Reading Skills, Writing, Speaking and Listening, and Language are addressed and embedded strategically throughout the unit of study. These standards cross cut with STEM, Arts, and Social Studies content.

- **DODEA** Social Studies Standards (www.dodea.edu/Curriculum /socialStudies/upload/08stn_SS_grdK.pdf)

  - **K.2** Put events in their own and their families' lives in temporal order

  - **K.5** Retell stories that illustrate honesty, courage, friendship respect, responsibility, and the wise judicious exercise of authority, and explain how the characteristics in the stories show these qualities

  - **K.9** Explain why people work

- **NGSS** Science and Engineering Standards for Kindergarten (www.nextgenscience.org/sites/default/files/AllTopic.pdf)

  - **K-LS1-1** Use observations to describe patterns of what plants and animals (including humans) need to survive

  - **K-ESS2-2** Construct an argument supported by evidence for how plants and animals (including humans) can change the environment to meet their needs

  - **K-ESS3-1** Use a model to represent the relationship between the needs of different plants or animals (including humans) and the places they live

- All eight practices of science and engineering are addressed and embedded strategically throughout the unit

  1. Asking questions (for science) and defining problems (for engineering)
  2. Developing and using models
  3. Planning and carrying out investigations
  4. Analyzing and interpreting data
  5. Using mathematics and computational thinking
  6. Constructing explanations (for science) and designing solutions (for engineering)
  7. Engaging in argument from evidence
  8. Obtaining, evaluating, and communicating information

- Digital Media Literacy Competencies (bit.ly/learningtargetsmedialit)

  - *Access:* Develop listening and reading comprehension.
  - *Create:* Brainstorm and generate ideas.
  - *Act:* Participate in communities of shared interest to advance an issue.
  - *Reflect:* Reflect on products using audio recording.

Our Animals and Habitats inquiry study focused on caring for living things and learning about animals through investigation and research. The unit was composed of three shorter studies: Fish and Tadpoles, Owls, and Wolves. In each study, children explored fiction and nonfiction books about the animals, while learning how to differentiate between factual and fictional information. Overall, our aim was for students to understand that:

FIGURE 9.1 Kindergartners initiate their own writing projects.

- Like humans, animals are part of interdependent communities that are affected by, and adapt to, the environment that surrounds them.

- Humans can harm or help the environment through their presence. Humans have a responsibility to act as stewards, protectors, and advocates for the environment.

- Authors, illustrators, and other types of artists convey important messages, emotions, knowledge, and cultural representations through words and images that people use and apply to their own experience.

Through shared or independent research, people gather, organize, and analyze information about the world to think critically and gain new understandings.

Getting Started

Like our other units, we started this structured inquiry unit by talking about what we already knew and what we wondered about. In this case, we used the first two columns of a K-W-L Plus organizer to guide the conversation and help organize students' early ideas about how tadpoles grow into frogs. Next, in a whole-group read-aloud, we read the book *From Tadpole to Frog* by Wendy Pfeffer (2015). Over the course of the week, we engaged in multiple repeating readings, each time looking at the text for a different purpose. Students listened for enjoyment and shared personal connections with the group. I also explicitly taught several new vocabulary words, leaving time for students to discuss each word's meaning in the whole group and encouraging them to use those words naturally during center time.

While exploring the centers, the children independently and collaboratively practiced higher-order thinking strategies, such as recalling key ideas and applying concepts from the text. They worked to analyze and compare ideas across multiple texts and to create new texts that integrated these ideas. Vocabulary cards with pictures were provided in a variety of centers so children could reference and integrate new concepts into their play and conversations. Lastly, students discussed and recorded what they learned and what they wanted to know more about. At the end of the week, we researched some of their questions as a group and collaboratively discovered more about the life cycle of frogs (see Figure 9.2).

Video Retelling of the Life Cycle of a Frog
bit.ly/PDInquiryFrog

For the second week, I designed several experiences to link our past study of frogs with the upcoming study of fish. First, we read Leo Lionni's *Fish Is Fish* (1974), a fictional story about frogs and fish, and discussed how the ideas compared with information they learned from their research about frogs. Then, we kicked off our study of salmon with the nonfiction book *The Life Cycle of a Salmon* written by Bobbie Kalman (2006). This book was part of the recommended curriculum, but at first glance, I was surprised by what seemed to be an overwhelming amount of information for kindergartners. I was not sure my young learners would be able to handle such a difficult text. However, their positive reactions and eagerness to learn more blew me away!

We explored this text together for a full two weeks, moving through the content at a pace somewhat set by my students' curiosities, so as not to rush through ideas they found interesting. By dividing this text up over several days, students had optimal time to zoom in and think deeply about the content as well as about the differences between fact and fiction. When reading, we used an idea web (see Figures 9.3A and 9.3B) to organize the knowledge they were building together. Students also spontaneously included instructional vocabulary in their

FIGURE 9.2 Researching the life cycle of frogs

collaborative conversations with classmates about a salmon's life cycle, confirming their understanding and their ability to apply their new knowledge to answer each other's questions.

As we continued to talk about salmon, the block center offered students the opportunity to add other features to their woodland habitat. Students independently and collaboratively added an estuary and a river for the salmon to travel through, ideas they learned about in the text. Then, they decided to act out the life cycle and journey of a salmon and shared their video recordings (recording with an iPad) for feedback.

To expand their writing skills, students were also encouraged to use index cards to label everything in the woodland (see Figure 9.4). Finally, we invited an expert in to show students how to dissect and examine a salmon head more closely (see Figure 9.5)—this definitely made a lasting impression and prompted all kinds of new wonderings!

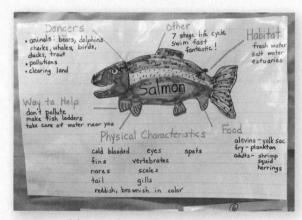

FIGURE 9.3A Salmon graphic organizer

FIGURE 9.3B Digital retelling of the salmon life cycle

FIGURE 9.4 Woodlands habitat with a river for the salmon

FIGURE 9.5 Salmon dissection

Digging Deeper

As we transitioned from learning about fish and their habitats to investigating owls and wolves, we continued to explore sets of fictional and nonfictional books about each kind of animal. Read-alouds of each new text and interesting questions like Why is the hierarchy in the wolf pack important? or What is the relationship between the pictures and the text in this story? were paired with occasional turn-and-talks with a partner before students shared their thinking with the whole group. These joint conversations offered regular opportunities to build and extend students' vocabulary while honing their ability to make predictions, visualize, and summarize to determine the central ideas—all important literacy outcomes on the end-of-year assessments.

In the STEM center, students used tools to dissect owl pellets and then created individual and whole-class data recording charts to help match animal bones (see Figures 9.6 though 9.9). Later, we met to share their discoveries about how the food an animal eats can provide information about its habitat.

As our inquiry continued, students turned their new knowledge into action in so many different ways. They built owl and wolf habitats in the block center, designed wolf dioramas using various materials, acted out wolf scenarios, created wolf dens in the woodland environment, and accessed other texts for inspiration when creating different art media.

During this time, students were also introduced to informative writing following our Get on the "Write" Informative Track writing rubric. Then, students collaboratively gathered information from various texts and integrated their ideas to write, draw, and/or dictate informational pieces that were shared in the classroom library (see Figures 9.6, 9.7, 9.8, and 9.9).

Using Technology to Extend Learner-Guided Inquiry

Of course, throughout our inquiry into the life cycle and habitats of frogs, fish, owls, and wolves, my students asked questions about lots of other animals. So, toward the end of our unit, I decided to set aside time for them to explore other animals of their choice. I gathered digital resources about the animals they were interested in and organized them into a Blendspace account on our classroom iPads. Fueled by their personal interests, students worked with partners to write informational pieces to share what they learned in their research (see Figures 9.10 and 9.11). In the short screencast linked to Figure 9.11, you can hear one kindergartner explaining, "Owls have facial disks."

FIGURE 9.6 Student-created nonfiction books about owls

FIGURE 9.7 Wolf habitat

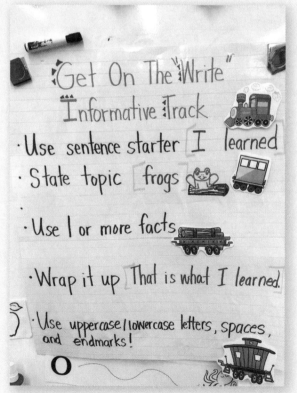

FIGURE 9.8 Kindergarten anchor chart for informative writing

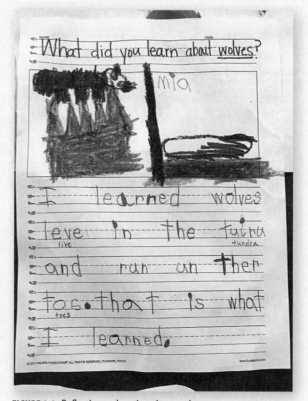

FIGURE 9.9 Reflection on learning about wolves

FIGURE 9.10 Kindergartner sharing information learned from owl research

FIGURE 9.11 Writing and discussing are an important part of research

As we ventured into the second year of using this curriculum, my team and I decided to explore a small set of digital tools to offer even more ways for students to creatively express their ideas. Two of the most popular apps students used to demonstrate their understanding of different texts during center time were Draw and Tell and Book Creator. We first introduced Draw and Tell to students because we felt it was easier for kindergartners to navigate. They used the app to draw or color their picture, and then to record themselves as they talked about their drawing. There's even an option to move images around the screen as they talk. Eventually, students progressed to using the Book Creator app to extend their thinking. When students were learning about the seven stages in a salmon's life cycle, for example, they decided to use Book Creator to help them organize their thoughts. This particular tool also makes it easy for young children to write, type, and audio record their voice.

Owls Have Facial Disks Video
bit.ly/PDInquiryOwls

Reflections and Next Steps

Two years ago, if someone had told me that my kindergartners would actually be able to engage with challenging informational texts in the ways I have described here, I don't think I would have believed them. Maybe a few children, perhaps, but certainly not the whole class! Through these PDI experiences, students were able to demonstrate what they learned in ways that aligned with their individual needs and preferences. Students who typically struggled with most paper-and-pencil tasks, for example, were able to shine during center time with opportunities to express their ideas in other ways. The increased time we focused on teaching vocabulary knowledge made a significant impact on student's understanding of key concepts, as noted by parents as well. Overall, pairing our repeated read-alouds with time for supported conversation, extended study, and reflection greatly improved students' comprehension, as observed in their writing, retellings, audio/video recordings, and acting out of stories in the imagination station. All of my kindergartners were actively engaged and motivated to learn more about animals and their habitats, and their growing knowledge provided solid ground for further study.

I also decided not to worry about where to fit technology into our plans the first time around. My colleague and I chose to intentionally focus our year 1 efforts on designing rich and regular opportunities for each core set of inquiry practices and modeling inquiry-based values and behaviors as often as possible. When children's questions led us beyond content in the books we were reading, a logical next step was to help them access multimedia online sources using our iPads.

In year 2, as my students' background knowledge grew and they became more independent, their desire and ability to digitally record their work happened quite naturally. In turn, I began to see the power of inquiry to foster comprehension and learning, and I grew more confident in moving beyond recording students with my cellphone. I used Blendspace to organize digital resources that helped students follow their curiosities, and I explored several digital apps for creating and reflecting on content. Thinking back, I let student needs and interests guide my reasons for selecting certain technologies, and it actually worked pretty seamlessly!

Finally, as I revisit elements in the PDI self-reflection tool (described in Chapter 3), I'm pleased with my own progress. The focused time and explicit language woven into our "thinking and feedback protocol" enabled me to model and scaffold opportunities for my kindergartners to regularly discuss, analyze, and reflect on their readings, their experiences, and their actions. Reading and writing routines (e.g., rereadings, retellings, journaling, and giving feedback) not only fostered comprehension and learning but also created natural opportunities for my students to document, celebrate, and easily share their important work with others.

Organizing the environment with different centers encouraged students to interact with materials and with each other in many different ways; requiring work in the STEM center ensured access to important content while time to freely explore other centers fostered choice making and reflection about their own strengths and preferences. And, to my surprise, more often than not, students were owning their interests, directing their thinking, and excitedly moving toward learning with intent. Next year, I'm ready to explore other digital texts and tools that may extend their learning (and my teaching) even further.

Personal Digital Inquiry in Fourth Grade— Tornadoes

In Chapter 7, I (Beth) shared a bit about the fourth graders I worked with during a daily reading group that met in the library, where I worked as a library media specialist. Other than the units we did in our group, these students had limited opportunities to engage with aspects of PDI. Wondering and discovering were not synonymous with school, and curiosity was not cultivated while sitting in a chair and desk. In addition, the questions they generated were often limited by their vocabulary, by what they thought they knew, or by gaps in their prior knowledge and experiences.

Prior to actually digging into the research for their PDI projects, I set out to plan and teach three instructional activities. Each activity was designed to stimulate knowledge building and deeper thinking around the guiding questions, which in turn prepared the students to generate additional questions to guide their own inquiries.

Building Background Knowledge

While reading the novel *Night of the Twisters* by Ivy Ruckman (2003) which took place over a three-week period, additional information about tornadoes was shared with students through the use of video clips, nonfiction books, and website articles. Slowly, I could see students building their background knowledge and becoming more intrigued with tornadoes. The students reminded me that engagement is a key to prompting wondering and discovery. It's difficult to generate authentic questions about something you don't care about, but tornadoes are a hot topic in Kansas, and the descriptions, action, and suspense of the novel piqued my students' curiosity. During our time of reading, viewing, exploring, and talking, the students spontaneously generated many interesting questions, which we recorded and collected for our upcoming project work:

- What is the difference between a twister and a tornado?
- What is the strongest tornado to hit Kansas?
- Why should people go into the bathtub during a tornado if they don't have a basement?

As students gained more knowledge, whether from reading the novel or informational texts or viewing videos, their questions reflected their new knowledge.

- What is the Fujita scale?
- How does a tornado form?
- What is the difference between a tornado and a hurricane?

Based on all of this great curiosity, I decided to extend our tornadoes unit by adding a PDI component. I allotted two weeks, or ten class sessions, to the project. Two inquiry questions guided our research: What conditions create a tornado? What effects do tornadoes have on the land, structures, and people? (See Table 9.2 for the complete PDI planning guide.)

As a group we moved together at the same pace from one activity to the next, as I guided students through the inquiry process according to this schedule:

Day 1:   Activate background knowledge from novel.

Day 2:   Review questions previously asked, generate additional questions, select question.

Day 3:   Model and practice locating information in a print or digital book or article.

Day 4:   Model and practice locating information from an image.

Day 5:   Model and practice locating information from a video.

Day 6:   Continue locating information and take notes individually.

Day 7:   Discuss options for creating project. Model Google Slides. Begin creating projects.

Day 8:   Create projects.

Day 9:   Practice giving oral presentations with each other.

Day 10: Share projects with second graders.

Throughout my planning and instruction, I kept in mind that our class inquiry was guided by the school district's fourth-grade English language arts standards plus a yearlong study of the regions of the United States as part of the social studies curriculum. Our tornado unit presented information about Tornado Alley, located primarily within the Midwest region of the country. I wanted my students to understand that tornadoes are not unique to Kansas and that other states have similar climate and weather conditions conducive to tornadoes.

In addition to studying tornadoes and tornado safety and learning about gathering information from sources to share with others, I also wanted the students to share their projects with an audience beyond me or even each other. So we made plans to give oral presentations to a second-grade class. The district English language arts curriculum design map called for second graders to "ask and answer questions about what a speaker says in order to clarify comprehension, gather additional information, or deepen understanding of a topic or issue" (Topeka Public Schools 2018). In addition, the district science standards included Earth's Systems as one of the four science units for second grade. Beyond meeting standards, presenting the tornado projects to second graders gave the fourth graders the opportunity to teach important tornado safety tips that may, one day, save the life of a student and their family.

Getting Inspiration from a Text

Next, after finishing the novel, I asked the students a question: "What clues does the environment give us that a tornado is possible?" Together we created a list of clues that let people know the conditions were right for a tornado. Next, students were asked to find text evidence in the novel to support the elements on the list. While creating this list together, using the interactive whiteboard, we discussed our own personal experiences with seeing these same clues in the weather in our community. Our descriptions included:

- warm and muggy
- clouds building fast
- wind whipping trees
- greenish look of the sky
- be careful or the wind will blow you over
- black and snarly sky

Generating this list of phrases served as a way to develop vocabulary and concepts associated with tornadoes that students could use when generating questions for their PDI projects. At the beginning of the activity, I would think aloud about what I knew about tornadoes and how what I knew related to what I read in the text. Through my modeling, I worked to keep the focus on finding connections within the text, rather than on sharing our own tornado stories, although a few personal

TABLE 9.2

PERSONAL DIGITAL INQUIRY (PDI) PLANNING GUIDE
Tornadoes (Grade 4): Created by Beth Dobler, Topeka, KS

INQUIRY QUESTIONS: What conditions create a tornado? What effects do tornadoes have on the land, structures, and people?

SET EXPECTATIONS FOR TEACHING AND LEARNING	PLAN AUTHENTIC OPPORTUNITIES FOR PERSONAL DIGITAL INQUIRY

SET EXPECTATIONS FOR TEACHING AND LEARNING

Knowledge Outcomes:

Students will ...

- recognize the weather factors that lead to a tornado
- identify the ways scientists study tornadoes and the aftermath
- identify the regions of the United States and the states within Tornado Alley
- compare and contrast fiction and nonfiction about a similar topic
- increase their ability to access and comprehend information presented as text, video, and image
- recognize ways to organize information into a cohesive form
- determine important details from text, video, and image sources
- recognize ways to organize information into a cohesive form

Action Outcomes:

Students will ...

- determine important details from text, video, and image sources
- record information in an interactive notebook
- create a paper or digital project to present information
- orally share information and poster with younger students

Content Standards:

- Topeka Public School District Standards for Social Studies, ELA, and Technology
- American Association of School Librarians Standards Framework for Learners

Digital Standards:

- Digital Media Literacy Competencies

(See next page of table for details.)

PLAN AUTHENTIC OPPORTUNITIES FOR PERSONAL DIGITAL INQUIRY

- **Wonder & Discover:**
- Draw from fiction to trigger questions about tornadoes. Record for later use.
- Provide background information by providing vocabulary definitions (i.e., Fujita scale, wind speed, funnel).
- Brainstorm questions about tornadoes and facilitate students selecting a question of interest.

Collaborate & Discuss:

- View and discuss video and text news reports of the tornado in Greensburg, Kansas in 2007.
- Share personal tornado stories. Discuss tornado safety.
- Discuss responses to the question: What clues does the environment give us that a tornado is possible?
- Model and discuss ways to determine important details from various sources (print article or book, video, image) by using close reading and viewing strategies to develop a deeper understanding.

Create & Take Action:

- Use a classroom digital space to access digital resources for the project.
- Create a project to share information about tornadoes. Choose between print and digital project.
- Prepare for oral presentations to younger students by talking through ways to explain complex concepts in easy-to-understand ways.
- Orally present projects to younger students.

Analyze & Reflect:

- Analyze information and use an interactive notebook to record important details.

TABLE 9.2 (*continued*)

MAKE PURPOSEFUL CHOICES ABOUT DIGITAL TEXTS AND TOOLS (Experiences to Deepen Learning Across the PDI Knowledge Continuum)				
← Lower-Order Thinking				Higher-Order Thinking →
Acquire Knowledge Teacher curates print and digital resources on tornado question topics. Digital resources are shared with students in class digital space (Google Classroom) for easy access.	**Build Knowledge** Teacher models the process of reading or viewing and identifying important details within a text, video, and image.	**Express Knowledge** Learners have the option of creating a digital project. Teacher explains and models use of Google Slides and how to copy and paste an image.	**Reflect on Knowledge** At various points during the unit the group pauses in their research to share what they are learning and their processes for learning.	**Act on Knowledge** All learners share projects with younger students.

Standards
- Topeka Public School District 4th Grade Year-Long Course and Grade Level Standards (http://www.tpscurriculum.net/standards /standards.cfm).

Social Studies
- **SS.4.1.01:** Identifies and compares information from primary and secondary sources and recognizes historical perspective.
- **SS.4.4.18:** Identifies and describes the physical components, patterns, and processes of the Earth's atmosphere, land, water, and biomes.

ELA-Reading—Informational
- **LA.04.RI.7:** Interpret information presented visually, orally, or quantitatively (e.g., in charts, graphs, diagrams, time lines, animations, or interactive elements on Web pages) and explain how the information contributes to an understanding of the text in which it appears.
- **LA.04.RI.10:** By the end of the year, read and comprehend informational texts, including history/social studies, science, and technical texts, in grades 4–5 text complexity band proficiently, with scaffolding as needed at the high end range.

ELA-Writing
- **LA.04.W.5:** With guidance and support from peers and adults, develop and strengthen writing as needed by planning, revising, and editing.

ELA-Speaking and Listening
- **LA.04.SL.1:** Engage effectively in a range of collaborative discussion (one-on-one, in groups, and teacher led) with diverse partners on grade 4 topics and texts, building on others' ideas and expressing their own clearly.

Technology
- **4.3.C:** Validate and evaluate the new information based on previous experience and knowledge.
- **4.3.E:** Find similar ideas from multiple sources.

AASL Standards Framework for Learners
(www.standards.aasl.org/wp-content/uploads/2017/11/AASL -Standards-Framework-for-Learners-pamphlet.pdf.)
- Learners participate in an ongoing inquiry-based process by engaging in sustained inquiry.
- Learners gather information appropriate to the task by organizing information by priority, topic, or other systematic scheme.
- Learners select and organize information for a variety of audiences by integrating and depicting in a conceptual knowledge network their understanding gained from resources.

Digital Media Literacy Competencies
(bit.ly/learningtargetsmedialit).
- Access: Develop skills for identifying important information from multimedia sources.
- Analyze: Utilize close reading and viewing strategies to understand information on a deeper level.

connections were helpful. It seems in Kansas everyone has either been close to a tornado or knows someone else who has, so personal stories are abundant.

At times students felt their personal experiences overrode the descriptions we found in the book, and I gently steered the students back to the phrases in the text. One student, Gavin, said he had been in a tornado as a baby, and he remembered it being very loud. Another student, Aaron, said he saw on TV that a tornado can pick up a two-ton building. It's hard to know if these tornado descriptions were from Gavin's and Aaron's own experiences or not, which is why I emphasized the importance of remaining close to the text descriptions.

Brainstorming Topics for Inquiry

As a group, we brainstormed a collection of questions from which students could select one for further study in their PDI project. First, I posted questions that students had already asked during our novel study, and then I posed a few questions of my own. When writing my own questions, I did a think-aloud to model where my questions came from—my own thoughts and wonderings prompted by the novel and from informational texts or videos we had seen together. Then I invited students to add more questions by writing each one on a note card and adding it to our display. As each student added a question, I asked for an explanation of what had prompted their question. I did this to help the students recognize that useful questions are often connected to what we have seen, heard, or experienced and may stem as much from what we do know as from what we do not know.

Next, the students each selected a question to guide their inquiry and then began searching for information. Two students, Tanessa and Amy, decided to either reword their question or start again with a different question when it became difficult to locate useful information they could understand. In this way, an inquiry question becomes a fluid tool for guiding a learner to seek more information.

Our inquiry process was of the modeled/structured variety (see Chapter 2), as I modeled ways to gather information and make notes from three types of resources (texts, images, and videos) and how to pull the notes together across their sources to create a project. The students then applied these skills to resources connected with their own inquiry questions. Since these fourth graders were new to inquiry, I wanted to keep their attention on the process of "getting smarter" rather than the product. So I modeled this by sharing lots of information about the process while we were working and revealing details about the project as teasers with phrases such as "Be sure to record the source of your information because you will need this for your project."

Collaboratively Analyzing and Discussing Their Discoveries

Although students chose their inquiry question as individuals, there were many opportunities for collaboration and discussion throughout the inquiry unit. One important characteristic of modeled/guided inquiry is the teacher working through the inquiry process alongside the students. After I modeled and thought aloud about analyzing the texts and recording information in my interactive notebook, my next step was to work with the students as a group to continue this process for my inquiry question. Together we analyzed the article, image, or video to determine which facts were important to include in our notes and where to place these on our labeled diagram or four-square note-taking page. Once we identified information, we talked through together what to do next and why. During strategic points in the inquiry process, I built in time for students to also discuss with each other, using structured discussion activities, such as turn-and-talk and round-robin. Discussions centered around their analysis of the article, image, or video and the specific information they found important and how the ideas were recorded in their interactive notebook. Then we returned to a whole-group discussion to analyze our thinking, talking through the strategies that seemed to work well or not so well.

Creating and Reflecting on the Products of Our Inquiry

When it came time to share what they learned, the students first returned to their notes collected from viewing their book or article, image, and video connected to their own inquiry questions. Notes were kept in an interactive notebook, in which students could write, sketch, label, list, and annotate information. All students were given time to review their notes, think about what they had learned about their inquiry question, and write a sentence to be shared aloud that explained one thing they learned from the project (see Figure 9.12).

Next, students were asked to write four more sentences that summarized ideas learned during their research, which would become the basis for the content of their presentation. I wanted a draft of this content to be in place before the students decided on the format of their presentation, so the important process of synthesizing information did not get lost in the excitement of designing a creative product.

FIGURE 9.12 Pausing to review notes gives students a chance to think more deeply.

Students were then ready to consider options for the format of their project, which we called a "teaching tool" since it would be used to teach others about tornadoes. I had learned from my experience as both a teacher and a student that building choice into a project often creates stronger interest and motivation. For this project, each student had a Chromebook, so Google Slides was a familiar option, although I soon discovered those who chose that option had varying skill levels with using Google Slides or Google Docs (see Figures 9.13, 9.14, 9.15). Some students preferred to create a paper poster, using a piece of chart paper (see Figure 9.16). Encouraging students to choose the format of how they expressed their ideas naturally invited an opportunity to reflect on their own strengths and preferences as well as their willingness to take risks and try something new.

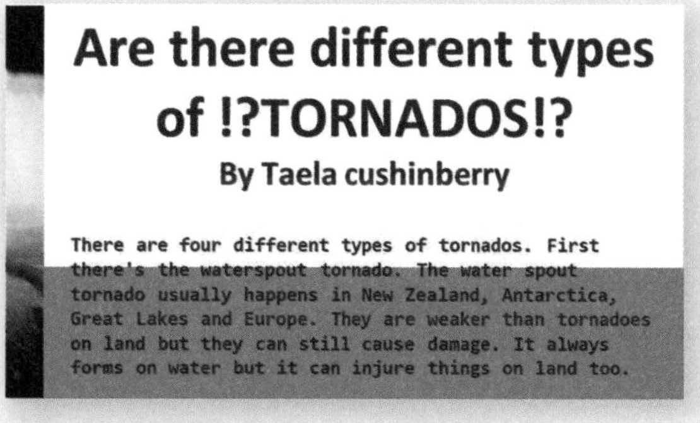

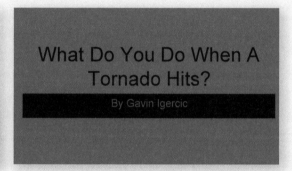

FIGURE 9.13 Creating a project to share with others

FIGURE 9.14 Inquiry presentation begins with a question.

The Tornado Hit!

On May 4, 2007 an EF5 tornado hit Greensburg, Kansas. It was a horrific night when that tornado hit. The tornado itself was 1.7 miles wide and was moving at 205 miles per hour. It was extremely rare for that EF5 to hit. Families were all crying from the deaths, rain/thunder, and devastation of their town. Being exact, 11 people died others were either injured or in shelter. The police department, the ambulance, and the fire department all came to try and calm down Greensburg. This tornado went down at 9:00 at night it was pitch black so people weren't as aware of this EF5 but when they were they saw all of the devastation. When it ended 95% of the town was demolished. Wreckage everywhere and the worst part is that it took sooooo long to rebuild everything. It was such a good looking town before this EF5 hit. The tornado had power and devastation.

Source: http://www.kansas.com/news/weather/tornado/article985720.html

FIGURE 9.15 Writing about a tornado

It was also at this point that I shared a rubric for evaluating the projects (see Figure 9.17). Since it was our first time using a rubric together, I kept the rubric fairly simple, using the headings of good quality and just so-so quality. The fourth graders gave their presentations to a group of second graders. Before giving their presentations, our group discussed the qualities of an effective presentation and the students practiced with each other. Even so, several admitted being nervous, and one opted out of the oral presentation.

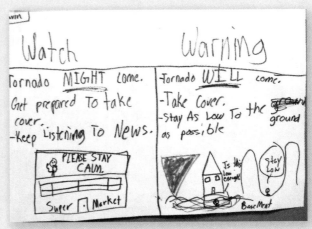

FIGURE 9.16 Paper chart project

Name Gavin +8/8

Tornado Project Rubric

	Good Quality	Just So-So Quality
Notes in your notebook (3 points)	List facts about your topic from books or a website +3	Notes in notebook are missing.
Teaching Tool (3 points)	Create a teaching tool with images, correct spelling and capital letters (Google slides, paper poster) +3	Teaching tool is sloppy, with misspellings.
Presentation (2 points)	Share your project with others using a clear, loud voice. +2	Share your project in a very quiet voice that others can't hear.

Comments:

Good attention to spelling and punctuation.
You seemed very comfortable speaking in front of the 2nd graders.
Thanks for showing the tornado shelter house. I had not seen this before

FIGURE 9.17 Project rubric

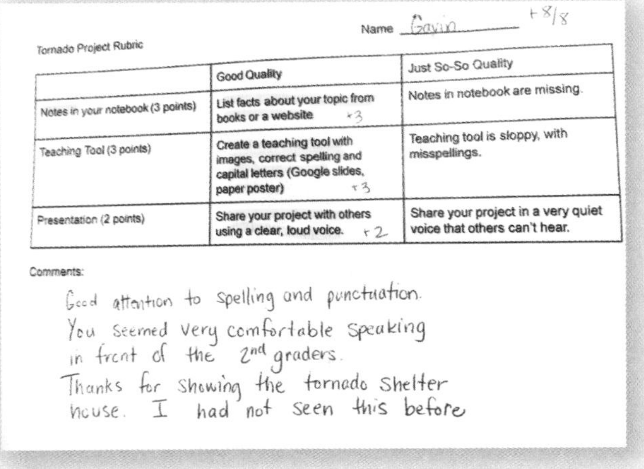

Fostering Knowledge Building and Creative Action

Our use of technology in this inquiry unit centered on two purposes: acquiring and building knowledge and then acting on that knowledge. Along the way, students knew that they were building knowledge for a purpose beyond their own understanding. Having this broader goal encouraged students to think more deeply about information as they considered it from the perspective of a younger learner. I nurtured the development of this perspective through questions and thinking prompts:

- Think about how you could explain the Fujita scale to younger students.
- What do younger students need to know about staying safe during a tornado?
- How can we describe the intensity of a tornado without scaring the younger students too much?
- Would younger students understand that word, phrase, or idea?

Looking at information through the eyes of another coaxes the learner into thinking of ideas twice—once for their own knowledge and once for their audience. For students who were just developing the habits of inquiry, this really stretched their thinking, but it was also very motivating. Two of the fourth graders had a sibling or cousin in the second-grade class, and others knew younger students from the bus or after-school program. Being seen as a knowledgeable other became important to the fourth graders and provided motivation if their stamina began to wane.

Reflections and Next Steps

For me, this inquiry unit was a bit like that old adage of building the airplane while still flying it. Although the spirit of PDI aligned with my philosophy of teaching, I was not yet confident in how to put all of the pieces together into a cohesive unit. Also, my students did not have a history of inquiry-based teaching to help guide this process. I found it helpful to give myself permission to fail with grace—if it came to that point. I did let the students know we were trying something new and why. This frankness seemed to rally them to give more effort, although it didn't take much because they were also eager to try something new. Surprisingly, sharing my desire to make my teaching more engaging brought the students and me together toward a common goal. It felt like the students recognized and appreciated my attempts at providing more meaningful activities and showed their appreciation by being more actively engaged than with typical lessons.

Embedding voice and choice into the inquiry unit, through choosing an inquiry question, resources, and project format, seemed to be a key to our success. My group of twelve fourth graders consisted of varying personalities and learning preferences, as with any group of learners. Since I was not their regular classroom teacher, and only saw the students for forty-five minutes a day, I had to develop a relationship with each one in different ways. Offering choices not only let me get to know their learning preferences but also let the students know that I valued each one as a learner with unique learning needs, which went a long way to developing trust, which led to loyalty.

I wish I had built more reflection in this unit. We informally reflected on the inquiry process and our learning through class discussions, but I did not give students any structured reflection activities. Although I believe in the power of reflection in learning, it felt like all of my energies went into planning for and facilitating the inquiry activities. Reflection was an afterthought—but now it's on my list of goals for next time. In the past, I have found that areas where I am less skilled improve because they are at the front of my mind. My own reflection brings my challenges to the foreground, and I give them more attention. I imagine this could be true for students, too.

Personal Digital Inquiry in First Grade— Open Inquiry

Opening Up Inquiry

In April, I (Karen) told my students: "Remember how we worked together as a class to study plants in the fall, and then in the winter you learned about geography, and then we studied about what makes elephants special? Through these projects, you learned all about the inquiry process: making discoveries, collaborating, taking action, analyzing, and reflecting. Well, now that you have had all that practice, I think you are ready to take the next step. Using everything you have already learned about inquiry, I would like for you now to choose your very own topic to research, so you can really study about something you love."

As I spoke, I watched my first graders follow along first with fervent nods, then with big smiles, and finally quiet cheers. Some already knew exactly what they wanted to study, while others thought reflectively about what to choose. Five children instantly chose dragons. Another wanted to study plants, another George Washington. Two students wanted to learn about monkeys. Two children decided to study bunnies, and another two weren't sure. Three agreed to study sharks. Several students were interested in pandas. One wanted to study football; another was curious about cheetahs.

The most excited students were my small band of dragon lovers. These five students had been finding books on this subject in the library on their own, talking about them during their free time, looking it up on our research sites on the computer, and hoarding any resources they could find. Although I had planned for the class to do an inquiry project of their own choosing this year, their healthy and delightful obsession made me realize just how ready they were for it. I wanted to channel this energy into an opportunity to teach them how to better explore and study their personal interests. It would be a chance to build on what we had already learned throughout the year, by investigating the things they enjoyed. I set aside three weeks of a daily one-and-a-half-hour literacy block time for this class project. (See the complete PDI planning guide for this project in Table 9.3.)

TABLE 9.3

PERSONAL DIGITAL INQUIRY (PDI) PLANNING GUIDE
Open Inquiry (Grade 1): Created by Karen Pelekis, Scarsdale, NY

GUIDING QUESTION: How will you learn about, and teach others, about a topic that you choose?

SET EXPECTATIONS FOR TEACHING AND LEARNING	PLAN AUTHENTIC OPPORTUNITIES FOR PERSONAL DIGITAL INQUIRY

SET EXPECTATIONS FOR TEACHING AND LEARNING

Knowledge Outcomes:
Students will...

- discover personal interests by selecting a topic to study
- read digital and nondigital informational text focusing on learning about a self-selected topic
- research a self-selected topic to gain new understandings
- collaborate with others to learn more
- write about topic using both digital and nondigital tools
- create a project to teach about their topic
- reflect on their findings
- compare and contrast the findings of other students

Action Outcomes:
Students will...

- learn to collaborate with others
- respect the responses of others
- belong to a community of learners
- communicate information with others
- create and share a project to teach others

Content Standards:
- Common Core State Standards (CCSS) in Reading, Writing, Listening & Speaking

Digital Standards:
- Digital Media Literacy Competencies
(See next page of table for details.)

PLAN AUTHENTIC OPPORTUNITIES FOR PERSONAL DIGITAL INQUIRY

Prerequisite Knowledge
- Understand the inquiry process from previous studies; practice with digital and nondigital resources and tools; have familiarity with reading and writing digital and nondigital informational text.

Wonder & Discover:
- Explore topics and questions of personal interest; discover a topic of interest to research and understand more deeply.

Collaborate & Discuss:
- Explore, analyze, talk about, and organize new knowledge gained from a multimedia collection of resources; work together with a partner or small group to discuss research on topic of interest; discuss what to make for a project and how to make it.

Create & Take Action:
- Choose a topic of interest to study and research; decide what to make for a project and how to make it; create a project, using digital and nondigital resources, to share findings with and teach multiple audiences.

Analyze & Reflect:
- Describe how new content was learned; evaluate accuracy, clarity, layout, and detail in their projects; receive feedback from peers and parents; analyze connections between projects; and reflect on learning.

TABLE 9.3 *(continued)*

DIGITAL EXPERIENCES TO DEEPEN LEARNING				
(Options for Purposeful Use of Technology)				
← Lower-Order Thinking				Higher-Order Thinking →
Acquire Knowledge	**Build Knowledge**	**Express Knowledge**	**Reflect on Knowledge**	**Act on Knowledge**
Teacher shows online resources, including videos, for students to learn background information on topic of choice, if needed.	Students research topics using online resources to build on knowledge and decide what information to include in their projects. Sometimes, students will need assistance with research.	Students work individually, in pairs, or in small groups to create a project on their selected topic using creativity software (Pixie) or other digital or nondigital tools.	Collaborative pairs/groups evaluate their projects, using what they have learned from previous inquiry projects.	Students create projects for a hallway bulletin board to share with the school. They also share them with their kindergarten buddy class, fifth-grade buddy class, and parents to teach others and answer questions.

Common Core State Standards:

Reading:

- **CCSS.ELA-LITERACY.RI.1.5** Know and use various text features (e.g., headings, table of contents, glossaries, electronic menus, icons) to locate key facts or information in a text.
- **CCSS.ELA-LITERACY.RI.1.6** Distinguish between information provided by pictures or other illustrations and information provided by the words in a text.
- **CCSS.ELA-LITERACY.RI.1.7** Use the illustrations and details in a text to describe its key ideas.
- **CCSS.ELA-LITERACY.RI.1.10** With prompting and support, read informational texts appropriately complex for grade 1.

Writing:

- **CCSS.ELA-LITERACY.W.1.2** Write informative/explanatory texts in which they name a topic, supply some facts about the topic, and provide some sense of closure.
- **CCSS.ELA-LITERACY.W.1.5** With guidance and support from adults, focus on a topic, respond to questions and suggestions from peers, and add details to strengthen writing as needed.
- **CCSS.ELA-LITERACY.W.1.6** With guidance and support from adults, use a variety of digital tools to produce and publish writing, including in collaboration with peers.
- **CCSS.ELA-LITERACY.W.1.7** Participate in shared research and writing projects (e.g., explore a number of "how-to" books on a given topic and use them to write a sequence of instructions).
- **CCSS.ELA-LITERACY.W.1.8** With guidance and support from adults, recall information from experiences or gather information from provided sources to answer a question.

Speaking & Listening:

- **CCSS.ELA-LITERACY.SL.1.1** Participate in collaborative conversations with diverse partners about grade 1 topics and texts with peers and adults in small and larger groups.
- **CCSS.ELA-LITERACY.SL.1.1.A** Follow agreed-upon rules for discussions (e.g., listening to others with care, speaking one at a time about the topics and texts under discussion).
- **CCSS.ELA-LITERACY.SL.1.1.B** Build on others' talk in conversations by responding to the comments of others through multiple exchanges.
- **CCSS.ELA-LITERACY.SL.1.1.C** Ask questions to clear up any confusion about the topics and texts under discussion.
- **CCSS.ELA-LITERACY.SL.1.2** Ask and answer questions about key details in a text read aloud or information presented orally or through other media.
- **CCSS.ELA-LITERACY.SL.1.3** Ask and answer questions about what a speaker says in order to gather additional information or clarify something that is not understood.
- **CCSS.ELA-LITERACY.SL.1.4** Describe people, places, things, and events with relevant details, expressing ideas and feelings clearly.
- **CCSS.ELA-LITERACY.SL.1.5** Add drawings or other visual displays to descriptions when appropriate to clarify ideas, thoughts, and feelings.

Digital Media Literacy Competencies
bit.ly/learningtargetsmedialit

- *Access:* Listening and reading comprehension
- *Analyze:* Compare and contrast resources
- *Create:* Brainstorm and generate ideas; compose creatively using language and image; work collaboratively.

Initially, it was a little overwhelming for me, and I wondered what I was getting myself into, especially with the wide range and number of topics. To make this project more manageable I decided to work with the dragon group first, since it was the biggest and most committed to the topic. This group, with their self-identified joint interest in dragons, would lead the way for the rest of the class. I figured the others might change their minds after some initial research. So, I left the other groups to work more independently, reading books on their topics selected from the school library, and conducting research online using PebbleGo or World Book Online for Kids.

Komodo Dragon Group Leads the Way

The dragon group quickly realized that they wanted to focus on something real that was related to their topic, rather than something imaginary. They wholeheartedly immersed themselves in studying the closest thing they could find: Komodo dragons. To gather information, they watched videos, read books, and listened to online resources read aloud to them (using digital text-to-speech tools). After wondering and discussing, they wanted to create a way to depict just how large a Komodo dragon was.

Their decision for a project was interesting to me. It revealed how they had been listening throughout the year, because I would always show my students the actual size of anything we read. For example, when we were studying elephants earlier in the year, we used yardsticks to see how large African and Asian elephants were. I did this because I had been particularly influenced by a speech I heard author Seymour Simon give at a conference. He stated the need to have students physically see facts to understand them more completely. He stressed the benefits of making comparisons and analyzing diagrams—which I now see as critically important to the elements of analysis and reflection.

So the kids went right to the yardsticks and measured out how many feet long a Komodo dragon would be. I also encouraged them to see how big they were in comparison to the yardsticks. Lying down on the floor next to them, they were surprised to find that a Komodo dragon was equal to about two and a half first graders (see Figure 9.18).

The group needed to decide what they wanted their Komodo dragon to look like for their project. Using instructions on how to draw a Komodo dragon from the Internet they found a simple way to recreate the idea for their dragon. Since it would be challenging to create a ten-foot-long picture, the kids practiced on

How to Draw a
Komodo Dragon
bit.ly/drawdragon

regular-sized paper until they felt comfortable drawing it (see Figure 9.19).

The group wanted to make their project out of craft paper from a large bulletin board roll, since it was the only way to have a continuous sheet of paper. We estimated the amount that needed to be pulled out, and they happily went down to the basement to get it with me. We returned to the classroom, and they measured out the paper with yardsticks.

Then they collaboratively worked together to sketch the larger-scale drawing on the paper. I needed to help them manage the paper a bit and coordinate the combined drawing efforts over such a large space. The students eagerly cut it out, and then they decided to add on a tongue. Their Komodo dragon was a little rudimentary, but it was their own. They even displayed the dragon on our bulletin board with an extended measuring tape underneath to show the actual size (see Figure 9.20).

Next, the students reviewed their previous research to write about it. The group was cohesive and generally got along well. I watched the students to see whether they were agreeing with each other and being fair about decision mak-

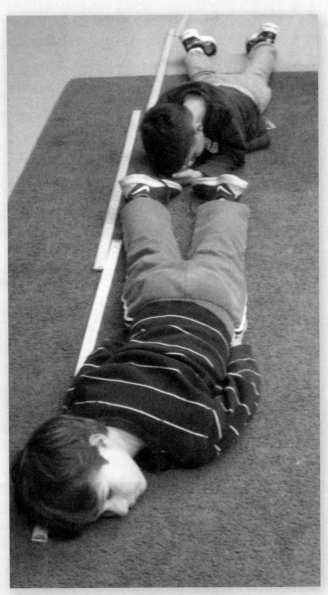

FIGURE 9.18 Students use yardsticks to determine the relative size of a Komodo dragon.

ing. There were only a few times that I needed to step in to make sure that everyone's voice was being heard and that students had fair turns at the computer. Using the creativity software Pixie, they assembled their favorite facts and photographs with picture backgrounds (see Figure 9.21). With this digital tool, it was easy for them to make corrections, change the pictures and text, and rearrange the components.

FIGURE 9.19 Student practice drawing of Komodo dragon

FIGURE 9.20 First graders help to create a life-size Komodo dragon.

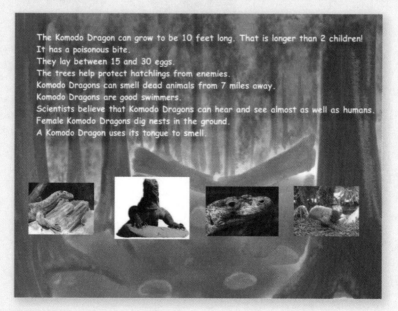

The Komodo Dragon can grow to be 10 feet long. That is longer than 2 children!
It has a poisonous bite.
They lay between 15 and 30 eggs.
The trees help protect hatchlings from enemies.
Komodo Dragons can smell dead animals from 7 miles away.
Komodo Dragons are good swimmers.
Scientists believe that Komodo Dragons can hear and see almost as well as humans.
Female Komodo Dragons dig nests in the ground.
A Komodo Dragon uses its tongue to smell.

FIGURE 9.21 Page of a write-up on Komodo dragons by a small group of first-grade students

They liked experimenting with different font colors, background options, and photo choices. Using this digital tool made it simpler for them to collaborate and make decisions together, because they could switch around options and writing to see which ones to choose without having to worry about erasing a paper or ungluing a picture. The group worked on this project for several periods, so it was convenient that they could access the program themselves and get right to work. They even wrote parts of their digital book during their free time. While other groups required teacher assistance, this group was able to mostly work independently, and I mainly provided targeted feedback. Since this was an open inquiry exploration, the students focused on research and discovery; they were asked to select and create their own combination of mixed-media projects.

Another World's Largest

Meanwhile, other students were taking note of the Komodo dragon activities. The student studying plants was intrigued with the idea that the dragon group was studying the world's biggest lizard, and set out to discover what the world's biggest flower was. Along the way, two other students became engaged in this study. The child who was studying George Washington switched to this group. Another student, still studying sharks, joined in as a consultant, having actually seen the world's biggest flower on a trip to Indonesia. This child shared firsthand knowledge with the pair on how the flower smelled like it was rotten, and how it attracted flies and insects. Our resident expert also offered detailed commentary when we watched YouTube videos I found about the plant.

In the spirit of the Komodo dragon, the team set out to create a life-size flower, complete with markings and a raised center. They used colored bulletin board paper and worked for a long time cutting out small shapes of orange and yellow to more accurately recreate the petals. They were patient and willing to put in whatever time they needed for cutting, pasting, and cleaning up after themselves after each session. The display was complete with a yardstick positioned next to the flower to show its actual size (see Figure 9.22).

Having made the flower authentic in size, color, and shape, the group wanted to also include the

FIGURE 9.22 Life-size rendition of the world's largest flower

FIGURE 9.23 Close-up of the center of the flower, including the spikes inside and the yellow fly on the side

pointy spikes in the center. Since they knew that the flower was smelly to attract insects and other animals, they attached a drawing of a fly near the middle (see Figure 9.23).

Just like the Komodo dragon group, the students decided to write about their research and findings. The group was so proud of their artwork that they decided to include a description of how they designed their flower. As with the written work for all of my students, the team focused on the content rather than the spelling. I always remind them that it is more important that they get down their ideas first and not let spelling a word interfere with their writing. We went through and corrected the spelling together afterward, since the product would be shared with others (see Figure 9.24). They were a hardworking team, with members that enjoyed the inquiry process and creating their product.

The World's Biggest Flower
Rafflesia Arnoldii

This is the world's biggest flower. It is named Rafflesia Arnoldii. It is a famous plant from Indonesia. The flower is red, orange, yellow, and brown and has dots all over the petals. The flower smells like a dead animal. It smells bad because insects and animals will come to the flower and then the flower will eat them. On our flower we added a fly on the plant to show this. We also added spikes in the center of our flower because the flower contains spikes in the middle.

This is the world's biggest flower. It is up to 3 feet long and can weigh up to 24 pounds. It is as long as a yard, which is three feet or 36 inches.

One yard = 3   feet = 36 inches

To make the flower, the first thing we did was cut the petals out of red paper. We measured each petal to make sure the flower would be 3 feet. We cut the center of the flower out of orange paper and glued the petals around it. We added orange and yellow spots to the petals. We used model magic to make the 3D spikes in the center of the flower and colored them brown and orange.

FIGURE 9.24 Write-up on world's biggest flower by first-grade students

World's Oldest Chimpanzee

Meanwhile, the pair of students studying monkeys also became interested in finding some kind of world's record about their topic and in their research came across the oldest chimpanzee, who at the time was Little Mama. To better explain her life, they carefully created a time line showing some important events they researched about the monkey's personal history: when she was born, when she moved to Florida, and her seventy-fifth birthday. Little Mama was an interesting study, and the pair wrote up a short report about her life (see Figure 9.25).

A More Common Theme Emerges

The student researching cheetahs was excited to learn that it was the world's fastest land animal and that it fit in with this popular "world's most" theme. But everyone else's topic was not easily recognized as the world's best in some way. The students did, however, start to see a different connection between the largest flower and largest reptile and the oldest chimp and the fastest animal: they jointly discovered that size, speed, and age could all be measured. Suddenly, seemingly unrelated topics had more similarities than was originally realized. Now the football topic could be compared to a cheetah, because both had the element of speed. With a little bit of research, we discovered that when a good kicker punts a football, it travels as fast as a running cheetah.

What About Weight?

The students were excited about our new common theme, so the pair writing their book about bunnies wanted to find some way to include measurement in their topic. They were interested in finding a different kind of measurement and were not inspired by the information they saw in their books or the digital resources I permitted them to use independently. So the students and I researched the topic online together, and the pair decided to write about the world's heaviest bunny. At the same time, the panda group was busy learning from the information and photographs found in several books, and each student chose a favorite page to

> ### The World's Oldest Chimpanzee
> #### *Little Mama*
>
> The world's oldest living chimpanzee was born in 1940 in Africa. She lives in a safari park in West Palm Beach, Florida. She lived there since 1967. Her name is Little Mama. She is 74 years old. Most Chimpanzees live from ages 40-60, but this one is 74 years old! She is small and weighs about 100 pounds.
>
> Little Mama's birthday is on Valentine's Day. On her birthday, she likes to eat cake, pie, and soda because she likes sugar a lot.

FIGURE 9.25 Sharing information about the chimpanzee

recreate. The team members painstakingly looked for details to include in their artwork and wanted to illustrate the interesting facts they found. They were very committed to their project and looked forward to displaying their pictures on the bulletin board and then putting them together to make a book. They were the only group not very interested in finding a measurement idea, although they were fine with the other students wanting the main theme of the bulletin board to be measurement. I intervened and did a bit of searching to find a way to possibly fit the panda group into this measurement theme. The group loved the video I found on the world's smallest panda, and they incorporated it in their display, including hanging paper clips that matched the same weight as the smallest baby panda. The shark trio explored weight as well, and found a comparison weight. In this way, each group found a way to integrate a measurement component into their existing work.

Honoring Open Inquiry While Finding a Common Theme

I considered this to be an open inquiry study and did not want to compromise that. Students still did their own projects on the topics of their choice and displayed their work on the bulletin board. Most of the students were surprised and excited, however, that even though they had chosen a wide range of topics, there was still a common thread that they had discovered that tied them all together. This higher-level understanding made their inquiry work stronger.

The class chose to use "Measurement" as the title of the bulletin board (see Figure 9.26). As a result, some groups did have to create an additional measurement component for the bulletin board that they would not have otherwise included. To me, as their teacher, it was worth the trade-off. These combined projects also served as a comprehensive study of measurement, an important math topic that is often skimmed over in our curriculum. The students were able to appreciate how measurement is part of our lives in many different ways. It deserved the inquiry work we did, and the students learned how it could be related to their personal interests.

After their creations were made, the students then turned their knowledge into action by teaching their kindergarten buddy class all about their projects, explaining what they had made, and answering questions from both their fifth-grade buddies and their parents. Students from other classes were also able to study the projects as they were displayed on the hall bulletin board.

FIGURE 9.26 Bulletin boards can be a teaching tool for other students

Reflections and Next Steps

Overall, this group-based, open inquiry project with my first graders was very rewarding and meaningful for the students and for me. One of the students who researched the oldest chimpanzee actually went to see her in Florida. Although I had all of these students several years ago, some of them still talk with me about the Komodo dragons and fondly remember the large one they made in our class. Although this inquiry study lasted several days longer than I had originally planned and there was a lot going on all at once, it was worth it. Ultimately, what made this experience special and more powerful is that students took notice of what other students were doing, and they inspired each other. By finding common themes, they discovered similarities in their different topics and looked for connections across their interests. It became our collective class inquiry, rather than several separate projects.

As I reflect on why this open inquiry study worked well, certainly one factor that helped was the combination of enthusiastic, cooperative students. In thinking now about what was effective instructionally, I believe the students benefited from prior inquiry studies that gradually released responsibility to them (as we discussed in Chapter 2): a modeled plant study in the fall, a structured geography study in the winter, a guided elephant study in the early spring, and then this open inquiry later in the spring.

The fall plant study included lots of modeling, experiments, hands-on experiences, collaboration, shared writing pieces, analysis, and personal responses. This became the groundwork for sparking an interest in inquiry work, research, and discovery, while establishing classroom routines and learning expectations for the year. For this study, each of the students made a biology journal, with the first half of the book dedicated to recording their plant studies and the second half reserved for their chicken life cycle study at the end of the year. The class had easy access to these books and used them throughout the year, which helped them remember both what they had learned about plants and about the elements of inquiry.

In addition to reinforcing this content beyond the fall, the sequence of units helped students compare and contrast their understanding of the plant life cycle to the animal life cycle. The students finished the second half of their biology journals at the end of the year with an animal life cycle study, when they learned about chicks. In the future, I think it will be critical to pay more attention to how I set up my units so students have the foundational skills they need and there is more planned release of responsibility throughout the year.

One concern I had during this inquiry study was what to do about students who picked a topic and worked alone; I encouraged them to make an individual choice, but that meant not working collaboratively on the same subject with other students. To foster opportunities for more experiences working with others, I asked these students to partner up with classmates when conducting research, and in some cases, I paired them up with others creating similar inquiry products. I wondered, though, if it was more important for them to have them collaborate than it was for them to research their first choice of topic. The students who worked together on the same topic overall had a richer experience, and now with my understanding of the elements of inquiry, I will find ways to ensure open inquiry is a collaborative experience, maybe by having them list their top three ideas.

Since implementing this open inquiry unit, our writing curriculum has changed, so now each student writes one long (about ten pages) and detailed book about a self-selected nonfiction topic. It is more of a writing assignment than a research project, and the writing expectations are much more extensive and rigorous. Now that I am more familiar with this new curriculum, I am finding ways to mesh it with inquiry practices. Beyond writing, there are new curriculum demands across all subject areas, and I first need to give myself time to learn these expectations and standards. Once I do, I am ultimately aiming to use the PDI framework to help integrate all of this learning into a more cohesive classroom experience for my students, with inquiry at the core.

Afterword

Looking Back and Thinking Ahead

So here we are—three educators circling back in our own inquiry process to reflect on where we've come and what we've learned about how to design engaging learning spaces with an aim toward student-directed learning. We began our journey by sharing our vision of PDI, why it matters, and how it has impacted the students and teachers with whom we've worked. We put forth a series of questions to guide our thinking (and hopefully yours) and introduced a number of resources to support your planning and implementation of PDI: these include the PDI framework, the PDI self-assessment tool, the PDI questioning tool, the PDI knowledge continuum, and the PDI planning guide.

Along the way, we provided examples and think-alouds to demonstrate how teachers have flexibly integrated intentional teaching practices and classroom routines that cultivate deep learning, active participation, and creative expression, with and without digital texts and tools. We shared stories about how these experiences have helped young children gradually grow into intentional and self-directed learners in a range of different contexts. And most important, we have come to appreciate both the excitement and the challenges of exploring how to implement inquiry-based approaches to teaching and learning in today's elementary school classrooms. We truly hope these stories and supports have helped pave the way for you to follow your own motivations for exploring PDI with your students.

As we explained at the outset, we do not claim to know all of the answers. Instead, our hope is that you'll be inspired to collaborate with others to facilitate real and sustainable change in your teaching that also empowers children to pursue and share their inquiries with others. Guided by Kouzes and Posner's (2012) five practices of exemplary leadership (listed in bold on page 216–217) and our experiences with hundreds of teachers and librarians at our annual Summer Institute in Digital Literacy at the University of Rhode Island (see Hobbs and Coiro [2016] and www.digiuri.com), we leave you with a few ideas for how to continue your own journey while also aiming to inspire others at your school.

Network and learn with others at the annual Summer Institute in Digital Literacy at the University of Rhode Island.

Model the Way. We encourage you to continue asking questions with your students about things that matter to you and to them. This can help to strengthen relationships with students and creates natural opportunities to talk, think deeply, and consider ways of acting on new ideas. As Beth shared earlier, "Sharing my desire to make my teaching more engaging brought my students and me together toward a common goal . . . learning."

Inspire Shared Vision. Create opportunities for students to develop their role as active learners by inviting them into the conversation about how to accomplish shared expectations for teaching and learning. Explore a small set of digital texts and tools that offer diverse ways for you and your students to build, express, and reflect on new ideas. Over time, these jointly constructed experiences help create a vision for how to connect with and engage young learners in your unique context.

Challenge the Process. Recognize that not every day will be easy and sometimes you will make mistakes. We encourage you to find a colleague who shares your passion for learning new things and taking some risks. Be aware of your strengths and seek out others who are strong in different areas. Align your inquiries to meaningful standards while challenging your students to be active knowledge producers, critical thinkers, and responsible citizens. Take small, but purposeful, steps and use your students' positive reactions to fuel the next phase of your work.

Enable Others to Act. "Everyone learns from everyone!" is the motto we share at the Summer Institute in Digital Literacy. This idea empowers educators to share what you know and to be comfortable seeking support from others when you don't know. One way to explore this idea in your classroom is to create regular opportunities for students to develop their own voices and make choices as part of a safe learning community. Like Karen, you can turn to outside experts in your school and neighborhood to share with children insights beyond your expertise. These experiences will help you navigate your role in guiding and supporting inquiry and help students practice and shape their own emerging identities as self-directed learners.

Encourage the Heart. Although this recommendation comes last, in some ways, it's the most important. Taking time to celebrate your successes (big and small) and to share them with others in your school community (inside and outside your building) is powerful. We spend so much time encouraging our students, we often forget to step back and take time to reflect on and recognize our own accomplishments. Planning and implementing inquiry-based practices in elementary school is hard work; reflecting on and sharing the rewards for you and your students is an integral part of the PDI process.

In summary, implementing PDI experiences requires carefully building a culture of inquiry in your classroom community and intentionally aligning your teaching with meaningful goals for learning and action while guiding students to pursue their own inquiries. Writing this book has helped the three of us (as coauthors) achieve an important personal goal: to better articulate the potential of PDI in diverse contexts while reflecting on the complexities encountered along the way. This tangible product of our inquiry offers us a solid reference to help others envision a range of authentic examples of how elementary school teachers design PDI opportunities to meet their unique hopes and needs. Our hope is that whether you work alone or with others, planning for PDI can now be an easier and achievable goal for you.

APPENDIXES

Digital Considerations

Before you get into the nitty-gritty of selecting specific digital tools, the following considerations will be helpful as you plan for using digital tools to enhance your classroom inquiries:

Digital Device Considerations

- What devices do you and your students have access to from your classroom and/or in the library (e.g., individual iPads, an iPad cart, Chromebooks, laptops, or some combination of these)?

- When will the devices actually be ready for you to use with students? For new devices, you might expect a lag time of almost six to eight weeks to set up new programs, install class or student passwords, assign students to apps, and so on. You might expect similar delays if you've asked to have a new app installed on current devices. In either case, you should have a "paper plan" ready for your inquiry experiences until things are set up.

- How many students will be using each device? How will this number influence your grouping and scheduling practices?

- How will digital resources be shared across the devices? For example, when one student saves a photo on one device, what steps are needed for that student to share this photo with a partner working on another device?

Accessing Digital Programs and Applications

- What digital tools do you already have access to in your district and how are elementary school teachers using them?

- Are there limits to how many students or teachers can use certain tools at the same time?

- What is the process for exploring or requesting new digital tools in your school or district? Who are the necessary contacts?

- Once a particular program or app has been installed on a device, how easy will it be for students to access it on a regular basis? Will students need a log-in and user password? Will they have to enter this each time they use the app? Some interfaces (e.g., Seesaw) allow students to log in once and then they can move between the different tools within the interface (e.g., draw, write, take photos, comment).

Specific Tool Features and Considerations

- What is your level of familiarity with the tool? Has your district provided professional development for this tool, or are you comfortable getting started with less support from others?

- Does the tool require a special browser or certain settings for the features to work as designed?

- How easy is the tool for students to use independently or with minimal support from an adult? If it's too complicated for most students, it might be better to steer them toward something less complicated. If a few students have experience with the tool, you might designate them as class experts and direct others to them for support.

- Does the tool have a classroom management feature to help organize students and/or their work? Several apps have added these features to their interfaces, although many charge for the management support. Are these features worth the cost?

- Can students (or their family members) access the programs from their home devices? Are students able to borrow devices to occasionally take them home? If not, how will this impact the time students need to complete their work?

- Make it a point to understand the features (both strengths and weaknesses) of the program in terms of how to access files, upgrade to new versions, and share files from one version to another after updates have been made. Planning ahead for these changes will help avoid a lot of frustration.

- Is the tool free, or is there a paid version? Are there important benefits to paying for a subscription, or do you only need the free features?

- Try to select tools that allow students to do multiple things. It's much easier to introduce students to a single interface that has several features, rather than overwhelming them with multiple tools that can only be used for one thing.

PERSONAL DIGITAL INQUIRY (PDI) PLANNING GUIDE	
INQUIRY QUESTION:	
SET EXPECTATIONS FOR TEACHING AND LEARNING	**PLAN AUTHENTIC OPPORTUNITIES FOR PERSONAL DIGITAL INQUIRY**
Knowledge Outcomes: (Subject-specific or multidisciplinary)	**Wonder & Discover:**
	Collaborate & Discuss:
Action Outcomes: (e.g., collaborate, start conversations, raise awareness, take action, change minds)	
	Create & Take Action:
Content Standards: (CCSS, ALA, etc.)	**Analyze & Reflect:**
Digital Standards: (ISTE, Digital Media Literacy Competencies, etc.)	

MAKE PURPOSEFUL CHOICES ABOUT DIGITAL TEXTS AND TOOLS
(Experiences to Deepen Learning Across the PDI Knowledge Continuum)

← Lower-Order Thinking   Higher-Order Thinking →

Acquire Knowledge	**Build Knowledge**	**Express Knowledge**	**Reflect on Knowledge**	**Act on Knowledge**
Learn passively, receive (digital) information given or modeled by others	Learners (use technology to) connect new information to prior knowledge	Learners (use technology to) share their new knowledge with others	Learners (use technology to) reflect on and evaluate their inquiry processes and products	Learners (use technology to) translate their knowledge into action

Digital Tools* Mentioned in This Book

		Page
Alphabet Organizer	tinyurl.com/yc58wcn	71
Apple Notes	tinyurl.com/y8r7jjkt	65
Book Creator	bookcreator.com	191
Creative Commons	search.creativecommons.org	59, 122
Draw and Tell	tinyurl.com/gkuvbfs	191
Diigo	diigo.com	62
Easy Annotate	tinyurl.com/y6etbr9h	58
Evernote	evernote.com	58
Explain Everything	explaineverything.com	58, 180
Flipgrid	flipgrid.com	62, 180
Glogster	edu.glogster.com	63
Google Classroom	classroom.google.com	47, 102, 119, 123, 158, 197
Google Docs	google.com/docs/about	40, 58, 62, 64, 200
Google Slides	google.com/slides/about	65, 194, 197, 200
Jing	techsmith.com/jing-tool.html	104, 157
Kidspiration†	inspiration.com/Kidspiration	63
Notability	gingerlabs.com	65
Padlet	padlet.com	58, 63
Pages (Apple)†	apple.com/pages	58
PicCollage	pic-collage.com	166
Pixie†	www.tech4learning.com/pixie	40, 63, 66, 71, 73, 205, 207
Popplet	popplet.com	58, 166, 167
Screencastify	screencastify.com	104, 157
Screencast-O-Matic	screencast-o-matic.com	157
Seesaw	web.seesaw.me	47, 58, 62, 63, 133-136, 166, 178, 180, 221
ShowMe	showme.com	58
Stationery Studio†	tinyurl.com/ydf5p7ww	63
Storyboarder	wonderunit.com/storyboarder	58
ThingLink	thinglink.com	58
Wixie†	wixie.com	63, 66, 73, 131, 140
YouTube	youtube.com	70, 136, 176, 209

*Direct links to all of these digital tools can be found on our website.

†At the time of printing, only paid versions of this tool were available while other tools had a version that was free.

Digital Texts* Mentioned in This Book with Uses Across Grade Levels

*Direct links to all of these digital texts can be found on our website

†At the time of printing, only paid versions of this digital text were available while

other texts had a version that was free.

PERSONAL DIGITAL INQUIRY SELF-REFLECTION TOOL	
Imagine if someone stepped into your classroom on any random day and stayed for at least an hour. How likely would this visitor notice each of the following actions described here? For each statement, assign a rating between 5 and 1 using the following scale. 5 = Hard to miss it 4 = Highly likely to notice 3 = Hit or miss depending on the circumstances 2 = Not very likely to notice 1 = I doubt anyone would notice	

EXPECTATIONS	Rating
1. I stress to students that solving problems and developing understanding, not only acquiring knowledge, are the goals of classroom activity and lessons.	
2. I make a conscious effort to communicate to students that using or acting on what they learn in creative ways is valued.	
3. I actively establish a set of expectations for student independence so my students are not dependent on me to answer all questions and direct all activity.	

LANGUAGE	Rating
1. I try to notice and name the thinking and learning occurring in my classroom, saying things like, "Alex is generating specific questions to guide his inquiry" or "Letitia is reflecting on whether or not that document sharing tool was useful."	
2. I give specific, targeted action-oriented feedback (oral or written) that guides students toward taking initiative in future efforts and actions, rather than generic praise comments ("good job," "great," "brilliant," "well done").	
3. I use inclusive, community-building language, talking about what "we" are learning and "our" inquiry, while listening and clarifying ideas generated by the group.	

Adapted from the Cultures of Thinking Self-Assessment Tool from *Creating Cultures of Thinking: The 8 We Forces Must Master to Truly Transform Our Schools* by Ron Ritchhart ©2015. Reprinted by permission of Wiley Publishing.

TIME	Rating
1. I make a conscious effort to weave time for building relationships into everyday routines and project schedules.	
2. I provide the time and space for students to listen, reflect on their own ideas, extend the ideas of others, and share their contributions.	
3. I try to sequence activities in ways that allow students to make connections and build on what they learned previously to anticipate what they might learn in the future.	

MODELING	Rating
1. I display open-mindedness, taking risks, reflecting on my learning, and a willingness to consider alternative perspectives.	
2. I demonstrate my own curiosity, passion, and interest to students.	
3. My students and I regularly ask questions and explain our thinking as we discover new things and solve problems together.	

OPPORTUNITIES	Rating
1. I focus students' attention on discovering, discussing, analyzing, and reflecting on meaningful connections between their work and important ideas in their worlds outside of school.	
2. I provide students with opportunities to direct their own learning and become independent learners.	
3. I encourage students to use or act on their creative learning products to start conversations, raise awareness, take action, or change minds in their classroom, learning community, or beyond.	

Adapted from the Cultures of Thinking Self-Assessment Tool from *Creating Cultures of Thinking: The 8 We Forces Must Master to Truly Transform Our Schools* by Ron Ritchhart ©2015. Reprinted by permission of Wiley Publishing.

(continues)

ROUTINES	Rating
1. I use explicit routines and flexible structures to organize age-appropriate lessons that ensure we can all use technology to help us learn (e.g., use digital devices, find digital resources, work in shared documents, publish work).	
2. I set up ways to regularly document, share, and celebrate our important work with peers, families, the local community, and, when appropriate, with relevant audiences in the real world.	
3. I regularly share with students the purpose(s) for learning with or without technology and explain how the skill sets we are using can help to inspire curiosity, answer questions, and think deeply about our world.	
	Rating
1. I ensure that all students show a genuine interest in and respect for each other's thinking. Students are pushed to elaborate on their thinking beyond a simple answer or statement. Ideas may be critiqued or challenged, but people are not.	
2. I view students as partners in learning and encourage them to share what they know or have learned with multiple audiences whenever possible.	
3. I listen in on groups and allow them to make mistakes and collaboratively grapple with ideas, rather than always inserting myself into the process.	
ENVIRONMENT	Rating
1. I arrange the physical and digital learning spaces of my classroom to facilitate thoughtful interactions, collaborations, and discussions that vary flexibly to accommodate learner needs.	
2. My wall displays and planned activities are ongoing and flexible to invite sustained inquiry and connections across lessons and topics throughout the year.	
3. A visitor can easily recognize what I care about and value with respect to learning.	

REFLECTIONS

Which PDI practices am I especially proud of at this point in the year and why?

Which PDI practices are not as likely to be noticed at this point and why?

Which PDI practice(s) would I most like to focus on next and why?

What are my next steps to get started?

Adapted from the Cultures of Thinking Self-Assessment Tool from *Creating Cultures of Thinking: The 8 We Forces Must Master to Truly Transform Our Schools* by Ron Ritchhart ©2015. Reprinted by permission of Wiley Publishing.

PERSONAL DIGITAL INQUIRY QUESTIONING TOOL

Use this space and guiding questions to brainstorm initial ideas for how you might integrate opportunities for each set of PDI practices into your inquiry unit. Aim to create flexible ways for students to depen their understanding of learning outcomes and incorporate their own voice and choice into howthey engage with the ideas.

GUIDING QUESTIONS:

How will learners analyze content to build their understanding of challenging information, and how will they reflect on their choices and their learning at multiple points in their inquiry process?

How will learners engage with content and hands-on experiences to activate their wonderings and discover more about their inquiry topic?

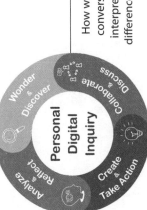

How will learners express their interests and new understandings through creative work designed to start conversations, raise awareness, take action, or change minds in their community or beyond?

How will learners collaboratively engage in joining conversations around shared interests to discuss interpretations, make connections, and negotiate differences in thinking?

Consider how digital texts, tools, and other technologies may be used to support and/or facilitate each of these inquiry practices.

References

Alberta Learning. 2004. *Focus on Inquiry: A Teacher's Guide to Implementing Inquiry-Based Learning.* https://archive.org/details/focusoninquirylearn04albe/page/n3

Almasi, Janice. 1995. "The Nature of Fourth Graders' Sociocognitive Conflicts in Peer-Led and Teacher-Led Discussions of Literature." *Reading Research Quarterly* 30 (3): 315–351.

American Association of School Librarians. 2018. *AASL Standards Framework for Learners.* https://standards.aasl.org/wp-content/uploads/2018/08/180206-AASL-framework-for-learners-2.pdf.

Benest, Frank. 2011. "Learning with Intent: A Strategy for Adaptive Change and Self-Renewal." *Public Management,* October, 18–21. http://www.frankbenest.com/Learning%20with%20Intent.pdf.

Bennett, Sue, Karl Maton, and Lisa Kervin. 2008. "The 'Digital Natives' Debate: A Critical Review of the Evidence." *British Journal of Educational Technology* 39 (5): 775–786.

Bereiter, Carl, and Marlene Scardamalia. 1989. "Intentional Learning as a Goal of Instruction." In *Knowing, Learning, and Instruction: Essays in Honor of Robert Glaser*, ed. Lauren B. Resnick. Hillsdale, NJ: Erlbaum.

Boss, Suzie, and Jane Krauss. 2007. *Reinventing Project-Based Learning: Your Field Guide to Real-World Projects in the Digital Age.* Eugene, OR: International Society for Technology in Education.

Boston Public Schools. 2014. *Focus on K2: An Integrated Approach to Teaching and Learning.* http://bpsearlychildhood.weebly.com/uploads/1/0/1/3/10131776/focus_on_k2_guiding_documents2.pdf.

Bray, Barbara, and Kathleen McClaskey. 2016. *How to Personalize Learning: A Practical Guide for Getting Started and Going Deeper.* Thousand Oaks, CA: Corwin.

Brown, John Seely. 2000. "Growing Up: Digital: How the Web Changes Work, Education, and the Ways People Learn." *Change: The Magazine of Higher Learning* 32 (2): 11–20.

Bruce, Bertram B., and Ann Peterson Bishop. 2008. "New Literacies and Community Inquiry." In *Handbook of Research in New Literacies*, ed. Julie Coiro, Michelle Knobel, Colin Lankshear, and Donald J. Leu. Mahwah, NJ: Erlbaum.

Brunelle, Lynn. 2018. *Turn This Book into a Beehive! And 19 Other Experiments and Activities That Explore the Amazing World of Bees.* New York: Workman.

Bukowiecki, Elaine M., and Marlene P. Correia. 2010. *Informational Texts in Pre-kindergarten Through Grade-Three Classrooms.* New York: Rowman & Littlefield.

Cannon, Janell. 2005. *Crickwing.* New York: Voyager Books.

Casey, Leo. 2013. "Learning Beyond Competence to Participation." *International Journal of Progressive Education* 9 (2): 45-60.

CAST. 2018. *The UDL Guidelines* Version 2.2. http://udlguidelines.cast.org.

Cervantes, Angela. 2015. *Gaby, Lost and Found.* A Wish Novel. New York: Scholastic.

Churches, Andrew. 2008. *Bloom's Digital Taxonomy.* Available http://www.ccconline.org/wp-content/uploads/2013/11/Churches_2008_DigitalBloomsTaxonomyGuide.pdf .

Clarke, Grant, Karen Gill, Catherine Sim, Lillian Patry, and Yael Ginsler. 2014. *Engaging School Districts in Evaluative Thinking and Research-Based Inquiry to Advance 21st Century Teaching and Learning.* Paper presented at annual meeting of American Educational Research Association, Philadelphia, PA.

Coiro, Julie. 2015. "The Magic of Wondering: Building Understanding Through Online Inquiry." *The Reading Teacher* 69 (2): 189–193.

———. 2016. "Let's Get Personal: Balancing Talk with Technology to *Truly* Personalize Learning." *Literacy Today* 33:(4) 6–7.

Collins, Allen, John Seely Brown, and Ann Holum. 1991. "Cognitive Apprenticeship: Making Thinking Visible." *American Educator* 15 (3): 6–11.

Committee on Developments in the Science of Learning. 2000. *How People Learn: Brain, Mind, Experience, and School.* Washington, DC: National Academy Press. Available online at https://www.nap.edu/read/9853/chapter/1.

Common Sense Education. n.d. *Digital Citizenship: Everything Educators Need to Empower the Next Generation of Digital Citizens.* https://www.commonsense.org/education/digital-citizenship.

Cooper, Kristy S. 2013. "Eliciting Engagement in the High School Classroom: A Mixed Methods Examination of Teaching Practices." *American Educational Research Journal* 51 (2): 363–402.

Cornett, Claudia. 2010. *Comprehension First: Inquiry into Big Ideas Using Important Questions.* Scottsdale, AZ: Holcomb Hathaway.

Covey, Stephen R. 1989. *The 7 Habits of Highly Effective People.* New York: Simon & Schuster.

Dewey, John. (1938) 1997. "Experience and Education." In *John Dewey: The Latter Works, 1938-1939*, ed. Jo Ann Boydston. Vol. 13. Carbondale: Southern Illinois University Press.

Dobler, Elizabeth, and Maya. Eagleton. 2015. *Reading the Web: Strategies for Internet Inquiry.* New York: Guilford.

Fisher, Douglas, and Nancy Frey. 2012. "Close Reading in Elementary Schools." *The Reading Teacher* 66 (3): 179–188.

Friesen, Sharon, and David Scott. 2013. *Inquiry-Based Learning: A Review of the Research Literature.* Prepared for the Alberta Ministry of Education. http://galileo.org/focus-on-inquiry-lit-review.pdf.

Fullan, Michael, and Maria Langworthy. 2014. *A Rich Seam: How New Pedagogies Find Deep Learning.* London: Pearson.

Gambrell, Linda. 2011. "Seven Rules of Engagement: What's Most Important to Know About Motivation to Read." *The Reading Teacher* 65 (3): 172–178.

Google. n.d. "Be Internet Awesome." https://beinternetawesome.withgoogle.com/en_us.

Harrington, Lisa. M. 2014. *It's a Good Thing There Are Bees.* Rookie Read-About Science. New York: Scholastic.

Harris, Judi, and Mark Hofer. 2009. "Instructional Planning Activity Types as Vehicles for Curriculum-Based TPACK Development." In *Research Highlights in Technology and Teacher Education*, ed. Cleborne D. Maddux. Chesapeake, VA: Society for Information Technology in Teacher Education (SITE).

Harvey, Stephanie, and Harvey Daniels. 2009. *Inquiry Circles in Action: Comprehension & Collaboration.* Portsmouth, NH: Heinemann.

Herron, Marshall D. 1971. "The Nature of Scientific Enquiry." *School Review* 79 (2): 171-212.

Hobbs, Renee, and Julie Coiro. 2016. "Everyone Learns from Everyone: Collaborative and Interdisciplinary Professional Development in Digital Literacy." *Journal of Adolescent and Adult Literacy* 59 (6): 546–549.

———. 2018. "Design Features of a Professional Development Program in Digital Literacy." *Journal of Adolescent & Adult Literacy* 50 (3): 304–313.

Hobbs, Renee, and David Cooper Moore. 2013. *Discovering Media Literacy: Teaching Digital Media and Popular Culture in the Elementary School.* Thousand Oaks, CA: Corwin.

How to Draw Animals. 2010. "How to Draw a Komodo Dragon." http://www.howtodrawanimals.net/how-to-draw-a-komodo-dragon.

Jenkins, Henry, Ravi Purushotma, Margaret Weigel, Katie Clinton, and Alice J. Robison. 2009. *Confronting the Challenges of Participatory Culture: Media Education for the 21st Century.* Cambridge, MA: MIT Press. Available online at https://www.macfound.org/media/article_pdfs/JENKINS_WHITE_PAPER.PDF.

Kalman, Bobbie. 2006. *The Life Cycle of a Salmon.* New York: Crabtree.

Kellow, Jan-Marie. 2006. *Inquiry Learning in an ICT-Rich Environment.* https://goo.gl/Bmv1qb.

Kouzes, James M., and Barry Z. Posner. 2012. *The Leadership Challenge: How to Make Extraordinary Things Happen in Organizations.* 5th ed. San Francisco: John Wiley & Sons.

Kuhn, Deanna, John Black, Alla Keselman, and Danielle Kaplan. 2000. "The Development of Cognitive Skills to Support Inquiry Learning." *Cognition and Instruction* 18 (4): 495–523.

Lionni, Leo. 1974. *Fish Is Fish.* New York: Dragonfly Books.

Marsh, Laura. 2016. *National Geographic Readers: Bees.* Washington, DC: National Geographic Society.

McAndrews, Shannon. 2015. *AVID Elementary: Foundations Implementation Resource.* San Diego, CA: AVID.

McClaskey, Kathleen. 2019. "Continuums: The 7 Elements of Learner Agency." http://kathleenmcclaskey.com/continuums/.

———. 2017. "Crosswalk of Learner Agency Across the Stages." http://kathleenmcclaskey.com/crosswalk-of-learner-agency-across-the-stages/.

McLoughlin, Maureen, and Glenn L. DeVoogd. 2004. *Critical Literacy: Enhancing Students' Comprehension of Text.* New York: Scholastic.

McTighe, Jay, and Grant Wiggins. 2012. *Understanding by Design Framework.* https://www.ascd.org/ASCD/pdf/siteASCD/publications/UbD_WhitePaper0312.pdf.

———. 2013. *Essential Questions: Opening Doors to Student Understanding.* Alexandria, VA: ASCD.

Meyer, Anne, David H. Rose, and David T. Gordon. 2014. *Universal Design for Learning: Theory and Practice.* Wakefield, MA: CAST Professional Publishing

Moline, Steve. 2012. *I See What You Mean: Visual Literacy K–8.* 2nd ed. Portland, ME: Stenhouse.

MrBrownThumb. 2013. "How to Pollinate an Amaryllis Flower." https://www.youtube.com/watch?v=Td6J0A1QiAc.

National Geographic. 2012. "Pictures: Colored Honey Made by Candy-Eating French Bees." https://news.nationalgeographic.com/news/2012/10/pictures/121011-blue-honey-honeybees-animals-science/#close.

Next Generation Science Standards Lead States. 2013. "Appendix D: All Standards, All Students: Making the Next Generation Science Standards Accessible to All Students." *Next Generation Science Standards: For States, by States.* Washington, DC: National Academies Press.

Pauk, Walter, and Ross J. Owens. 2010. *How to Study in College.* 10th ed. Boston: Wadsworth.

Pearson, P. David, Taffy E. Raphael, Vicki L. Benson, and Christina L. Madda. 2007. "Balance in Comprehensive Literacy Instruction: Then and Now." In *Best Practices in Literacy Instruction,* ed. Linda B. Gambrell, Lesley Mandel Morrow, and Michael Pressley. 2nd ed. New York: Guilford.

Pfeffer, Wendy. 2015. *From Tadpole to Frog* (Let's Read-and-Find-Out Science 1). New York: HarperCollins.

Pink, David H. 2009. *Drive: The Surprising Truth About What Motivates Us.* New York: Riverhead Books.

Prensky, Marc. 2001. "Digital Natives, Digital Immigrants, Part II: Do They Really Think Differently?" *On the Horizon* 9 (6): 1–6. https://www.marcprensky.com/writing/Prensky%20-%20Digital%20Natives,%20Digital%20Immigrants%20-%20Part2.pdf.

———. 2011. "H. Sapiens Digital: From Digital Immigrants and Digital Natives to Digital Wisdom." *Innovate: Journal of Online Education* 5 (3): Article 1. Available online at http://nsuworks.nova.edu/innovate/vol5/iss3/1.

Ritchhart, Ron. 2015. *Creating Cultures of Thinking: The 8 Forces We Must Master to Truly Transform Our Schools.* San Francisco: John Wiley & Sons.

Rothstein, Dan, and Luz Santana. 2011. *Make Just One Change: Teach Students to Ask Their Own Questions.* Cambridge, MA: Harvard Education Press.

Ruckman, Ivy. 2003. *Night of the Twisters.* New York: HarperCollins.

Saavedra, A. R., and V. D. Opfer. 2012. "Learning 21st Century Skills Requires 21st Century Teaching." *Phi Delta Kappan* 94 (2): 8–13.

Sacher, L. 1998. *Holes.* New York: Farrar, Straus & Giroux.

Spinelli, J. 1999. *Maniac Magee.* New York: Little, Brown Books for Young Readers.

Thomas, Doug, and John Seely Brown. 2011. *A New Culture of Learning: Cultivating the Imagination for a World of Constant Change.* Lexington, KY: CreateSpace.

Topeka Public Schools. 2018. *English Language Arts Curriculum Design Maps.* http://www.tpscurriculum.net/standards/pacingGuides.cfm. http://www.tpscurriculum.net/standards/standards.cfm

Vasquez, Vivian. 2010. *Getting Beyond "I Like the Book": Creating Spaces for Critical Literacy in K–6 Classrooms.* 2nd ed. Newark, DE: International Reading Association.

Watanabe-Crockett, Lee. 2017. "15 of the Best Reflective Questions Learners Can Use for Debriefing Learning." *Wabisabi Blog.* https://globaldigitalcitizen.org/15-reflective-questions-debriefing-learning?mc_cid=1f13afcf38&mc_eid=2d975f311b.

Webb, Norman L. 2002. *Alignment Study in Language Arts, Mathematics, Science, and Social Studies of State Standards and Assessments for Four States.* Washington, DC: Council of Chief State School Officers.

Wubbels, Theo, Perry den Brok, Jan van Tartwick, and Jack Levy. 2012. "Introduction to Interpersonal Relationships in Education." In *Interpersonal Relationships in Education: An Overview of Contemporary Research*, ed. Theo Wubbels, Perry den Brok, Jan van Tartwick, and Jack Levy. Rotterdam, The Netherlands: Sense Publishers.

Zhang, Shenglan, Nell K. Duke, and Laura M. Jimenez. 2011. "The WWWDOT Approach to Improving Students' Critical Evaluation of Websites." *The Reading Teacher* 65 (2): 150–158.

Index